FAMILY HEALTH
PSYCHOLOGY

Series in Applied Psychology: Social Issues and Questions

Stevan Hobfoll, *Editor-in-Chief*

IN PREPARATION

FAMILY HEALTH PSYCHOLOGY

Edited by

T. John Akamatsu
Mary Ann Parris Stephens
Stevan E. Hobfoll
Janis H. Crowther

Kent State University
Kent, Ohio

Routledge
Taylor & Francis Group

LONDON AND NEW YORK

FAMILY HEALTH PSYCHOLOGY

First published 1992 by Hemisphere Publishing Corporation

2 Park Square, Milton Park, Abingdon, Oxon OX14 4RN
711 Third Avenue, New York, NY 10017, USA

Routledge is an imprint of the Taylor & Francis Group, an informa business

First issued in paperback 2016

Copyright © 1992 Taylor & Francis

This book was set in Times Roman by Hemisphere Publishing Corporation. The editors were Marly Davidson, Heather Jefferson, and Deena Williams Newman; the production supervisor was Peggy M. Rote; and the typesetter was Phoebe Carter. Cover design by Michelle Fleitz. Printing and binding by Braun-Brumfield, Inc.

A CIP catalog record for this book is available from the British Library.

⊚ The paper in this publication meets the requirements of the ANSI standard Z39.48-1984(Permanence of Paper).

Library of Congress Cataloging-in-Publication Data

Family health psychology / edited by T. John Akamatsu . . . [et al.].
    p.   cm. — (Series in applied psychology)
    Based in large part on the 1991 Forum on Health Psychology which took place in April at the Inn at Honey Run in the Amish country of central Ohio.
    Includes bibliographical references and index.

    1. Clinical health psychology.   2. Family psychotherapy.
I. Akamatsu, T. John.   II. Kent Psychology Forum (1991): Inn at Honey Run)   III. Series: Series in applied psychology (New York, N.Y.)
R726.7.F36   1992
155.9'24—dc20   92-6333
                                                  CIP

ISBN 978-1-56032-247-4 (hbk)
ISBN 978-1-138-96957-5 (pbk)
ISSN 1048-8164

To my wife, Sharon, whose support and child care made completion of this project possible.—T.J.A.

To Jack, whose love and support have sustained me in times of difficulty, and have helped me enjoy the good times even more.—M.A.P.S.

To my friend, Shosh Shoham, and my son's little friend, Re'ut Shoham.—S.E.H.

To my sister, Patty Hughes, whose presence and support help keep me healthy.—J.H.C.

CONTENTS

CONTRIBUTORS

T. JOHN AKAMATSU, Applied Psychology Center, Department of Psychology, Kent State University, Kent, Ohio 44242.

THOMAS L. CAMPBELL, Departments of Family Medicine and Psychiatry, University of Rochester, Rochester, New York 14620.

SARAH L. CLARK, Department of Psychology, Kent State University, Kent, Ohio 44242.

JAMES C. COYNE, Departments of Family Practice and Psychiatry, University of Michigan Medical School, Ann Arbor, Michigan 49109-0708.

JANIS H. CROWTHER, Applied Psychology Center, Department of Psychology, Kent State University, Kent, Ohio 44242.

DENNIS DROTAR, Case Western Reserve School of Medicine and Metrohealth Medical Center, Cleveland, Ohio 44109-1998.

JENNIFER A. DRULEY, Department of Psychology, Kent State University, Kent, Ohio 44242.

VERONICA FISKE, Departments of Family Practice and Psychiatry, University of Michigan Medical School, Ann Arbor, Michigan 49109-0708.

DAVID S. GOCHMAN, Raymond A. Kent School of Social Work, University of Louisville, Louisville, Kentucky 40292.

STEVAN E. HOBFOLL, Applied Psychology Center, Department of Psychology, Kent State University, Kent, Ohio 44242.

JANE JACOBS, Center for Family Research, George Washington University, School of Medicine, Washington, DC 20037.

search, and the concept of the Forum evolved as one means of achieving these goals. Unlike most research meetings and conferences where large registration and broad topic coverage are sought, the Forum seeks to limit participation to a small number of invited researchers and active professionals whose shared expertise is focused on a specific topic. The intent is to foster intense and free-flowing discussions of research, theory, and practice in various arenas of applied psychology.

The 1991 Forum on Family Health Psychology was the third in a series of Forums that emphasizes families and health. The first Forum in 1989, chaired by Mary Ann Parris Stephens, focused on stress and coping in later-life families. The second Forum in 1990, chaired by Janis H. Crowther, examined individual and family factors in the etiology of bulimia nervosa.

The 1991 Forum was chaired by T. John Akamatsu, and co-chairs were Mary Ann Stephens, Stevan Hobfall, and Janis Crowther. The 10 scholars who were invited were: Thomas Campbell (University of Rochester, School of Medicine), James Coyne (University of Michigan, School of Medicine), Dennis Drotar (Case Western Reserve School of Medicine and Metrohealth Medical Center), David Gochman (Raymond A. Kent School of Social Work, University of Louisville), Jane Jacobs (George Washington University, School of Medicine), Susan Jones (Kent State University, School of Nursing), Anne Kazak (Children's Hospital of Philadelphia), Gerald Koocher (Children's Hospital and Havard School of Medicine, Boston), Michael C. Roberts (University of Kansas), and Gillian Walker (Ackerman Institute for Family Therapy). Graduate students from the Department of Psychology at Kent State University who participated were: Sally Clark, Jennifer Druley, Kathy Laing, Kathy Moore, and Mary Jean Petron. Other invitees included Kathy Cole-Kelly (Case Western Reserve University), Antoinette Graham (University Hospitals of Cleveland), Vanessa Jensen (Cleveland Clinic Foundation), Diana Morris (Case Western Reserve University, School of Nursing), William Smucker (Family Practice Center, Akron, Ohio), and Thomas Webb (Children's Hospital Medical Center of Akron, Ohio).

The 1991 Forum took place over a four-day period in April at the Inn at Honey Run in the Amish country in central Ohio. As has been the case in previous Forums, the sequestered and very comfortable atmosphere gave rise to lively and productive interactions among the diverse group of participants involved. A truly collaborative and interdisciplinary effort resulted, which we believe is reflected in the content of the current volume.

Because this edited volume offers a unique compilation of research findings and applied issues, it will be of interest to researchers and clinicians who are interested in families and health and illness. The book could serve as a text in a graduate level course on health psychology as a companion to a traditional text, or as a primary text for an advanced course on Family Health Psychology. The interdisciplinary nature of the subject matter should also make the volume appealing to several academic and professional disciplines, including psychology, medical sociology and social work, nursing, family medicine, and family therapy.

T. John Akamatsu
Mary Ann Parris Stephens
Stevan E. Hobfoll
Janis H. Crowther

ACKNOWLEDGMENTS

We acknowledge the contributions of several people whose efforts and resources made this volume possible. We are very grateful to the Ohio Board of
Regents, whose Academic Challenge Award funded the Applied Psychology
Center and its mission of promoting applied psychological research. We thank
Seymour Sarason and Camille Wortman, whose ideas and encouragement about
the Forum Series were invaluable to its creation. We also thank our colleagues
in the Department of Psychology at Kent State University who provided emotional support and encouragement in the development of the Forum concept and
in the preparation of this volume. Special thanks are extended to Judy Jerkich,
for her secretarial assistance and personal involvement in these activities, and to
Norma Akamatsu, whose helpful comments and assistance in editing were invaluable.

FAMILY HEALTH PSYCHOLOGY: INTRODUCTION AND OVERVIEW

T. John Akamatsu
Kathleen A. Laing
Kent State University

Although still in a formative stage of development, there is a growing body of literature documenting the interrelationships between family factors and health and illness in psychology (e.g., Turk & Kerns, 1985) and in medicine (e.g., Henao & Grose, 1985; Ramsey, 1989). In psychology, the disciplines of health psychology and pediatric psychology have begun to recognize and address such factors. In a similar manner, the development of family medicine as a recognized discipline is indicative of the growing interest and attention to family factors.

In this chapter, we provide a historical overview of the growth of family factors as an area of interest and its subsequent influence on the study of health and illness in an attempt to provide a common background for the chapters that follow. The chapter begins with a brief overview of health psychology. We have adopted a health psychology perspective in contrast with a behavioral medicine or pediatric psychological approach. Although there is a good deal of overlap between these disciplines, we felt that the health psychology model allows focus on the full range of contributions from psychology (in contrast with behavioral medicine) and allows attention to both adults and children (in contrast with a pediatric orientation). The focus of this volume is on physical health and illness, although mental health issues are also addressed as they relate to physical factors.

HEALTH PSYCHOLOGY

References to a partnership between medicine and psychology and a recognition of the influence of the mind on the body in understanding disease can be found in ancient literary documents from Babylonia and Greece (Gentry & Matarazzo, 1981; Matarazzo & Carmody, 1983). With the advent of physical medicine in the seventeenth century, however, a dualistic viewpoint developed in which the mind and body were believed to function separately and independently. This mind–body dualism was further strengthened in the nineteenth century by the discovery that microorganisms caused certain diseases. However, many diseases could not be explained on a strictly physiological basis, and in the early twentieth century the field of psychosomatic medicine emerged. Although psychosomatic medicine classified illness as arising from either psychological or physiological processes, it represented a return to a recognition of mind–body interaction in illness. More recently, empirical evidence has begun to accumulate that suggests that biological, psychological, and social factors contribute, in varying degrees, to all forms of health and illness. Thus a biopsychosocial model has replaced the traditional psychosomatic medicine model of illness, and a collaborative relationship between medicine and psychology has been reinstated (Engel, 1977; Gentry & Matarazzo, 1981).

Emergence of Health Psychology

Health psychology as a field emerged and rapidly expanded from the mid-1970s to the mid-1980s. Gentry (1984) identifies several trends during that time that probably contributed to the development and rapid expansion of health psychology. First, there was a general recognition that the traditional biomedical model failed to adequately explain health and illness. Second, behavioral science research was maturing, including the application of learning theories to disease etiology and illness behavior. Third, although the prevalence of life-threatening infectious diseases had declined greatly, life-threatening chronic illnesses that were clearly associated with life-style factors were becoming increasingly prevalent. Fourth, there was a general increase in concern with quality of life and prevention of illness. Finally, in part due to the continual treatment required by chronic illnesses, the cost of health care was increasing rapidly. Thus alternatives to the traditional health care system were being sought.

Within this climate, the American Psychological Association (APA) appointed the Task Force on Health Research in 1973 to "collect, organize, and disseminate information on the status of health behavior research" (APA, 1976, p. 270). On the basis of their review, the Task Force concluded, "Up to the present time, American psychologists have not been attracted in large numbers to the problems of health and illness as fruitful areas for both basic and applied research activity; nor have these psychologists perceived the potentials for their work in effecting improvements in health maintenance, illness prevention, and health care delivery" (APA, 1976, p. 271). The Task Force also developed a roster of psychologists who were interested in conducting health research, and in 1975 a group of these psychologists organized as a section, the Section on

Health Research, under the auspices of the Division of Psychologists in Public Service. The number of psychologists interested in this new area of specialization grew very rapidly. Thus separate division status within APA was sought, and in 1978 the Division of Health Psychology (Division 38) was established. A divisional journal, *Health Psychology,* was established a year later (Rodin & Stone, 1987).

Although the formation of Division 38 solidified the emergence of an organized field of health psychology, psychologists previously had been active in these areas. For example, the Division of Rehabilitation Psychology was established in 1958 to address research and practical issues in rehabilitative aspects of health psychology. The Society of Pediatric Psychology was established in 1968 to represent a professional and scientific subspecialty with health psychology based on the ages of patients served. Traditionally, both mental and physical health issues have been addressed by pediatric psychologists. The *Pediatric Psychology Newsletter,* established in 1969, became the *Journal of Pediatric Psychology* in 1976.

Psychologists have also played an active role in the formation of scientific and professional organizations outside of their own discipline. For example, in the late 1970s, psychologists were instrumental in the formation of the field of behavioral medicine (Robin & Stone, 1987), an interdisciplinary field concerned with the integration of behavioral and biomedical sciences relevant to health and illness (Schwartz & Weiss, 1978a, 1978b). Psychologists currently constitute one half to one third of the membership in the Society for Behavioral Medicine and the Academy of Behavioral Medicine Research (Robin & Stone, 1987). The professional organizations named above address all aspects of health and illness and thus illustrate the expansion of the psychologist's role as a health professional in contrast with only a mental health professional (Matarazzo & Carmody, 1983).

Definition and Scope of Health Psychology

The Division of Health Psychology adopted the following as a working definition:

> *Health psychology is the aggregate of the specific educational, scientific, and professional contributions of the discipline of psychology to the promotion and maintenance of health, the prevention and treatment of illness, the identification of etiologic and diagnostic correlates of health, illness, and related dysfunction, and the improvement of the health care system and health policy formation. (Matarazzo, 1980, p. 815)*

Health psychology draws on all traditional areas of psychology, including clinical, cognitive, social, personality, physiological, developmental, and industrial. In addition, all theoretical orientations within psychology are represented in health psychology, including systems, existential, behavioral, social learning, and psychodynamic perspectives. Finally, as in the discipline of psychology, a broad range of activities fall within the purview of health psychology, such as clinical practice, basic and applied research, health promotion and prevention, administration, health policy formation, and teaching and supervision. Thus the numerous subspecialties, theoretical orientations, and professional and scientific activities of the discipline of psychology are utilized to address health- and illness-related issues.

Content areas within health psychology include virtually every aspect of health and illness, ranging from biobehavioral pathways of physical illness to public health-risk reduction. More specifically, health psychology addresses health care delivery issues, such as health care systems design, provider–patient relationships, and stresses on, and of, health care professions. Health psychology also attends to patients, addressing such issues as adherence to treatment regimens, preparation for medical procedures, and psychological processes that are induced by and maintain physical illness. In addition, psychosocial factors such as stress, coping, and social support are considered as well as the influence of ethnicity, socioeconomic status, gender, and racial patterns in health and illness. Health psychology also incorporates efforts to keep individuals out of the health care system through health promotion and health habit modification. Finally, health psychology addresses these issues across the entire spectrum of physical illnesses, from migraine headaches to AIDS.

Health Psychology Within an Interdisciplinary Context

Much has been written about the suitability of psychologists, particularly clinical psychologists trained within a scientist-practitioner model, to make significant contributions to health and illness issues (e.g., Hartman, 1981; Matarazzo & Carmody, 1983). Matarazzo and Carmody (1983) suggest that clinical psychologists have expertise in experimental design, methodology, and quantitative analysis as well as knowledge and experience in such areas as human development, psychopathology, behavior change, motivation, and psychological assessment and intervention. However, contributions from experimental, physiological, and social psychology are also well recognized (Matarazzo & Carmody, 1983).

Given the broad scope of health psychology, no single discipline can incorporate training and experience in all relevant phenomena. Advances in health psychology are dependent on collaboration among professionals, not only within the discipline of psychology but also between psychology and other behavioral and biomedical disciplines. Moreover, for collaborative relationships among diversely trained professionals to be successful, the professionals involved must have a basic understanding of their counterpart disciplines' theories, concepts, and techniques relevant to the particular health and illness issues being addressed. To contribute to an understanding of health and illness, health psychologists need to collaborate with, and have an appreciation of the unique skills, perspectives, and approaches of, a wide variety of health-related professionals.

Health-relevant disciplines include, but are not limited to, medicine, nursing, nutrition, epidemiology, pharmacology, health education, sociology, and anthropology. Whether health psychology realizes its potential for making significant contributions to the health status of the nation is dependent on health psychologists having the requisite content knowledge and process skills to collaborate effectively with these other health-related disciplines (Weiss, 1987).

GROWING INTEREST IN THE FAMILY

Seminal work involving family issues has roots in sociology, social work, and psychiatry (Broderick & Schrader, 1981; Ransom, 1989). The earliest studies of families were undertaken within the discipline of sociology (e.g., Burgess, 1926; Cooley, 1902/1964), which drew attention to the interactive and reciprocal influence of social groups, including the family, on individual personality development. The centrality of the family's role in transmitting societal influences to the individual and the systemic nature of families were also recognized. Thus groundwork was laid for the future emphasis on the family (Ransom, 1989).

From the mid-1950s on, when family therapy began, interest in the family has burgeoned to its current status as a major influence in the mental health area. Divergent models of treatment have developed that share the assumption that the family system is of primary importance and is the appropriate unit of intervention and that emphasize circular patterns rather than linear causality. In a recent survey of practitioners, systems theory was described as one of the four dominant theoretical orientations used by respondents (Jensen, Bergin, & Greaves, 1990). It is fair to say that present-day emphases on family issues owe a great deal to developments in family therapy.

Family Systems Theory and Family Therapy

The origins of family systems theory and its application in family therapy are complex and diverse. Clinical observations regarding the relapse of successfully treated schizophrenics when they returned to their family environments (e.g., Haley, 1959) as well as empirically based observations of dysfunction in the families of schizophrenics (e.g., Lidz, Cornelison, Fleck, & Terry, 1957; Wynne, Ryckoff, Day, & Hirsch, 1958) led to an interest in the family, particularly communication styles, in the development and maintenance of schizophrenia and, later, other types of psychopathology. Research that pointed to the importance of the context in controlling behavior (Minuchin, 1974) also contributed to a growing interest in family factors.

Theoretical contributions of functionalism, general systems theory, and cybernetics to family systems theory have been discussed thoroughly by Nichols and Schwartz (1991). Although different family theorists have emphasized different components of these theories, there is general agreement on some basic tenets underlying family systems theories and the approaches to family therapy based on them.

First, it is generally recognized that the whole is more than the sum of its parts (von Bertalanffy, 1968). That is, the family system is more than just its individual members. The nature of the interactions between family members, the rules that govern these interactions, and repetitive patterns of interaction need to be considered (Nichols & Schwartz, 1991). Moreover, the structural organization within the family is an important aspect of the system (Minuchin, 1974). The system has an existence of its own and thus is the appropriate target of intervention.

Second, emphasis is placed on the contextual elements within the family or from larger systems (e.g., society) that have an influence on behavior shown by family members (Minuchin, 1974). Such contextual elements are often another target of intervention in family therapy.

Third, the importance of understanding the homeostatic mechanisms (Jackson, 1957), the adjustment of the family system to changing internal or environmental stress, is emphasized in many family therapies. In particular, the homeostatic function of the symptom shown by the identified patient in protecting the system has been an important focus in family therapy.

Fourth, the notion of circular causality (Bateson, 1968) is central in family therapy approaches. As opposed to traditional models based on linear causality, systemic perspectives emphasize the reciprocal and interactive pattern of behaviors that influence and are influenced by subsequent behaviors. The implications that ensue are of such significance that circular causality has been hailed as the essential component of a new epistemology (Hoffman, 1981).

Lastly, the importance of the family life cycle (Carter & McGoldrick, 1989), predictable stages in the development of the family, is another basic tenet of many family systems approaches.

Currently, numerous versions of family therapy exist and, to one extent or another, share the basic tenets described above. Levant (1980) suggests that models of family therapy can be distinguished from one another on the basis of the degree to which they emphasize (a) intergenerational factors (e.g., Bowenian and psychoanalytically based therapies), (b) current patterns of interaction that maintain the presenting problem (e.g., structural, strategic, and behavioral therapies), and (c) expression of affect within the therapy session (e.g., experiential and Gestalt therapies).

Nichols and Schwartz (1991) suggest that by the 1980s these divergent models had developed to a point at which evaluation and reappraisal were possible. Traditional family therapies were criticized for being too technique-oriented and pragmatic, thus losing sight of broader issues. Although criticized as antipragmatic (e.g., Coyne, 1982), a constructivist movement has developed within family therapy. The constructivist perspective, in contrast with the functionalism, pragmatism, and logical positivism characteristic of traditional family therapies, emphasizes the importance of focusing on the family's view of reality rather than imposing the therapist's theoretically determined reality on the family. There is a consequent shift in emphasis away from behavioral factors toward recognition of the importance of the meaning of events, symptoms, and so forth, among family members. The therapist's role is viewed as one of collaborator with the family, as opposed to the traditional directive, power-oriented figure who holds responsibility for change in family members. The models of White (White & Epston, 1990) and deShazer (1988) are the leading examples of the constructivist position. Although the long-term influence of the constructivist perspective on family therapy in general is not clear at this point, it represents the "cutting edge" of family therapy today (Nichols & Schwartz, 1991).

Family Therapy and Illness

Family theorists and therapists have directly addressed health and illness issues. Minuchin's work (Minuchin, 1974; Minuchin et al., 1975) with psychosomatic illness is often cited and has helped bridge the gap between family-oriented treatment of psychopathology and physical illness. Families who foster the development of psychosomatic illness were thought to be characterized by enmeshment, overprotectiveness, rigidity, lack of conflict resolution, and involvement of the sick child in parental conflict. Although the research has been questioned in recent years (e.g., Coyne & Anderson, 1988), its role in linking family therapy and physical illness cannot be disputed.

Whereas Minuchin's work identified characteristics of families at risk for the development of psychosomatic illness, Pratt (1976) identified characteristics of the "energized family," thought to be resistant to the development of physical illness. Such families are characterized by varied and frequent family interactions, established community ties, encouragement of autonomy, creative problem solving that uses family skills and objectives, and ability to adjust to role changes within the family. Thus flexibility (as opposed to rigidity) and independence (as opposed to enmeshment) appear to distinguish energized from psychosomatic families.

Another direct application of family therapy to physical illness has been developed and elaborated in the Chronic Illness project at the Ackerman Institute for Family Therapy (e.g., Penn, 1983; Walker, 1983). Application and adaptation of principles of family therapy to families with a chronically ill member has been the goal of this project, with particular emphasis on structural aspects of the family system.

Families and Psychology

Because psychologists were not predominant in the early stages of the development of family therapy, psychologists with interests in researching family issues or in doing family therapy were often viewed by their colleagues as being unscientific or at least overly influenced by less empirically oriented disciplines. Yet, interest in family matters grew and the ascendence of family concerns in psychology in general was given formal recognition with the formation of the Division of Family Psychology (Division 43) in 1984 and with the initiation of the *Journal of Family Psychology* in 1987 (Kaslow, 1987). Researchers and practitioners interested in family issues who previously were affiliated with nonpsychological organizations such as the American Association for Marriage and Family Therapy (AAMFT) found a home within the American Psychological Association. Division 43 has worked to establish criteria for training within the specialty area and to define and establish new settings, formats, and models for the provision of skills necessary for clinical work and research in the family area. It is clear that family considerations have gained significant status in psychology

Families and health psychology

The potential importance of family factors in health psychology is reflected in some of the major theories used by health psychologists. In particular, stress and coping models (e.g., Hobfoll, 1988; Lazarus & Folkman, 1984) can easily incorporate family factors in that family members may be viewed as sources of both stress and support affecting the individual. Stress and coping models have been expanded to include specific family variables (e.g., Wallander, Varni, Babani, Benis, & Wilcox, 1989; see Drotar, Chapter 12). Reiss (1981, 1982) has also identified characteristics of families who are resistant to the effects of stress, in particular the stress of illness in a family member (See Jacobs, Chapter 9). Moreover, the social ecological model (Bronfrenbrenner, 1979; see Kazak, Chapter 8) includes the family as an important component in a concentric model of environmental influences on a child. Thus it is not surprising that, within the area of health psychology, family factors have also recently come to the forefront.

Roberts and Wallander (1992) have collected articles that deal with family factors that were published in a special issue of the *Journal of Pediatric Psychology*. They note that within child health care a shift has occurred from an almost exclusive focus on the parents to an almost exclusive focus on the child. More recently, another shift toward recognition of the importance of the family context as a whole has stimulated a good deal of research.

In addition, major advocacy groups in health care issues for children, such as the Association for the Care of Children's Health (ACCH; Shelton, Jeppson, & Johnson, 1987) and the Select Panel for the Promotion of Childrens' Health (Harris, 1981), have emphasized the importance of family factors in the health of children (Roberts & Wallander, 1992).

In a similar vein, in the health psychology area, Drotar et al. (1989) have called for greater emphasis on "child health psychology." Family influences on the health of children and adolescents such as family mediation of health behavior and outcomes, the impact of changes in family structure on health, the impact of child illness and handicap on the family, and the impact of family maltreatment were identified as areas of priority for research and clinical intervention.

Family systems theory influences on health psychology

Within health psychology, family systems considerations have also begun to gain recognition. Turk and Kerns (1985) have made pioneering efforts in calling attention to family systems issues in the area of behavioral medicine. In this edited volume, chapters exploring family interfaces with health issues across the life span are presented. Kerns and Turk (1985) highlight the importance of interdisciplinary examination of this area and the need for an empirically test-able, integrative systems model to extend research on families and health. They note that empirical knowledge based on family systems theory has been quite limited. Studies based on biopsychosocial models (e.g., Engel, 1977), which incorporate both biological and psychosocial factors, have been descriptive rather than explanatory in terms of transactional influences between family and health variables.

In pediatric psychology, Fiese and Samaroff (1989) provided a theoretical framework for understanding the family context. On the basis of a transactional model, these authors suggest that a given outcome is a result of the interplay between the child and the environment over time. Thus the child's behavior has an influence on, and is influenced by, parental and other environmental agents. Identification of family paradigms, stories, and rituals fosters an understanding of the way in which the family regulates itself. Interventions based on this transactional model are also discussed.

Families and Medicine

With the establishment of family practice as a specialty area in 1969, the impor-tance of family issues in medicine seemed to have been given recognition. However, Ransom and Vandervoort (1973) suggest that a distinction should be drawn between family practice and family medicine. Family practice entails delivery of primary care involving integration and synthesis of varied areas of medicine and comprehensive care provided to all age groups by a physician. In contrast, family medicine incorporates the view that the family can be considered the unit of treatment, with an emphasis on relational aspects of family members in the etiology and maintenance of disease. Ecological considerations involving individual family members, the family system, and the family's relation to other environmental influences are also seen as important.

Ransom (1985) reports on early projects investigating family factors and health and traces the evolution of family considerations within medicine. The Peckham Experiment (Pearse & Crocker, 1943) involved the development of a neighborhood center providing social, recreational, and educational resources to allow study of health factors in families. This project viewed the family as the unit of study and first delineated ideas of emergent quality—the notions that the family functions as more than the sum of its individual members, that it has a life cycle of its own, and that it has a hierarchical organization within it. Another early study of family functioning and health, the *Patient's Have Families Project* (Richardson, 1945), also delineated concepts akin to current family therapy concepts such as family homeostasis, enmeshment and disengagement, and triangulation (Ransom, 1985). In spite of these early attempts at identifying family systems concepts, the focus on the individual as the unit of treatment has prevailed, even with the development of the family practice speciality. Ransom (1985) indicates that the importance of family background is the only way in which family issues play a role in family practice.

More recently, family systems issues have been incorporated directly into medical practice. Ramsey (1989) presents a very comprehensive volume covering numerous aspects of family systems in medicine and suggests that the investigation of the interaction of the family system with the nervous, endocrine, and immune systems in producing or altering the course of illness is at the core of "the science of family medicine." The publication of *Family Medicine: The Medical Life History of Families* (Huygen, 1982) and *Family Therapy and Family Medicine: Towards the Primary Care of Families* (Doherty & Baird, 1983) and the establishment of the journal, *Family Systems Medicine* in 1983 are further indications of the growing emphasis on family systems issues in the practice of medicine (Ransom, 1985). In terms of treatment, the discipline of family systems medicine (see Campbell, McDaniel, & Seaburn, Chapter 13) uses the expertise of both medical and family practitioners in the treatment of illness.

As can be seen in the foregoing discussion, the roots of present-day interest in family health issues are varied and diverse. To a certain extent, these literatures have evolved independently of one another. It is clear that an integrative approach could do much to facilitate future developments in this area of study.

THE PURPOSE OF THIS VOLUME

The chapters in this volume are based on presentations made at the third Kent Psychology Forum held in April 1991. In organizing this conference and volume, a course-of-illness format was used to ensure coverage of the full range of possibilities in examining family influences on health and illness. Pre-illness issues are addressed in Section I (Families and Prevention) of this volume to provide coverage of family influences on health cognitions (Gochman, Chapter 3) and prevention of physical and mental health problems (Roberts & McElreath, Chapter 4). Koocher and MacDonald (Chapter 5) discuss prevention issues associated with the families of children with life-threatening or terminal illness.

Section II (Families and Illness) examines family and marital factors as they relate to chronic illness. A social ecological approach to family research in chronic pediatric illness (Kazak, Chapter 7) and a family systems view of chronic illness (Jacobs, Chapter 8) are presented. Marital issues in coping with chronic illness (Coyne & Fiske, Chapter 9) and the relationship between marital conflict/divorce and illness (Jones, Chapter 10) are also addressed.

Family issues in treatment are discussed in Section III (Families and Intervention). Expansions from the existing pediatric psychological literature to treatment in the family context are discussed by Drotar (Chapter 12). Campbell, McDaniel, and Seaburn (Chapter 13) discuss the development and practice of family systems medicine. Lastly, Walker (Chapter 14) describes and discusses the uses of family therapy with families of patients with AIDS.

In selecting these participants, an attempt was made to have an interdisciplinary mix to ensure that divergent approaches were represented and to be responsive to Kerns and Turk's (1985) conclusion that such a framework is important. Thus participants had backgrounds in the areas of health and pediatric psychology, social work, family medicine, and nursing. Both traditional and family systems viewpoints are represented among participants; most contributors are both researchers and practitioners, and several are practicing family therapists. Thus the selection of participants and topic areas also ensured coverage of both research and applied issues in this volume.

One purpose of this volume is to provide a current review of research and applied topics from a variety of perspectives in the area of families and health. More important, the conference setting, which used a sequestered format and limited participation to invited contributors and a small number of graduate students and local experts, allowed participants to interact with one another and discuss individual presentations. Thus a unique opportunity for dialogue among professionals with divergent perspectives was possible. On the final day of the conference, general discussion designed to integrate the material presented and identify directions for future work provided ideas that truly distinguish this volume from others dealing with families and health and illness. Participants were directed to consider future developments in three areas: theoretical considerations, research strategies and directions, and intervention. In so doing, it was expected that participants could help to define and delineate issues relevant to the definition of a new subspeciality, family health psychology. This material is presented in Chapter 15 of this volume.

REFERENCES

American Psychological Association Task Force on Health Research. (1976). Contributions of psychology to health research. *American Psychologist, 31*, 263-274.

Bateson, G. (1968). *Mind and nature.* New York: E.F. Dutton.

Broderick, C. B., & Schrader, S. S. (1981). The history of marriage and family therapy. In A. S. Gurman & D. P. Kniskern (Eds.), *Handbook of family therapy* (pp. 5-35). New York: Brunner/Mazel.

Bronfrenbrenner, U. (1979). *The ecology of human development.* Cambridge, MA: Harvard University Press.

Burgess, E. W. (1926). The family as a unity of interacting personalities. *Family, 7*, 3-9.

Carter, E., & McGoldrick, M. (Eds.). (1989). *The changing family lifecycle: A framework for family therapy* (2nd ed.) Needham Heights, MA: Allyn & Bacon.

Cooley, C. H. (1964). *Human nature and the social order.* New York: Schoken Books. (Original work published in 1902).

Coyne, J. (1982). A brief introduction to epistobabble. *Family Therapy Networker, 6*, 27-28.

Coyne, J., & Anderson, B. J. (1988). "Psychosomatic family" reconsidered: Diabetes in context. *Journal of Marital and Family Therapy, 14*, 113-123.

deShazer, S. (1988). *Clues: Investigating solutions in brief therapy.* New York: Norton.

Drotar, D., Johnson, S. B., Iannotti, R., Krasnegor, N., Matthews, K. A., Melamed, B. G., Millstein, S., Peterson, R. A., Popiel, D., & Routh, D. K. (1989). Child health psychology. *Health Psychology, 8*, 781-784.

Engel, G. L. (1977). The need for a new medical model: A challenge for biomedicine. *Science, 196*, 129-136.

Fiese, B. H., & Samaroff, A. J. (1989). Family context in pediatric psychology: A transactional perspective. *Journal of Pediatric Psychology, 14*, 293-314.

Gentry, W. D. (Ed.). (1984). *Handbook of behavioral medicine.* New York: Guilford.

Gentry, W. D., & Matarazzo, J. D. (1981). Medical psychology: Three decades of growth and development. In C. K. Prokop & L. A. Bradley (Eds.), *Medical psychology: Contributions to behavioral medicine* (pp. 5-15). New York: Academic Press.

Haley, J. (1959). The family of the schizophrenic. *American Journal of Nervous and Mental Diseases, 129*, 357-374.

Harris, P. R. (1981). *Better health for our children: A national strategy.* Washington, DC: U.S. Government Printing Office.

Hartman, L. M. (1981). Clinical psychology: Emergent trends and future applications. *Journal of Clinical Psychology, 37,* 439–445.

Henao S., & Grose N. P. (Eds.). (1985). *Principles of family systems in family medicine.* New York: Brunner/Mazel.

Hobfoll, S. E. (1988). *The ecology of stress.* Washington, DC: Hemisphere.

Hoffman, L. (1981). *Foundations of family therapy.* New York: Basic Books.

Huygen, F. J. A. (1982). *Family medicine: The medical life history of families.* New York: Brunner/Mazel.

Jackson, D. (1957). The question of family homeostasis. *Psychiatric Quarterly Supplement, 3,* 79–90.

Jensen, J. P., Bergin, A. P., & Greaves, D. W. (1990). The meaning of eclecticism: New survey and analysis of components. *Professional Psychology: Research and Practice, 21,* 124–130.

Kaslow, F. W. (1987). Trends in family psychology. *Journal of Family Psychology, 1,* 77–90.

Kerns, R. D., & Turk, D. C. (1985). Behavioral medicine and the family: Historical perspectives and future directions. In D. C. Turk & R. D. Kerns (Eds.), *Health, illness, and families: A life-span perspective* (pp. 338–353). New York: Wiley-Interscience.

Lazarus, R. S., & Folkman, S. (1984). *Stress, appraisal, and coping.* New York: Springer.

Levant, R. F. (1980). A classification of the field of family therapy: A review of prior attempts and a new paradigmatic model. *American Journal of Family Therapy, 8,* 4–16.

Lidz, T., Cornelison, A., Fleck, S., & Terry, D. (1957). Intrafamilial environment of the schizophrenic patient: II. Marital schism and marital skew. *American Journal of Psychiatry, 114,* 241–248.

Matarazzo, J. D. (1980). Behavioral health and behavioral medicine: Frontiers for a new health psychology. *American Psychologist, 35,* 807–817.

Matarazzo, J. D., & Carmody, T. P. (1983). Health psychology. In M. Hersen, A. E. Kazdin, & A. S. Bellack (Eds.), *The clinical psychology handbook* (pp. 657–682). New York: Pergamon.

Minuchin, S. (1974). *Families and family therapy.* Cambridge, MA: Harvard University Press.

Minuchin, S., Baker, L., Roseman, B., Liebman, T., Milman, L., & Todd, T. (1975). A conceptual model of psychosomatic illness in children. *Archives of General Psychiatry, 32,* 1031–1038.

Nichols, M. P., & Schwartz, R. C. (1991). *Family therapy: Concepts and methods* (2nd ed.). Needham Heights, MA: Allyn & Bacon.

Pearse, I. H., & Crocker, L. (1943). *The Peckham Experiment: A study of the living structure of society.* London: Allen & Unwin.

Penn, P. (1983). Coalitions and binding interactions in families with chronic illness. *Family Systems Medicine, 1,* 16–25.

Pratt, L. (1976). *Family structure and effective health behavior: The energized family*. Boston: Houghton-Mifflin.

Ramsey, C. N. (1989). *Family systems in medicine*. New York: Guilford.

Ransom, D. C. (1985). The evolution from an individual to a family approach. In S. Henao & N. P. Grose (Eds.), *Principles of family systems in family medicine* (pp. 5–23). New York: Brunner/Mazel.

Ransom, D. C. (1989). Development of family therapy and family theory. In C. N. Ramsey (Ed.), *Family systems in medicine*. New York: Guilford.

Ransom, S. C., & Vandervoort, H. E. (1973). The development of family medicine: Problematic trends. *Journal of the American Medical Association, 225*, 1098–1102.

Reiss, D. (1981). *The family's construction of reality*. Cambridge, MA: Harvard University Press.

Reiss, D. (1982). The working family: A researcher's view of health in the household. *American Journal of Psychiatry, 139*, 1412–1420.

Richardson, H. B. (1945). *Patients have families*. New York: Commonwealth Fund.

Roberts, M. C., & Wallander, J. L. (1992). Family issues in pediatric psychology: An overview. In M. C. Roberts & J. L. Wallander (Eds.), *Family issues in pediatric psychology* (pp. 1–24). New York: Earlbaum.

Rodin, G., & Stone, G. (1987). Historical highlights in the emergence of the field. In G. C. Stone, S. M. Weiss, J. D. Matarazzo, N. E. Miller, J. Rodin, C. D. Belar, M. J. Follick, & J. E. Singer (Eds.), *Health psychology: A discipline and a profession* (pp. 15–26). Chicago: University of Chicago Press.

Schwartz, G. E., & Weiss, S. M. (1978a). Behavioral medicine revisited: An amended definition. *Journal of Behavioral Medicine, 1*, 249–251.

Schwartz, G. E., & Weiss, S. M. (1978b). Yale Conference on Behavioral Medicine: A proposed definition and statement of goals. *Journal of Behavioral Medicine, 1*, 3–12.

Shelton, T., Jeppson, E., & Johnson, B. (1987). *Family centered care for children with special health care needs: An overview*. Washington, DC: Association for the Care of Children's Health.

Turk, D. C., & Kerns, R. D. (Eds.) (1985). *Health, illness, and families: A life-span perspective*. New York: Wiley-Interscience.

von Bertalanffy, L. (1968). *General systems theory*. New York: George Braziller.

Walker, G. (1983). The pact: Caretaker-parent/ill child coalition in families with chronic illness. *Family Systems Medicine, 1*, 6–29.

Wallander, J. C., Varni, J. W., Babani, L., Benis, N. T., & Wilcox, K. T. (1989). Family resources as resistance factors for psychological maladjustment in chronically ill and handicapped children. *Journal of Pediatric Psychology, 14*, 157–173.

Weiss, S. M. (1987). Health psychology and other health professions. In G. C. Stone, S. M. Weiss, J. D. Matarazzo, N. E. Miller, J. Rodin, C. D. Belar, M. J. Follick, & J. E. Singer (Eds.), *Health psychology: A discipline and a profession* (pp. 61–74). Chicago: University of Chicago Press.

White, M., & Epston, D. (1990). *Narrative means to therapeutic ends.* New York: Norton.

Wynne, L. C., Ryckoff, I., Day, J., & Hirsch, S. I. (1958). Pseudomutuality in the family relationships of schizophrenics. *Psychiatry, 21,* 205–220.

I

FAMILIES AND PREVENTION

2

OVERVIEW

Jennifer A. Druley
Kathleen A. Moore
Kent State University

On the surface, prevention of illness looks easy. If behavioral risk factors associated with an illness are known, one simply has to convince people to stop engaging in the faulty practices and the likelihood of developing the illness will be reduced significantly. However, this assumes that the antecedents are identifiable and that the factors operative in the persuasion process are obvious. Even if you can identify antecedents and convince people of the value of preventive practices, behavioral change is not ensured. Moreover, even if individuals are convinced to change their immediate behavior, long-term change is not guaranteed.

On the surface, using the family as a unit of analysis seems easy. One simply studies the individual members, then aggregates the findings, producing a more complete, richer data set. Yet, the family is a complicated, dynamic system. Each individual interacts with other members and thus affects and is affected by them. Questions concerning conceptualization of the family abound. It is clear, that studying familial processes is actually far from easy.

Given the inherent difficulties involved in both types of research, why would anyone propose to study them together simultaneously? The three chapters in this section validate this fusion as well as confirm its necessity.

The following three chapters examine different facets of illness prevention. The three chapters differ from most other discussions of prevention in that they place prevention in the specific context of the family. Both the role of cognitions (see Gochman, Chapter 3) and behaviors (see Roberts & McElreath, Chapter 4) in prevention are examined. Basic research issues are presented in Chapter 3 on health cognitions and in Chapter 4 on the prevention of physical and mental health problems. Applied issues are addressed in Chapter 5 on families coping with life-threatening illness. The authors highlight major empirical findings and conceptual issues, present problems with existing research, and set agendas for future study.

In Chapter 3, Gochman discusses family health cognitions or what he terms, "the great unknown." Gochman's sociological perspective of the family is found in the cross-cultural flavor of his presentation. Unlike most Eurocentric perspectives taken in the traditional literature, findings from the United States, Africa, Australia, and Saudi Arabia are presented.

Gochman presents what he calls a pastiche of studies that explore health cognitions in families. First, the impact of cognitions on the use of health services, personal health actions, and health policies is examined. He concludes that there is little evidence that cognitions have an impact on these health-related behaviors. Next, he presents research on intergenerational links, including parent–child cognitions and characteristics. Evidence in regard to intergenerational links is also weak, although family intactness is one characteristic that seems to influence children's health cognitions.

Gochman suggests that although he would have preferred to present a mosaic of research, rather than a pastiche, this was not possible given the lack of depth, coherence, and organization found in this body of research. He sets an agenda for future research in this area, including a need for understanding the development of health cognitions and an improved conceptualization of the family. He cautions researchers against emphasizing the role of cognitions over behavioral determinants and against emphasizing family influences over other social variables (e.g., socioeconomic status). He contends that more theory-based research is needed and presents some promising models.

In Chapter 4 in this section, Roberts and McElreath discuss research on the prevention of physical and mental health problems. Although Gochman focuses primarily on family health cognitions, Roberts and McElreath focus more on family illness-preventive behaviors. They review family-based (namely, parent–child) research on preventing medical anxiety and pain, injuries, and obesity. Issues such as whether or not and when and how families should be involved in prevention are addressed. They critique past prevention research on several grounds, including the individualistic focus and the inattention to developmental influences.

In a similar manner to Gochman, they note that improved conceptualizations of the family are needed. Just as Gochman asserts that we need to go beyond demographics or family size and evaluating family factors, Roberts and McElreath argue that we need to go beyond the use of families simply as tools of convenience. We need to examine the complex roles that families may play in preventive behavior. In addition to extending our notions of the family, they call for better conceptualizations of prevention.

Roberts and McElreath also caution that health professionals should not assume or dictate too much (i.e., that they know what is best for all families; e.g., brush your teeth, wear your seat belt, and eat properly), especially because many evaluations of prevention interventions are either nonexistent or inadequate. Both Chapters 3 and 4 stress the potentially important role of the family in health research, yet warn against becoming overly family-focused. Roberts and McElreath suggest that the family is just one of many appropriate targets and vehicles for prevention programs.

Whereas Gochman and Roberts and McElreath examine factors predicting preventive health behavior (preventing illness or injury from developing), Chapter 5 focuses on preventing unsuccessful psychological adaptation after life-threatening or terminal illness has occurred. Many of the findings and notions in Chapters 3 and 4 are illustrated or supported in Chapter 5. Koocher and MacDonald not only recommend a family approach to clinical care but also deem it necessary for optimal adaptation.

Whereas Chapters 3, 4, and 5 all stress the importance of considering developmental factors in family health psychological research, Koocher and MacDonald's Chapter 5 contains the most extensive discussion. Children's developmental tasks, the development of cognitions (especially children's conceptions of death), and the developmental life cycle of the family are discussed.

Koocher and MacDonald also emphasize the need to consider the family environment in providing psychological care. Clinicians should appraise communication patterns, cohesion and support, and issues of control to ensure a comprehensive assessment and intervention. The authors also discuss issues relevant to the treatment of a terminally ill child in the home and stress the necessity of continued follow-up or after-care following the death of the child.

A recurrent theme in these chapters is that researchers should consider influences on the entire family, not just parent–child influences. This point is especially salient in Chapter 5, as Koocher and MacDonald note how the death of a child is troubling for the entire family, including the often neglected siblings. The siblings may not be able to turn to the parents for support because the parents are consumed by their own grief reactions.

Gochman's notion of cognitive mediation, which refers to the way in which cognitions of one family member influence another's, is illustrated in Koocher and MacDonald's discussion of children's conceptions of their illness and its potential consequences. They note how children often are not afraid of death until they learn (through parental cognitions, affect, or behaviors) that they should be feeling fear. A similar point is made by Roberts and McElreath, who note that parental anxiety is often associated with the child's anxiety levels.

In summary, all three chapters raise critical issues and present challenges to future studies involving family prevention. After completing this section of the book, the reader will be convinced not only of the benefits of using the family as a unit of analysis but also of its obvious necessity. Existing literature on family factors and prevention is at an early stage of development, and conclusive findings are not yet possible. The authors of these chapters have provided a greater understanding of what needs to be done, or at least considered, in conducting future research and in designing preventive interventions.

3

HEALTH COGNITIONS
IN FAMILIES

David S. Gochman
University of Louisville, Kentucky

THE DOMAIN OF HEALTH COGNITIONS

Cognition denotes "those personal thought processes that serve as frames of reference for organizing and evaluating experiences. Beliefs, expectations, perceptions, values, motives, and attitudes all provide the person with ways of filtering, interpreting, understanding, and predicting events" (Gochman, 1988c, p. 21). *Health cognitions* refers to beliefs, expectations, perceptions, values, motives, and attitudes that provide frames of reference for organizing and evaluating health, regardless of whether those cognitions have demonstrable empirical linkages with health status and regardless of whether they are objectively valid.

The domain of this chapter, health cognitions in families, denotes those cognitions that are related to health events that have relevance for an individual's family. It includes such topics as beliefs about illnesses of a family member, perceptions related to health procedures involving a family member, and behavioral expectations for a family or its members in relation to maintaining health and avoiding illness. To maintain a focus on the family, this chapter does not include discussions of cognitions in children and adolescents for which there is no family referent, or in cohorts of persons identified as parents, or mothers, for example, but with no reference to family.

The chapter begins with a review of what is currently known about health cognitions of family members and continues with what is known about intergenerational linkages. It concludes with an evaluation of current knowledge and an agenda for future research, including a proposal for an alternative way of thinking about such research.

HEALTH COGNITIONS OF FAMILY MEMBERS

Discussion and evaluation of early work on health cognitions of family members are available (e.g., Baranowski & Nader, 1985; Gochman, 1985, 1988a). More recent studies can be organized around beliefs about conditions and treatment (e.g., beliefs about the causes of cancer or asthma), role dimensions (e.g., a mother's involvement in work activity), and the impact of cognitions on other behaviors (e.g., parents' illness beliefs and use of immunizations).

Beliefs About Conditions and Interventions

Cognitions related to conditions and treatment include general beliefs related to health and illness as well as beliefs about specific conditions. The specific conditions discussed are cancer, asthma, and diarrhea. The interventions are oral rehydration therapy (ORT; discussed along with diarrhea) and immunizations.

Beliefs about health and illness

The illness of a hospitalized child generates parental perceptions of uncertainty. These perceptions contain ambiguity, lack of clarity, lack of information, and unpredictability (Mishel, 1983). These perceptions emerge from the novelty and complexity of medical technology, inadequate communication from physicians and nurses, and unknown prognoses. Parents who judged their child to be more seriously ill were observed to have higher levels of perceived uncertainty than those who judged their child to be less seriously ill (Mishel, 1983).

Complementing this report of a relatively complex conceptual structure is a simple narrative of how Zulu mothers define their children's health (Craig & Albino, 1982). Interview data revealed that their criteria for health were eating and playing behaviors: A sick baby is one who does not eat or play.

Cancer. Parents of children with acute lymphoblastic leukemia were found to have many theories of the cause of the disease. For example, interview data from an Australian sample revealed that more than half believed that it was environmentally determined; other parents believed that a previous infection caused it (McWhirter & Kirk, 1986).

In Saudi Arabia, where cancer is perceived as a "sly disease," commonly thought to be fatal and considered to be a taboo subject, most parents of children with cancer had an adequate, "biomedically valid" understanding about their child's cancer (Bahakim, 1987). However, they also believed that the future (i.e., prognosis) was in the "hands of Allah" and thus took few initiatives in finding out more about treatment alternatives. From these findings, Bahakim (1987) urges health professionals providing care for this population to take initiatives themselves in suggesting treatment procedures to parents.

Asthma. Having a child with an asthmatic condition does not necessarily have any appreciable impact on parental health beliefs. The parents of asthmatic children in an Australian sample differed from controls only in having higher levels of belief in an allergic etiology for the condition (Spykerboer, Donnelly, & Thong, 1986). They also had less negative, less pessimistic views of asthma (Donnelly, Donnelly, & Thong, 1987). The two groups of parents did not differ on other variables, and two thirds of both groups had surprisingly high levels of knowledge about asthma.

Diarrhea and oral rehydration therapy. High morbidity and mortality rates from diarrhea in developing countries have stimulated efforts to understand parental beliefs about this condition in the hopes of increasing acceptance of therapies and thus of decreasing the toll from diarrhea. A number of these studies has focused on ORT. Interviews with a random sample of Haitian mothers showed that, despite a diversity of beliefs about diarrhea, its causes, etiology, and treatment, more than two thirds of the respondents were knowledgeable about the therapy, and these tended to be more often urban than rural (Coreil & Genece, 1988). Although knowledge of ORT was not directly related to whether or not it was used, it was related to using it in the recommended way as well as to delay in starting the therapy: Mothers who were knowledgeable about ORT knew enough to wait until sufficient water loss had occurred before they initiated ORT. The interviews further revealed that folk beliefs about diarrhea may be less potent than had been thought, and do not uniformly dictate use or nonuse of ORT.

Folk beliefs often allow for contradictions and inconsistencies. Mothers in Swaziland, for instance, who were patients of traditional healers generally shared the traditional healers' beliefs that diarrhea is caused by sorcery or ancestral displeasure (Green, 1985). A minority of the mothers, however, would nevertheless take a child to a clinic first, and then to the traditional healer if the clinic treatment was ineffective. Mothers responding to a survey in Ethiopia held similar supernatural beliefs. Many of them believed diarrhea was caused by the "will of God" or sorcery (Sircar & Dagnow, 1988). Despite such beliefs, more than two thirds of these mothers used modern medical care and ORT. In contrast, mothers in rural Pakistan revealed in interviews that they believed diarrhea was a natural condition not requiring treatment (Mull & Mull, 1988).

Immunizations. Cognitions related to immunizations are a critical area for study because inappropriately low levels of children's immunizations exist in both developed and developing countries. For example, interviews in Gazankulu, South Africa, showed that most mothers consider measles to be natural and "essential for the normal development of their children" (Ijsselmuiden, 1983, p. 361). These mothers seek the injection primarily because they believe that it hastens the rash, the early appearance of which they believe is related to a better outcome. They apparently favor vaccination even though they do not understand it and do not perceive it in terms of prevention. Parental beliefs about the efficacy of immunizations were also found to be unrelated to immunization of children of Philippine villagers (Friede, Waternaux, Guyer, DeJesus, & Filipp, 1985). Instead, parents who were more active in the communal life of their villages were more likely to have their children immunized. The importance of valid cognitions as determinants of health actions is thus open to question.

Paradoxically, some of the more negative assessments of immunizations are found in developed countries. Many mothers, in a random sample on the outskirts of Milan, believed that a child must get measles and pertussis as part of their natural development (Profeta, Lecchi, DeDonato, & Fraizzoli, 1989). Complementing this, over a quarter of a random sample of Irish parents would not have their children vaccinated against measles, a number of them believing that the natural illness was better than the vaccine (Sze-Tho & Gill, 1982). These observations suggest the need for health professionals to know more about what a target population actually perceives or believes rather than simply making assumptions about them. Such knowledge may lead toward increasing acceptance of these procedures.

Parental Role Dimensions

Role dimensions related to health cognitions in families embrace both the broader and more traditional aspects of parental roles, such as the work role of the mother, and the newer role conceptions, such as the role of parents as health educators. There are few studies reported in this area, but these seem more likely to be derived from conceptual frameworks than is true of studies in other areas.

Role dimensions relevant to maternal beliefs about the quality of health services and to their perceptions of a child's illness and needs for treatment were examined in a field study interviewing single, working Canadian mothers (Semchuk & Eakin, 1989). Concepts such as role conflict—between the roles of "good mother" (nurturing responsibilities) and "good worker" (work responsibilities)—and role flexibility (ability to alter schedules to meet emergencies) were found to be related to health cognitions. Mothers who experienced greater conflict between these roles tended to perceive their children's illnesses as more stressful than mothers who experienced less conflict. Those with little role flexibility made use of services they perceived as less trusted, such as hospital emergency rooms. Those with greater role flexibility used services that were more trusted, such as family physicians and pediatricians. Maternal working conditions can thus be seen to be related to whether a child's condition is perceived as a crisis and to what type of care will be sought.

An injury-belief model has also been developed, focusing on variables such as a child's injury history, how much parents worried about injuries, their expectations that the child would be injured, and their beliefs that injuries were preventable. Parents' knowledge about safety skills, their beliefs in their own competence to teach these skills, their confidence in the efficacy of efforts to teach these skills, and their beliefs that teaching safety skills can prevent injury were found to be effective predictors of the degree of parental teaching about injury prevention (Peterson, Farmer, & Kashani, 1990).

Impact of Cognitions

The impact of, or relationship between, parental cognitions and other family characteristics can be considered in terms of use of services, personal health actions, and health policies. Much of the work in this area is derived from the health-belief model and models of locus of control. These are two major conceptual frameworks for predicting health actions from health cognitions. Indeed, the injury-belief model is itself derived from the health-belief model. The health-belief model emphasizes the role of a cluster of cognitions: (a) perceptions of vulnerability to health problems, (b) perceptions of the severity or seriousness of those problems, (c) perceptions of the efficacy of actions taken to prevent or control these problems, and (d) perceptions of barriers and costs in taking such actions. These perceptions are used to predict a variety of preventive, illness, and sick-role behaviors such as getting routine medical checkups and acceptance of medical regimens (e.g., Kirscht, 1988).

Locus of control models emphasize how people perceive themselves as being in control over events in their lives (internal locus of control) as opposed to perceiving that things that happen to them are capricious or subject to control by others (external locus of control). By itself, the locus of control concept has been observed less consistently in health activities (e.g., Lau, 1988) than has the health-belief model.

Use of services

High agreement was observed between parental and physician's perceptions of levels of urgency in relation to use of pediatric emergency services by a representative cross section of patients admitted to the Emergency Department at Minneapolis Children's Medical Center (Braunstein, Abanobi, & Goldhagen, 1987). Yet, other data obtained in the self-administered questionnaire and structured interviews of this study indicated that there was also agreement that most visits to such services were not urgent. Use of the emergency service was apparently not determined by a parental perception of pediatric medical emergency.

However, parental beliefs in the efficacy of therapy for otitis media (middle ear infection) and their general health motivation were related to compliance in appointment keeping for their children with otitis media in a walk-in clinic of Children's Hospital in Philadelphia (Casey, Rosen, Glowasky, & Ludwig, 1985). Furthermore, a sample of mothers of infants from both low- and middle-income families demonstrated that mothers who believed in their own control over their children's health were more likely to take their children for timely well-baby examinations and to have their children immunized (Tinsley & Holtgrave, 1989). This study also showed that degrees of belief in chance or powerful others did not predict these examination and immunization outcomes. Somewhat in contrast, whereas mothers' perceptions of their children's health status predicted use of a prepaid pediatric service, other maternal cognitions such as health locus of control, attitudes toward health providers, and satisfaction with pediatric care bore no relationship to use of the service (Horwitz, Morgenstern, & Berkman, 1988).

In a study of health-belief model variables in a high-risk population, mothers' health cognitions such as their beliefs in their children's susceptibility to health problems, in the severity of those problems, and in the benefits and effectiveness of well-baby services did not predict use of well-baby services as such. These factors did, however, predict having children immunized (Kviz, Dawkins, & Ervin, 1985). Beliefs in the efficacy of the immunizations were found to be the most important predictors.

A survey of Iowa parents' attitudes toward dental disease in preschool children revealed that 89% did not think that preschoolers would have dental problems and thus did not see the need for preschool dental care (Walker, Beck, & Jakobsen, 1984). Finally, observations of a sample of mothers in Scotland showed the existence of skeptical beliefs concerning proprietary medicines, together with varied attitudes about the role of pharmacists. These cognitions often led to the use of the pharmacist as an alternative to the physician, or as a first step toward later physician use in primary health care for children with minor complaints (Cunningham-Burley & MacLean, 1987).

Although cultural factors are implicit in some of the preceding discussions of cognitions about diarrhea, cancer, and immunizations in developing countries, the issue of cultural differences was not addressed directly. Few studies do so. In a study that deals explicitly with cultural differences as such, Canadian families from English backgrounds were found to emphasize "normalization" of a child with a disability (i.e., they preferred that the child not stand out as being different). They were thus more likely to accept advice from health professionals that encouraged rehabilitation. In contrast, Canadian families from Chinese backgrounds apparently accepted the nonnormality on its own terms, and emphasized the child's contentment or happiness, thus risking a clash with health professionals who wanted to "push" the disabled child and did not want to accept its differences. These families were less inclined to perceive the benefits of rehabilitation (Anderson & Chung, 1982).

Personal health actions

A survey of a random sample of Maryland parents with children under 5 years of age found that the best predictors of intention to use car safety seats were parental beliefs about the children's comfort and resistance and wasting time (Gielen, Eriksen, Daltroy, & Rost, 1984). Use of child restraints in automobiles was found to be linked to adult beliefs about their relative benefits and costs, in a questionnaire survey of occupants of motor vehicles in Australia (Webb, Sanson-Fisher, & Bowman, 1988). Parents who used a restraint were more likely to believe that they could afford one, that restraints were a safety factor and could prevent injuries, and were less likely to believe that they were a nuisance or bother. Parents of unrestrained children were more likely to believe that injuries could be prevented if the children were carried on their laps.

Parental beliefs about fluoride tablets were related to their use in a sample of Swedish preschool children (Widenheim, 1982). In cases in which parents believed that swallowing the tablets was dangerous, their children were not likely to take them. Overall, parents weigh the benefits that health educators emphasize but also consider costs that are based both on personal experience and untrue assumptions.

Health policy

About 90% of mothers surveyed in New Zealand held strong positive attitudes about legislating the use of car seat restraints and mandating pool fencing. Yet, fewer than half believed in legislating fluoridation (Fergusson, Horwood, & Shannon, 1983). One reason for this paradox is that the community surveyed had strong anti-fluoridation sentiments.

In a study with more experimental manipulation than most of those reported in this chapter, a socially deprived sample of mothers of nursery school children in Scotland were asked about attitudes toward a hypothetical vaccine as well as their attitudes toward tooth loss and preventive care (Kay & Blinkhorn, 1989). Levels of the vaccine's effectiveness and safety were systematically varied throughout the sample. Variation in the vaccine's risk was found to have a greater impact on its acceptability than was variation on the degree of protection it afforded. Moreover, mothers had more positive attitudes toward a vaccine than toward fluoridation, suggesting that parents want to have a role in determining their children's own health future. The data also reveal a skepticism about biomedical technology.

Summary

Although a few of the studies reflect conceptual frameworks or are derived from hypotheses, the far larger number is not. Although one can abstract to some degree from their findings, generalizations are, at best, limited.

Studies dealing with beliefs about health and illness reveal an appreciable amount of diversity, as well as complexity and heterogeneity, within cultural and subcultural groups. In developed, industrialized societies as well as in less industrialized, developing ones, cognitions about diseases reflect intertwinings of folk beliefs with beliefs that are congruent with, or derived from, biomedical technology. Moreover, holding folk beliefs about a condition need not be a barrier toward acceptance of scientific, biomedically valid technologies.

There is little convincing evidence that cognitions have important impacts on use of health services, personal health actions, or health policy. Moreover, neither of the two basic conceptual models of health cognitions, the health-belief model and the locus of control model, is an unequivocally strong predictor of health actions.

INTERGENERATIONAL LINKAGES

Although the family is presumed to be a major determinant of health cognitions, the most recent literature reviews (e.g., Bush & Iannotti, 1990; Lau, Quadrel, & Hartman, 1990) affirm earlier assessments (e.g., Baranowski & Nader, 1985; Gochman, 1985, 1988c) that knowledge about relationships between family characteristics and children's health cognitions is virtually nonexistent. Baranowski and Nader (1985) described this relationship as "almost ignored" (p. 53).

Whatever knowledge is available of such intergenerational linkages can be discussed under headings of parental characteristics and child cognitions, parental cognitions and child characteristics, and family and child cognitions.

Parental Characteristics and Child Cognitions

Fathers' occupation was related to the validity of youngsters' beliefs about heart disease and nutrition in a Texas sample (Burdine, Chen, Gottlieb, Peterson, & Vacalis, 1984). Students whose fathers had professional or managerial positions scored highest in nutritional knowledge.

Parental smoking behaviors generally were found to have no effect on children's beliefs about smoking, with the exception that those whose parents smoked were more likely to disagree that smoking "stops you feeling tired," "makes you out of breath," and more likely to agree that smoking makes your teeth yellow (Eiser, Walsh, & Eiser, 1986). However, parental smoking behaviors, in contrast with parental beliefs, did have an impact on youngsters maintaining nonsmoking, once they self-initiated smoking cessation (Hansen, Collins, Johnson, & Graham, 1985). In addition, parental attitudes toward smoking and their smoking behaviors have an interactive effect on the likelihood that their youngsters would smoke (Newman & Ward, 1989). When parents themselves smoked, their negative attitudes toward smoking, as these were perceived by their children, had a significant impact on increasing adolescent nonsmoking. The adolescent children of nonsmoking parents with indifferent attitudes were about as likely to smoke as those of smoking parents who disapproved of smoking. Parental cognitions in this case were more important predictors of adolescent smoking than was parental behavior.

Intactness of family structure, as measured by the presence of both parents in a home, in comparison with the absence of at least one parent, was related to youngsters' cognitions that parents would be upset if they smoked, that smoking was a health problem, and that they would ask permission to smoke (Nolte, Smith, & O'Rourke, 1983). Moreover, parental presence decreased the likelihood of youngsters believing that friends and family enjoyed smoking.

The importance of intact family structure, along with family characteristics such as parental intellectual ability and socialization techniques, was found to have an impact on children's illness orientations, such as the "correctness" of their beliefs about illness and doctors and their faking of illness (Lau & Klepper, 1988). Broken families, families in which punishment was used as a socialization technique, and parents who were lower in intellectual ability were observed to be determinants of less appropriate illness orientations in children. Moreover, the children's self-esteem was found to be the important mediating linkage between these family factors and such illness orientations.

Parental Cognitions and Child Behaviors

Mothers' beliefs about dental health seemed to be unrelated either to their children's toothbrushing behavior or preventive dental visits (Chen, 1986) or use of fluoride tablets in a Danish sample (Friis-Hasche et al., 1984). However, mothers' beliefs about seriousness of dental disease predicted children's flossing behaviors (Chen, 1986). It is suggested (Chen, 1986) that although mothers rarely communicate beliefs orally to children or influence them through "cognitive mediation," mothers' behaviors may be more visible to children and thus more a determinant of the children's behavior.

Parental Cognitions and Youngsters' Cognitions

Beliefs about health and illness

Linkages were observed between caregiver and child cognitions in relation to concerns about illness, attributions of illness, perceptions of vulnerability and of severity, health locus of control, and attitudes toward health-related risk behaviors, among school children in the District of Columbia, but none for perceptions of health status, medicine use, or the perceived medical and nonmedical benefits of medicine use (Bush & Iannotti, 1988). Moreover, whereas the youngsters' cognitions were observed to be relatively stable, older children had beliefs that were closer to those of their caregivers than did younger children on several variables, suggesting a possible, albeit weak, developmental effect.

Parental beliefs about the efficacy of exercise, diet, nonconsumption of alcohol, and seat belt usage were appreciably related to the beliefs of their university-student children (Lau et al., 1990). Health education priorities of pupils in urban, coeducational black, Indian, and white primary schools in Pretoria and Cape Town, South Africa, were found to be related to those of their parents and teachers (Ross & Van der Merwe, 1983).

On the other hand, no relationship between mothers' and children's beliefs was observed for any dimension of the Parcel and Meyer Health Locus of Control scale (Perrin & Shapiro, 1985). However, mothers of children with chronic conditions were lower on internality and higher in beliefs about powerful others than were mothers of healthy children. Nor were any linkages observed in a Texas sample between parental nutritional beliefs and children's beliefs (Touliatos, Lindholm, Wenberg, & Ryan, 1984).

Specific conditions and interventions

A group of New Zealand female anorexia nervosa patients and their mothers had more positive evaluations of sickness and pain and more negative evaluations of thinness than did a control, nonpatient-mother group (Hall & Brown, 1983). Although this study did not directly relate mother and daughter cognitions, it points to familial similarities in beliefs related to anorexic conditions.

More direct mother–daughter linkages were observed in other studies. Females with idiopathic scoliosis evaluated other people with scoliosis similarly to the way their mothers evaluated them (Kahanovitz & Weiser, 1989). Mothers and daughters were also observed to have relatively similar beliefs about menstruation (Stolzman, 1986). However, daughters were more similar to their friends on some of the menstrual attitudes and beliefs than they were to their mothers, suggesting the importance of social and peer influences on these cognitions.

Somewhat in contrast, Scottish families showed less intergenerational influence than might have been expected. Data from three generations—children, mothers, and grandmothers—showed that grandmothers' cognitions on health-related child care influenced maternal behavior to a minimal degree and that there was little intergenerational similarity in cognitions toward health and use of health services (Blaxter & Paterson, 1982).

Asthmatic children and their mothers in a large western Pennsylvania metropolitan area were found to have significantly similar perceptions of prognosis, level of chest pain, and breathing difficulty related to asthmatic attacks, but no intergenerational relationships were observed between thoughts about threats of asthma to children's lives (Khampalikit, 1983). Children and mothers were found to have similar, but more moderate, linkages between beliefs about impact of asthma on social life.

High levels of *intrafamilial transmission*, a concept denoting the degree to which a family member and a child or adolescent with cancer have similar cancer-related conceptions, were found among children and adolescents with cancer as well as their family member (usually the mother). High degrees of intrafamilial correlation were observed for knowledge about cancer, expectations of a future that generated enthusiasm, levels of reality in perceptions of the future, and expectations about resumption of social activities on leaving the hospital (Susman et al., 1982).

The only positive linkage found in a sample of obese youngsters and their parents was between parental and child beliefs about the threat of obesity (Uzark, Becker, Dielman, Rocchini, & Katch, 1988). Negative linkages were found between the children's beliefs about the threat of obesity and parents' perceptions of personal control, and between the children's perception of personal control over weight and parental perceptions of barriers or difficulty in weight reduction. Children believe they have less control to the degree that their parents perceive greater difficulty in managing weight. Parental and child attributions of obesity were related in four cases: lack of exercise, family problems, nervous tension, and medical problems; however, they were not related in seven other areas.

Yet linkages were not generally observed between parents' and their children's perceptions of seriousness, susceptibility, and efficacy in relation to dental disease and its treatment, except for beliefs in luck, fate, or chance (Cipes, 1985). However, parents who believed that dental disease was serious had children who believed in the efficacy of toothbrushing. Moreover, very little correlation was found between parents' own perceptions and their perceptions of parallel beliefs in their children.

In contrast with these reports of linkages—albeit sometimes modest—between parental and child cognitions, significant disparities were found between the perceptions of pediatric outpatients at a tumor institute and their parents about the amount of choice available in relation to tests and treatment, the helpfulness of additional information, and the effects on the condition of alcohol, smoking, and drugs (Levenson, Copeland, Morrow, Pfefferbaum, & Silberberg, 1983). Parents nearly always attributed greater importance to these dimensions than did their children.

Summary

Relatively few studies have attempted to demonstrate relationships between health cognitions and other family characteristics, or between one another. As a result, there is only spotty evidence pointing to any such relationships. Health cognitions in families can be seen to have only very limited relationships either to parental characteristics, to health actions, or to one another. To the degree that these limited findings permit generalizations, family intactness (i.e., a family in which two parents/caretakers are present) is one characteristic that has some importance in determining youngsters' health cognitions, particularly those related to smoking (Nolte et al., 1983) and more general beliefs about health and illness (Lau & Klepper, 1988). Otherwise, no consistent patterns or coherent relationships are observed.

Sallis and Nader (1988) note the paucity of documentation of mechanisms of family influence. Moreover, Dielman, Leech, Becker, Rosenstock, and Horvath (1982), noting that studies relating parental and youngsters' health beliefs have been relatively rare, were unable to demonstrate any relationships during their own investigation a decade ago. They asserted, "Child health beliefs are scarcely influenced by parental characteristics" (p. 63). In the intervening years there has been insufficient study to either confirm or refute their assertion.

EVALUATION OF CURRENT KNOWLEDGE

Current knowledge about family cognitions permits little meaningful generalization. The preceding narrative is a "laundry list"—a pastiche rather than a mosaic. There is not sufficient coherence in the body of research to begin even a pedestrian evaluation, except in the most superficial terms, of method, nature, size of sample, and so on. In terms of a sociology of knowledge (e.g., Hayes-Bautista, 1978), current data-based knowledge is lacking in depth, coherence, and organization. It reflects minimal effort at broadening samples and, with a few notable exceptions (e.g., Bush & Iannotti, 1990; Lau et al., 1990), rare focused replications that build on prior research, or specific theoretical or conceptual models.

Much of this research appears to be driven by clinical or applied interests (e.g., the need to assess, develop, or service delivery; e.g., Walker et al., 1984). These are legitimate and important concerns, but they do not lead to systematic development of a coherent body of knowledge. Even in areas in which some knowledge exists, there is an urgent need for systematic expansion. There is consensus that little is known about health cognitions in families (e.g., Bush & Iannotti, 1990; Lau et al., 1990) or about the mechanisms by which they are transmitted among family members (e.g., Sallis & Nader, 1988).

However, an increasing number of systematic studies on cognitions about specific conditions, particularly asthma and cancer (e.g., Perrin & Shapiro, 1985; Susman et al., 1982), offer promise of movement toward an increase in consistent, coherent understanding of how families perceive and evaluate these conditions and their treatment. Equally important from the perspective of increasing generalizable knowledge, a small number of research programs (e.g.,

Bush & Iannotti, 1988; Lau & Klepper, 1988; Lau et al., 1990) are moving toward complex and thoughtful integrations of conceptual frameworks and away from single-model approaches, such as the health-belief model or the locus of control model.

Simultaneously, there is movement toward testing hypotheses with greater specificity that compare the relative merits of conceptual models. The *enduring family socialization* model, which suggests that health cognitions are learned within the family during childhood, that parents have primary influence on these, and that the cognitions remain stable throughout adulthood, has been contrasted with the *lifelong openness* model, which suggests that health cognitions are influenced by several socialization agents and change throughout the life cycle (Lau et al., 1990). Each of these models integrates developmental concepts, such as life cycle and socialization within the family, with health behavior concepts. Longitudinal data provide limited support for each of these models and have led Lau and his colleagues (Lau et al., 1990) to propose a *windows of vulnerability* model, which suggests that parental influence will continue unless and until the youngster experiences other potent socializing agents during critical developmental periods.

However, much of the research presented here still remains exploratory, descriptive, and essentially atheoretical and nonconceptual. Although relationships exist between some parental cognitions and use of selected health services for children, very little can be said about parental cognitions and child health behaviors or child health cognitions.

AGENDA FOR FUTURE RESEARCH

A future research agenda for health cognitions in families would assign priority to exploring the origins and development of health cognitions, sharpening the conceptualization of the family, and approaching the topic from a perspective emphasizing basic research.

Origins and Development of Health Cognitions

Literature reviews summarizing and evaluating the increasing body of work on health cognitions in young populations (e.g., Burbach & Peterson, 1986; Gochman, 1985, 1992; Kalnin & Love, 1982; Lau & Klepper, 1988) confirm that nearly all of it has been conducted without reference to family context. Virtually nothing is known of the determinants, even of those cognitions such as perceived vulnerability and locus of control, that have been studied most frequently in younger populations. An enormous gap thus exists in knowledge about the determinants of these health cognitions, particularly those determinants involving the family.

Coupled with the need for greater knowledge and understanding about the origins of health cognitions is the need for greater knowledge and understanding about how they develop, their developmental changes, and possible differential patterns related to other personal, family, and social characteristics. The dearth of well-conducted, rigorous research in this area has been noted repeatedly (e.g., Bush & Iannotti, 1988; Gochman, 1985, 1988a, 1988b, 1992; Kalnin & Love, 1982; Lau & Klepper, 1988).

Questions arise about the importance of a range of family factors, including but not limited to parental health cognitions, family size, structure, role relationships, methods of child rearing, access to resources, health history, and linkages to the larger community. Moreover, the relative importance of family factors in the origins and development of such cognitions needs to be compared with the impact of friendship and peer groups, social relationships, and societal and cultural values and institutions. Basic research into the origins of family health cognitions and how they develop is thus a major challenge for the future and leads directly to the second area identified for future research—conceptualization of the family.

Conceptualization of the Family

Possibly, the failure to discover the roots of childrens' health behavior in family characteristics reflects an unfortunate combination of inadequate conceptualizations of the family, together with a very small number of studies conducted in this area. Research has seldom looked at the family as an entity or unit (i.e., as a social group or social system). More often than not, research has considered family solely in terms of some personal or demographic characteristic of one or both parents, or in terms of its size.

Future research into health cognitions should examine the family in terms of its characteristics as an integral social unit. Important family characteristics such as role structure, norms, values, and patterns of communication are critical areas for future investigation. Pratt's (1976) conception of the "energized family" is one of the few extant conceptual models that considers the family in this way, and studies based on her model, or similarly coherent ones, are sorely needed. The energized family is one in which members demonstrate regular interaction with one another and attempt to cope and to master their lives. Energized families show fluidity in internal organization, a sharing of power, flexibility in role relationships, and concern for and support of the growth of family members (Pratt, 1976).

The family and larger social units

Energized families also maintain contacts with the community to advance the interests of their members. Family linkages with larger social units such as friendship networks and the community and its institutions had been a focus for research through the early 1980s (e.g., Gochman, 1985), much of which related family use of health services and other overt health behaviors (health cognitions among them) to characteristics of communities and society. Finding such community linkages to be related to immunizations (Friede et al., 1985) reaffirms the need to look beyond the family itself for increasing understanding of a range of health-related behaviors. The family needs to be conceptualized as an integral social unit embedded in a context of other such units.

Measuring and conceptualizing the family

Promising new approaches to conceptualizing and measuring the family as a social unit are appearing in the literature. Focusing on family use of health services, a Family Utilization Index (Schor, Starfield, Stidley, & Hankin, 1987) uses rates of individual family members' use of different types of care (acute, chronic, psychiatric, and nonillness care) to construct average usage rates for families. This index is then used to determine variability in usage both within and between families. Individual usage can then be examined to see how much of it is determined by family patterns or norms. The index may be seen as a paradigm for assessing the degree to which cognitions within a family are consistent (i.e., normative).

The concept of *intrafamilial transmission*, referring to the degree of shared or similar conceptions about cancer within a family, and a related concept of *interfamily consensus*, referring to the degree of such shared conceptions in randomly selected pairs (Susman et al., 1982), can be used to assess the degree of family consensus on cognitions related to other conditions as well as to a broader range of health issues. Sallis and Nader (1988) introduce the concept of *family aggregation* to denote intrafamilial similarities in health variables compared with nonfamily similarities. In addition to these innovate conceptualizations and approaches to measuring the family as an integral social unit, the work of Lau et al. (1990) introduces the concept of *windows of vulnerability* to refer to periods in the family life cycle when the strength of the family's influence has the potential for diminishing.

Family health culture: Do family health cognitions exist?

Black (1985) uses the concept of *family health culture* to refer to the unique combination of family experiences, beliefs, perceptions of symptoms, and reactions to them, which apparently influences the way in which families seek care or treatment for their children. Black also raises questions about whether such family health cultures are homogeneous. Even within the family unit the likelihood exists that mothers, fathers, and children have different beliefs and attitudes.

The degree to which future research on such family health cultures demonstrates homogeneity (i.e., the degree to which they are normative) will suggest whether there is value in examining what might be termed *family health cognitions*. It may make no difference how one conceptualizes the family—if there is no consensus about health-related cognitions within a family unit. The absence of observed intergenerational linkages may be accounted for less by the manner of inquiry and more by the nature of the phenomenon. In the absence of any body of rigorous data, it is premature to conjecture on this.

Health Cognitions in Families as a Basic Research Focus

Laudable pragmatic objectives underlie almost all of the studies discussed in this chapter and a good deal of other research on health-related behaviors. However, when such pragmatic objectives are the primary driving forces in research process, they are likely to be barriers to generating data that lend themselves to generalizations, to increasing scientific knowledge, and to answering basic research questions.

One way of increasing the likelihood that future research, including the research agenda identified in this section, will be scientifically valuable (i.e., will generate a body of knowledge that has depth, coherence, and organization and that broadens understanding and increases generalizability) is to adopt a *health behavior research* perspective. Such a perspective (e.g., Gochman, 1988c, 1992) begins with the premise that health cognitions in families are interesting in their own right and are inherently worthy of serious scientific investigation. This means that they ought to be the focus of some basic scientific activity. Basic health behavior research thus complements research on risk-factor behavior and on health interventions and programs. As such, health cognitions are looked on in terms of their interrelationships as well as how they are determined by a variety of diverse personal and social processes. The behaviors, in this case family health-related cognitions, must be the primary focus, not the treatment, health promotion package, marketing attempt, or health education program; the behavior rather than the technology; the basics rather than the applications.

Health behavior research is inherently interdisciplinary and not the turf of any single discipline or profession. The ways in which health behavior research differs from behavioral medicine, behavioral health, and health psychology are discussed elsewhere (Gochman, 1988c, 1992).

SUMMARY

This chapter has identified some beginnings in understanding health cognitions in families and has evaluated existing knowledge in this area. Important future research directions are suggested, particularly regarding the origins and development of health cognitions, and the conceptualization and the role of the family. A *health behavior* perspective, emphasizing both basic research and inter-disciplinary efforts, offers maximum promise of increasing our knowledge of family health cognitions and of remedying gaps in this knowledge.

REFERENCES

Anderson, J., & Chung, J. (1982). Culture and illness: Parents' preceptions [sic] of their child's long term illness. *Nursing Papers, 14,* 40–52.

Bahakim, H. M. (1987). Muslim parents' perception of and attitude towards cancer. *Annals of Tropical Paediatrics, 7,* 22–26.

Baranowski, T., & Nader, P. R. (1985). Family health behavior. In D. C. Turk & R. D. Kerns (Eds.), *Health illness and families: A life-span perspective* (pp. 51–80). New York: Wiley.

Black, N. (1985). The "health culture" of families as an influence on the use of surgery for glue ear: A case-control study. *International Journal of Epidemiology, 14,* 594–599.

Blaxter, M., & Paterson, K. (1982). *Mothers and daughters: A three generational study of health attitudes and behavior.* London: Heineman.

Braunstein, J., Abanobi, O. C., & Goldhagen, J. L. (1987). Parental perception of urgency and utilization of pediatric emergency services. *Family Practice Research Journal, 6,* 130–137.

Burbach, D. J., & Peterson, L. (1986). Children's concepts of physical illness: A review and critique of the cognitive-developmental literature. *Health Psychology, 5,* 307–325.

Burdine, J. N., Chen, M. S., Gottlieb, N. H., Peterson, F. L., & Vacalis, T. D. (1984). The effects of ethnicity, sex and father's occupation on heart health knowledge and nutrition behavior and school children: The Texas Youth Health Awareness Survey. *Journal of School Health, 54,* 87–90.

Bush, P. J., & Iannotti, R. J. (1988). Origins and stability of children's health beliefs relative to medicine use. *Social Science and Medicine, 27,* 345–352.

Bush, P. J., & Iannotti, R. J. (1990). A children's health belief model, *Medical Care, 28,* 69–86.

Casey, R., Rosen, B., Glowasky, A., & Ludwig, S. (1985). An intervention to improve follow-up of patients with otitis media. *Clinical Pediatrics, 24,* 149–152.

Chen, M. S. (1986). Children's preventive dental behavior in relation to their mothers' socioeconomic status, health beliefs and dental behaviors. *Journal of Dentistry for Children, 53,* 105–109.

Cipes, M. H. (1985). Self-management versus parental involvement to increase children's compliance with home fluoride mouthrinsing. *Pediatric Dentistry, 7,* 111–118.

Coreil, J., & Genece, E. (1988). Adoption of oral rehydration therapy among Haitian mothers. *Social Science and Medicine, 27,* 87–96.

Craig, A. P., & Albino, R. C. (1982). Urban Zulu mother's views on the health and health care of their infants. *South African Medical Journal, 63,* 571–572.

Cunningham-Burley, S., & MacLean, U. (1987). The role of the chemist in primary health care for children with minor complaints. *Social Science and Medicine, 24,* 371–377.

Dielman, T. E., Leach, S. L., Becker, M. H., Rosenstock, I. M., & Horvath, W. J. (1982). Parental and child health beliefs and behavior. In D. S. Gochman & G. S. Parcel (Eds.), Children's health beliefs and health behaviors. *Health Education Quarterly, 9,* 60–77.

Donnelly, J. E., Donnelly, W. J., & Thong, Y. H. (1987). Parental perceptions and attitudes toward asthma and its treatment: A controlled study. *Social Science and Medicine, 24,* 431–437.

Eiser, C., Walsh, S., & Eiser, J. R. (1986). Young children's understanding of smoking. *Addictive Behaviors, 11,* 119–123.

Fergusson, D. M., Horwood, L. J., & Shannon, F. T. (1983). Attitudes of mothers of five-year-old children to compulsory child health provisions. *New Zealand Medical Journal, 96,* 338–340.

Friede, A., Waternaux, C., Guyer, B., DeJesus, A., & Filipp, L. C. (1985). An epidemiological assessment of immunization programme participation in the Phillippines. *International Journal of Epidemiology, 14,* 135–142.

Friis-Hasche, E., Bergmann, J., Wenzel, A., Thylstrup, A., Pedersen, K., & Petersen, P. E. (1984). Dental health status and attitudes to dental care in families participating in a Danish fluoride tablet program. *Community Dentistry and Oral Epidemiology, 12,* 303–307.

Gielen, A. C., Eriksen, M. P., Daltroy, L. H., & Rost, K. (1984). Factors associated with the use of child restraint devices. *Health Education Quarterly, 11,* 195–206.

Gochman, D. S. (1985). Family determinants of children's concepts of health and illness. In D. C. Turk & R. D. Kerns (Eds.), *Health, illness, and families: A life-span perspective* (pp. 23–50). New York: Wiley.

Gochman, D. S. (1988a). Assessing children's health concepts. In P. Karoly & C. May (Eds.), *Handbook of child health assessment: Biopsychosocial perspectives* (pp. 332–356). New York: Wiley.

Gochman, D. S. (1988b). Health behavior research: Present and future. In D. S. Gochman (Ed.), *Health behavior: Emerging research perspectives* (pp. 409–424). New York: Plenum Press.

Gochman, D. S. (1988c). Health behavior: Plural perspectives. In D. S. Gochman (Ed.), *Health behavior: Emerging research perspectives* (pp. 3–17). New York: Plenum Press.

Gochman, D. S. (1992). Here's looking at you kid! New ways of viewing the development of health cognitions. In E. J. Sussman, L. V. Feagans, & W. S. Ray (Eds.), *Emotion, cognition, health and development in children and adolescents* (pp. 9–23). Hillsdale, NJ: Erlbaum.

Green, E. C. (1985). Traditional healers, mothers and childhood diarrheal disease in Swaziland: The interface of anthropology and health education. *Social Science and Medicine, 20*, 277–285.

Hall, A., & Brown, L. B. (1983). A comparison of the attitudes of young anorexia nervosa patients and non-patients with those of their mothers. *British Journal of Medical Psychology, 56*, 39–48.

Hansen, W. B., Collins, L. M., Johnson, C. A., & Graham, J. W. (1985). Self-initiated smoking cessation among high school students. *Addictive Behaviors, 10*, 265–271.

Hayes-Bautista, D. E. (1978). Chicano patients and medical practitioners: A sociology of knowledge paradigm of lay-professional interaction. *Social Science and Medicine, 12*, 83–90.

Horwitz, S. M., Morgenstern, H., & Berkman, L. F. (1988). Factors affecting pediatric preventive care utilization in a prepaid group practice. *Pediatrician, 15*, 112–118.

Ijsselmuiden, C. B. (1983). Beliefs and practices concerning measles in Gazankulu. *South African Medical Journal, 63*, 360–362.

Kahanovitz, N., Weiser, S. (1989). The psychological impact of idiopathic scoliosis on the adolescent female: A preliminary multi-center study. *Spine, 14*, 483–485.

Kalnin, I., & Love, R. (1982). Children's concepts of health and illness—and implications for health education: An overview. In D. S. Gochman & G. S. Parcel (Eds.), Children's health beliefs and health behaviors. *Health Education Quarterly, 9*, 8–19.

Kay, E. J., & Blinkhorn, A. S. (1989). A study of mothers' attitudes towards the prevention of caries with particular reference to fluoridation and vaccination. *Community Dental Health, 6*, 357–363.

Khampalikit, S. (1983). The interrelationships between the asthmatic child's dependency behavior, his perception of his illness, and his mother's perception of his illness. *Maternal–Child Nursing Journal, 12*, 221–296.

Kirscht, J. P. (1988). The health belief model and predictions of health actions. In D. S. Gochman (Ed.), *Health behavior: Emerging research perspectives* (pp. 27–41). New York: Plenum Press.

Kviz, F. J., Dawkins, C. E., & Ervin, N. E. (1985). Mothers' health beliefs and use of well-baby services among a high-risk population. *Research in Nursing and Health, 8*, 381–387.

Lau, R. R. (1988). Beliefs about control and health behavior. In D. S. Gochman, (Ed.), *Health behavior: Emerging research perspectives* (pp. 43–63). New York: Plenum Press.

Lau, R. R., & Klepper, S. (1988). The development of illness orientations in children aged 6 through 12. *Journal of Health and Social Behavior, 29*, 149–168.

Lau, R. R., Quadrel, M. J., & Hartman, K. A. (1990). Development and change of young adults' preventive health beliefs and behavior: Influence from parents and peers. *Journal of Health and Social Behavior, 31*, 240–259.

Levenson, P. M., Copeland, D. R., Morrow, J. R., Pfefferbaum, B., & Silberberg, Y. (1983). Disparities in disease-related perceptions of adolescent cancer patients and their parents. *Journal of Pediatric Psychology, 8*, 33–45.

McWhirter, W. R., & Kirk, D. (1986). What causes childhood leukaemia? *The Medical Journal of Australia, 145*, 314–316.

Mishel, M. H. (1983). Parents' perception of uncertainty concerning their hospitalized child. *Nursing Research, 32*, 324–330.

Mull, J. D., & Mull, D. S. (1988). Mothers' concepts of childhood diarrhea in rural Pakistan: What ORT program planners should know. *Social Science and Medicine, 27*, 53–67.

Newman, I. M., & Ward, J. M. (1989). The influence of parental attitude and behavior on early adolescent cigarette-smoking. *Journal of School Health, 59*, 150–152.

Nolte, A. E., Smith, B. J., & O'Rourke, T. (1983). The relationship between health risk attitudes and behaviors and parental presence. *Journal of School Health, 53*, 234–240.

Perrin, E. C., & Shapiro, E. (1985). Health locus of control beliefs of healthy children, children with chronic physical illness, and their mothers. *The Journal of Pediatrics, 107*, 627–633.

Peterson, L., Farmer, J., & Kashani, J. H. (1990). Parental injury prevention endeavors: A function of health beliefs? *Health Psychology, 9*, 177–191.

Pratt, L. (1976). *Family structure and effective health behavior: The energized family.* Boston: Houghton-Mifflin.

Profeta, M. L., Lecchi, G. M., DeDonato, S., & Fraizzoli, G. (1989). Inchesta sulla applicazione delle vaccinazioni contro la pertosse e contro il morbillo in una citta dell'hinterland Milanese [Survey of the use of vaccination against measles and pertussis in a city of Milanese hinterland.] *Annali de Igiene, Medicina Preventiva e de Communita, 1*, 1173–1184.

Ross, M. H., & Van der Merwe, G. J. (1983). Health interests of schoolchildren, parents and teachers and their applications to health education in primary schools. *Central African Journal of Medicine, 29*, 185–188.

Sallis, J. F., & Nader, P. R. (1988). Family determinants of health behavior. In D. S. Gochman (Ed.), *Health behavior: Emerging research perspectives* (pp. 107–124). New York: Plenum Press.

Schor, E., Starfield, B., Stidley, C., & Hankin, J. (1987). Family health: Utilization and effects of family membership. *Medical Care, 25*, 616–626.

Semchuck, K. M., & Eakin, J. M. (1989). Children's health and illness behaviour: The single working mother's perspectives. *Canadian Journal of Public Health, 80,* 346–350.

Sircar, B. K., & Dagnow, M. B. (1988). Beliefs and practices related to diarrhoeal diseases among mothers in Gondar Region, Ethiopia. *Tropical and Geographical Medicine, 40,* 259–263.

Spykerboer, J. E., Donnelly, W. J., & Thong, Y. H. (1986). Parental knowledge and misconceptions about asthma: A controlled study. *Social Science and Medicine, 22,* 553–558.

Stoltzman, S. M. (1986). Menstrual attitudes, beliefs, and symptom experiences of adolescent females, their peers, and their mothers. *Health Care for Women International, 7,* 97–114.

Susman, E. J., Hersh, S. P., Nannis, E. D., Strope, B. E., Woodruff, P. J., Pizzo, P. A., & Levine, A. S. (1982). Conceptions of cancer: The perspectives of child and adolescent patients and their families. *Journal of Pediatric Psychology, 7,* 253–261.

Sze-Tho, R., & Gill, D. G. (1982). Measles virus and vaccination: A survey of parental attitudes. *Irish Medical Journal, 75,* 250–251.

Tinsley, B. J., & Holtgrave, D. R. (1989). Maternal health locus of control beliefs, utilization of childhood preventive health services, and infant health. *Journal of Developmental and Behavioral Pediatrics, 10,* 236–241.

Touliatos, J., Lindholm, B. W., Wenberg, M. F., & Ryan, M. (1984). Family and child correlates of nutrition knowledge and dietary quality in 10–13 year olds. *Journal of School Health, 54,* 247–249.

Uzark, K. C., Becker, M. H., Dielman, T. E., Rocchini, A. P., & Katch, V. (1988). Perceptions held by obese children and their parents: Implications for weight control intervention. *Health Education Quarterly, 15,* 185–198.

Walker, J. D., Beck, J. D., Jakobsen, J. (1984). Parental attitudes and dental disease in preschool children in Iowa. *Journal of Dentistry for Children, 51,* 141–145.

Webb, G. R., Sanson-Fisher, R. W., & Bowman, J. A. (1988). Psychosocial factors related to parental restraint of pre-school children in motor vehicles. *Accident Analysis and Prevention, 20,* 87–94.

Widenheim, J. (1982). A time-related study of intake pattern of fluoride tablets among Swedish preschoolchildren and parental attitudes. *Community Dentistry and Oral Epidemiology, 10,* 296–300.

4

THE ROLE OF FAMILIES
IN THE PREVENTION OF PHYSICAL
AND MENTAL HEALTH PROBLEMS

Michael C. Roberts
University of Kansas

Lisa H. McElreath
University of Alabama

Prevention refers to interventions taken to avoid the development of problems before they arise or to minimize the negative impact of problems early in their development (Roberts & Peterson, 1984b). Prevention is a simple concept captured in Benjamin Franklin's "an ounce of prevention is worth a pound of cure." However, the prevention concept becomes difficult to apply in practice. All too often, prevention of problems becomes lost in demands for rehabilitative or clinical services for those already experiencing problems. Merging prevention concepts, derived from child health psychology, pediatric psychology, and public health, with the concerns of a health psychology for families is the focus of this chapter. The domain of family health psychology should inherently involve both physical health and mental health of children and adults in the group defined as family. The ultimate goal of this field is the application of psychological knowledge and techniques to the limitation, reversal, or prevention of problems that limit the full enjoyment of physical and psychological health. Problems may range from obesity to injuries, smoking to substance abuse, and anxiety and pain to heart disease, for example.

Given the focus on family health psychology, we restrict discussion to how family issues affect or are affected by the physical health of its members. Our focus here is on psychological phenomena and their link to prevention of health-related problems (e.g., obesity and injuries) and to the prevention of negative psychological consequences arising from physical illness and its treatment (e.g., anxiety and distress). We provide examples of the family's role in selected prevention problems. Unfortunately, the research literature involving family systems affecting health is not well developed. Studies have focused on the individual rather than on the family unit per se. Prevention interventions rarely include family considerations, although some illustrative cases will be discussed. Finally, we outline a research agenda and discuss future trends in prevention within family health psychology.

PREVENTION CONCEPTS

Major studies, commissions, and reports all emphasize prevention and the role of behavioral concomitants of both physical and mental health of children and adults. The Select Panel for the Promotion of Child Health delineated prevention approaches for enhancing children's health (Harris, 1981). The Surgeon General's report, *Healthy People* (Califano, 1979), presented prevention goals that would enhance the quality of life for people of all ages. A more recent health report, *Healthy People 2000* (Stoto, Behrens, & Rosemont, 1990), continues to highlight the importance of prevention interventions. Among important health goals that are affected by family systems are prevention of obesity, injury, alcohol and other drug use, adolescent pregnancy, and illnesses such as AIDS, cancer, and heart disease.

When prevention action is taken to avoid development of a problem before one occurs, this is known as *primary prevention*. Examples of primary prevention would include inoculations against disease, fluoride in water to prevent dental cavities, proper nutrition, and use of seat belts. *Secondary prevention* is action taken once a beginning problem or its potential is identified in an individual or group so that further development of the problem is limited or reversed. Examples of secondary prevention would include intervention with children showing early signs of conduct disorder, low cholesterol diets for those with elevated levels, preparation for medical events for children scheduled for hospitalization, and parent training for potentially abusive parents. *Tertiary prevention* is usually held not to be prevention per se, rather it is viewed as rehabilitation or cure once a problem has had a negative effect and those affected are attempting to regain former functioning. The only preventive aspect of tertiary prevention is the inhibition of any further problems. In this chapter, we focus on primary and secondary prevention.

A developmental perspective has particular relevance to family-oriented prevention. A developmental perspective helps determine "(a) when during the life-span intervention and prevention services are most needed and for what kinds of problems, (b) when these services should be offered to maximize their efficacy and acceptance, and (c) what types of services might be most effective" (Roberts, 1986, p. 152). Additional concepts of prevention such as active versus passive prevention, individual versus population interventions, milestone or at-risk approaches, specific targeting and cost-benefit considerations are covered in other sources (Peterson & Roberts, 1986; Roberts, 1986).

THE FAMILY

The family as a cohesive constellation of members is an appropriate focus for health psychology because members develop, function, thrive, and demise within the family context. Researchers and theorists have asserted repeatedly the importance of families in terms of health behavior, especially through the interaction of parents and children (e.g., see Patterson, Tupp, Sallis, Atkins, & Nader, 1988). Family members influence each other (Sallis & Nader, 1988), and parents of young children and children of elderly parents in particular serve as "gate keepers" of health information as well as catalytic models for health behavior change. Patterson et al. (1989) cite considerable evidence of family influence in setting or changing children's health behavior through (a) "parental control of environmental variables," (b) "parental modeling of health behaviors," and (c) "direct parental instructional prompts" (p. 278). Parents and other significant family members influence children and other members reciprocally by modeling behavior (e.g., smoking, alcohol use, exercise, and nutritional habits) and choosing or modifying the environment in which family members interact. This latter aspect relates to choices of recreation (e.g., all-terrain vehicles, bicycles, boating, and swimming pools), availability of hazards (e.g., poisons, swimming pools, and firearms), implementation of safety devices (e.g., bicycle/motorcycle helmets and smoke detectors), limitations on child behavior (e.g., risk taking, opportunities for interaction with hazards or growth experiences), and providing rewards for safe or healthy behavior (e.g., buckling up and brushing teeth). Of course, these parental influences are themselves affected by financial factors, parents' own health behavior, modifiability of the environment, family structure, and the culture within which families function.

Most recent prevention work by health psychologists (both child and adult oriented) has focused on motivating individuals to take protective actions for themselves and on enhancing individuals' (usually children's) capacity to cope with traumatic situations. In many preventive interventions, parents or families are typically either ignored or deliberately bypassed by interventions that target the child directly. Only a few published projects include any role for parents or families.

This lack of empirical research may be due to a number of considerations. First, the developing nature of research may be used such that researchers just have not gotten around to families while attempting to establish the efficacy of prevention through the simpler case of targeting individuals directly. Second, child health psychologists have noted a recent trend toward enhancing children's ability to take responsibility for their own health (Roberts, Maddux, & Wright, 1984). This new orientation contrasts with past health education, which was directed at parents' actions on behalf of their children. Third, preventionists have recognized that general health education in the past was not as successful as intended. Newer health education combined with behaviorally based interventions appear more successful, but resistance to including broader messages to parents and families remains because of limited success of earlier health education efforts. A fourth reason for limited family prevention research is that it is easier to target children where they congregate, mostly in schools or in front of the television, than it is to find and gain the attention of parents. Families are often harder to reach than either children or parents separately. Finally, there is no comprehensive conceptualization for prevention and families. This lack may impede research efforts that integrate families in prevention activities. In many ways, the most recent prevention view, which focuses on the children's behavior, neglects the etiological sequence or antecedents leading up to the behavior and the consequences immediately following hazardous or injurious behavior (cf. Matheny, 1987; Patterson et al., 1988). Successful prevention needs a conceptualization that includes developmental information antecedent to the problem.

Moreover, work in prevention has not adopted a family system model such as that outlined by Turk and Kerns (1985) or Fiese and Sameroff (1989). Typically, researchers have not studied relationships or interactional patterns of family members with regard to health goals. In most cases, researchers have assumed a linear causality model of parent-to-child rather than a more complex cause and effect of dynamic interaction in which all parties affect each other reciprocally. Doherty and Campbell (1988) describe, for example, how various family members influence each others' health habits. This aspect of family influence is evident for such topics as the family dynamics of smoking, eating behavior and obesity, and cardiovascular risk change. Nevertheless, only a few interventions have used family-based activities as part of prevention. In one project, Patterson et al. (1989) found modest evidence of an aggregation of behavior change in families: "Findings suggest that family members are more likely to influence other family members of similar ages" (p. 288) and "families who participate together in a health promotion program tend to make similar modifications in their health habits" (p. 289). They interpret their findings as arguing against "targeting the 'gatekeepers' " or some other single family member in hopes that change by this person will generalize to all other family members. These data also suggest that specific intervention strategies need to be developed to "enhance intergenerational family influences" (p. 288). As Stunkard, Felix, and Cohen (1985) state, "Using children to help their parents change health behavior may well be without precedent. Using parents to help their children change their health behavior is almost as rare" (p. 174). Because so few studies were found using the entire family in prevention efforts, we focus also on studies involving parents and children in preventive behaviors.

Prevention of Medical Anxiety and Pain

The literature in pediatric psychology contains a wealth of research on intervention to prevent or ameliorate children's emotional and behavioral reactions to medical and dental settings, personnel, and procedures. Typically, the preventive approach involves preparation of the child for encountering and coping with the potentially stressful aspects of health care. This literature is fairly massive and those interested in its detail should consult summaries by Peterson and Mori (1988) or Elkins and Roberts (1983) on preparing children for hospitalization and medical/dental events. The typical approach in preparation is to provide a child with information through tours, instruction, modeling films, or tapes, or play therapy. Many such interventions have demonstrated some effectiveness in reducing children's medical fears. The typical preparation approach bypasses the parent. However, we believe that parents and siblings should be important in medical preparation for several reasons. First, parental anxiety is associated with the child's anxiety (Alexander, Powell, Williams, White, & Conlon, 1991) so that an intervention may be sabotaged inadvertently when preparation is directed only to the child. Second, usurption or deprivation of the parental role or perceptions of that role (Brazelton, 1975) may lead to parental resistance. Third, general or blanket preparation cannot take into account particular aspects of the child, whereas inclusion of parents may enhance individualization for better effects (Peterson & Mori, 1988).

In contrast with the arguments in favor of family systems intervention, there are some professionals who suggest that family involvement may interfere with interventions. For example, research has shown that children cry more when a parent is present than when absent during injections (Gross, Stern, Levin, Dale, & Wojnilower, 1983). However, other professionals counter that what is needed is better prepared parents either to be supportive and assist with the child or to be the agent of preparation for their own child. A limited amount of research has involved parents to demonstrate the positive effect of involving parents.

Skipper and Leonard (1968) directed their procedures at mothers to train them to prepare their children for medical procedures during hospitalization. The parent-prepared children did better on various physiological measures than those without the parent preparation. Roskies, Mongeon, and Gagnon-Lefebvre (1978) also illustrated the success of a program for training mothers to provide nurturing and normal care while their child was hospitalized. The study also found that mothers and fathers visited more and provided more psychological support even though only mothers were targeted. Visintainer and Wolfer (1975) demonstrated successful preparation by providing information and reassurance to both parent and child at particular stress points while the child was hospitalized. Families receiving this stress-point preparation were less anxious and the children exhibited less distress. Peterson and Shigetomi (1981) added coping skills training (relaxation and imagery) to an informational modeling procedure for parents and their children. The parents then rehearsed and coached the use of the coping skills during hospitalization. Children in the skills training group showed fewer disruptive behaviors than untrained children. These authors suggested that parents may feel more competent and have less anxiety when informed of what to expect and how to cope with the events for their child. In a similar manner, Meng and Zastowny (1982) provided parents with stress inoculation strategies so they could intervene with their children. This parent training increased their children's coping for medical events. Other research has similarly established that parents' training and involvement in assisting their children benefited all participants (Jay & Elliott, 1990; Naylor, Coates, & Kan, 1984; Zastowny, Kirschenbaum, & Meng, 1986). Professionals have also called for involvement by nonhospitalized siblings to decrease overall family distress, but empirical support is insufficient. Overall, the few projects reviewed here demonstrate that prevention interventions with families (parents and children) can be successful at ameliorating the psychological concomitants of health care. It is interesting that there seems to be minimal research on preparing children for a parent's illness and hospitalization.

Injury Prevention

Injuries are the single largest physical threat to children, more so now than diseases, and a major life threat to adults (Roberts & Brooks, 1987). A number of injury control strategies have been implemented for removing hazards or teaching strategies for avoiding injurious situations. Psychology has much to offer this field in a variety of ways (Roberts, 1986, 1991; Roberts, Elkins, & Royal, 1984). In this arena, however, recent attention has been directed primarily to the child—changing his or her behavior to act safely and avoid injuries.

Indeed, behavioral approaches to injury prevention have been proved effective for training children (see summary in Roberts, Fanurik, & Layfield, 1987). For example, preventionists have taught children safer pedestrian street crossing, emergency exiting skills, sexual abuse preventive behaviors, safety behaviors for latchkey children, and seat belt usage. In all of these, children have been trained, either individually or in groups, to exhibit safer behaviors.

Injury prevention interventions have largely bypassed parents and families. Fortunately, in a few instances, there has been attention to parental or familial roles of injury control. For example, the situation of children home alone without parental supervision poses potential for injury. Research has demonstrated that unsupervised children at home can be trained in home safety behaviors (e.g., safe habits, and responses to emergencies and strangers). These successful behavioral interventions have been implemented primarily by outside trainers (Peterson, 1984a, 1984b; Peterson & Mori, 1985). In an expansion on this basic research, parents have been trained to provide this type of home safety instruction for their children. For instance, a case study demonstrated that a mother could fairly successfully train safety skills to her son (Peterson, Farmer, & Selby, 1988). In a larger scale study, volunteer parents implemented safety training. Unfortunately, although there were some positive gains noted, the parents' program did not show the same consistent effects obtained with more intensively prepared trainers from outside the family (Peterson, Mori, Selby, & Rosen, 1988).

Other training programs for personal safety (such as those aimed at preventing abduction or abuse) have also focused on training children by teachers or professionals (e.g., Poche, Brouwer, & Swearingen, 1981). More recently, trained parents taught their children personal safety skills, successfully increasing their knowledge and skills (Miltenburger & Thiesse-Duffy, 1988).

Because motor vehicle collisions are the leading cause of death and injury to children, a great deal of effort has gone into increasing the use of car passenger safety devices (Roberts & Turner, 1984). Prevention efforts have included procedures directed at adults to increase their use of seat belts and at parents to increase use of seat belts or safety seats for their children. The health education literature indicates a multitude of car safety education programs directed at parents of newborns and young children (e.g., Greenberg & Coleman, 1982; Miller & Pless, 1977; Reisinger & Williams, 1978). Most of these attempts had limited success. In contrast, behaviorally based interventions in the form of rewards for parents when they safely secure their children were more successful (e.g., Christophersen & Gyulay, 1981; Roberts & Turner, 1986). A move to reward young children directly for buckling up also achieved some success (Roberts & Broadbent, 1989; Roberts & Layfield, 1987; Sowers-Hoag, Thyer, & Bailey, 1987). Greater seat belt use was also achieved with elementary school children rewarded with colorful lapel stickers and other prizes on arrival at school when securely buckled in the car. An important component in these projects was that to receive the reward, all passengers in the car, including the adults, had to be buckled. The observational data indicated that seat belt use of all passengers in the car increased (Roberts, Alexander, & Knapp, 1990; Roberts & Fanurik, 1986; Roberts, Fanurik, & Wilson, 1988). Thus child access to rewards for their behavior prompted parents and other family members to become safer as well. Injury prevention programs have also targeted parents and children and families for home safety (e.g., greater use of smoke detectors, lowered water heater temperatures, and greater electrical safety) with some demonstrated success (e.g., Barone, Greene, & Lutzker, 1986; Gallagher, Hunter, & Guyer, 1985; Tertinger, Greene & Lutzker, 1984; Thomas, Hassanein, & Christophersen, 1984).

The importance of injury prevention work with families is also borne out in surveys indicating a substantial lack of knowledge about hazards and how parents can successfully modify the environment or their behavior and that of their child. For example, an extensive survey demonstrated that parents reported inadequate knowledge of such dangers as pedestrian and bicycle injuries, burns, or drowning (Eichelberger, Gotschall, Feely, Harstad, & Bowman, 1990). On the basis of similar results from another survey, Peterson, Farmer, and Kashani (1991) suggest that the lack of awareness by parents "may explain why so few parents attempt to modify their child's environment to reduce hazards or the child's behavior by teaching safe behavior practices" (pp. 115–116). Indeed, the survey conducted by Peterson et al. (1991) revealed very poor knowledge of safety skills and how to make the children's environment safer. Most parents did not believe that their children were vulnerable to injury. This suggests to us that injury prevention should attend to (a) increasing knowledge of hazards and appropriate safety behavior, (b) increasing the competence of family members and their perceptions about their own ability to take effective action for preventing injury for the family, and (c) providing for effective intervention strategies for parents and families to implement. Because parents set the family's environment to a large degree and supervise the children in interaction with this environment, more effective targeting of families to remove hazards or provide better supervision seems particularly appropriate.

Childhood Obesity

Although childhood obesity is itself a health problem that necessitates treatment, it can also be conceptualized as a prevention issue. Obese children are at greater risk for becoming obese adults (Abraham, Collins, & Nordsieck, 1971; Hawk & Brook, 1979), and for obese children who become adults, treatment prognosis appears poor (Brownell & Wadden, 1986). Obese individuals are thought to be at greater risk than nonobese persons for such conditions as cardiovascular disease and diabetes. Several family variables have been documented as being related to child weight status, including parental encouragement and prompts to eat (Klesges et al., 1983), weight status of other family members (Garn, Bailey, Solomon, & Hopkins, 1981), and family cohesion and conflict (Beck & Terry, 1985). The unit for treatment intervention becomes the family, not just one individual such as the child (Harkoway, 1987). In light of this view, behavioral approaches to childhood obesity treatment sometimes involve family members, most notably, parents. For example, Aragona, Cassady, and Drabman (1975) reported that training parents in contingency contracting and reinforcement resulted in greater weight loss for their overweight daughters than a no-treatment control. However, these losses were not maintained at an 8-month follow-up.

Several researchers have explored the relative efficacy of parent involvement versus no parent involvement in behaviorally based weight loss programs (Epstein, Wing, Koeske, Andrasik, & Ossip, 1981; Kirschenbaum, Harris, & Tomarkin, 1984). For instance, children who participated in a multifaceted program tended to lose weight regardless of whether or not the parents participated in treatment (Epstein et al., 1981). However, children who had achieved nonobese status were better able to maintain their new weight if their parents had participated in the program with them. Kirschenbaum et al. (1984) found that both parents and children lost equal amounts of weight regardless of parental participation, and that both child-only and parent-plus child groups were superior to a no-treatment control. Children in both treatment groups maintained their losses at 1-year follow-up; however, parents in the child-only group did not maintain their losses.

Treatment components (e.g., exercise, nutrition education, or behavior modification) are often added to programs to determine their effectiveness. For example, children and their parents lost more weight in diet-only or diet-plus-exercise groups than in a no-treatment control (Epstein, Wing, Koeske, & Valoski, 1987). Parents in the exercise group maintained losses better, whereas no group differences in maintenance were found for the children. Other programs have trained parents in problem-solving techniques or general child management skills with enhanced effects on maintenance of weight loss (Graves, Meyers, & Clark, 1988; Israel, Stolmaker, & Andrian, 1985).

Only a few studies have documented treatments involving adolescents and their parents. Brownell, Kelman, and Stunkard (1983) compared the relative efficacy of separate parent and child groups, child groups only, and parent and child in the same group, in a treatment program involving behavior modification, social support, nutrition education, and exercise. For these adolescents and their parents, the separate parent and child groups lost significantly more weight than the other two groups. At follow-up, they continued to lose weight, whereas the other two groups did not maintain their treatment losses. Although further studies need to be done in this area, this finding does point to the possibility that developmental differences (younger child vs. adolescent) exist in the effects of parental involvement on child weight loss.

As noted in the above studies, a significant problem in child weight treatment is the difficulty in maintaining treatment gains over long periods. Better long-term child outcomes were associated with targeting and reinforcing of parent and child, or parent and child engaging in reciprocal reinforcement (Epstein, McCurley, Wing, & Valoski, 1990). Greater weight changes are obtained for overweight nonparticipating siblings if parents and children were targeted for weight loss (Epstein, Nudelman, & Wing, 1987). This may be related to the connection between parents' weight status and children's weight loss maintenance. In this regard, children of nonobese parents maintained their relative weight losses significantly better than children of obese parents (Epstein, Wing, Valoski, & Gooding, 1987). Genetics may be related to behavioral factors in this situation.

Overall, it appears that family involvement in the treatment of childhood obesity does lead to some desirable outcomes. There are possible developmental differences in how children respond to the presence of their parents in treatment. For example, the work of Brownell et al. (1983) and Israel et al. (1985) suggests that younger children might benefit more from parents' direct restructuring of the environment, whereas older children might need more social support than actual environmental intervention.

Summary Comments

Before turning to an outline agenda for further research for family roles in prevention, we offer a few observations. The studies reviewed here in hospitalization, injuries, and obesity do not demonstrate the superiority of involving families but rather the potential benefit from such involvement in some circumstances. In other cases, individual-focused intervention may be the most effective. One cannot conclude from the current literature that prevention through families is better or worse than targeting children directly and bypassing parents. In all situations, for prevention gains to occur, generalize, and be maintained, family considerations will of course play a role. Some prevention areas will require integration of families because family values and behavior will be inherently involved. For example, prevention of sexually transmitted diseases (e.g., AIDS) or teenage pregnancy will involve the family's religious and philosophical values intrinsically. Religious values may also play a role in immunization and medical care. In a similar manner, the use of alcohol and other substance use will necessarily be influenced by family attitudes and behavior. Other prevention targets may be less complex but still necessarily involve familial roles such as seat belt usage or toothbrushing.

Decisions by families to engage in prevention activity, as with any health care decision, involve consideration of moral and religious issues as well as financial concerns. The transactional perspective offered by Sameroff and Chandler (1975) and Fiese and Sameroff (1989) may be adapted for this discussion. This model involves family and parent interaction such that each person adapts to or is affected by the interaction. The outcome—in this case, preventive behavior—is not exclusively caused by one or the other party in the interaction but by the history of interactions over time (cf. Valsiner & Lightfoot, 1987).

Research Agenda for Family Roles in Prevention

It is clear that more research needs to be done into the multitude of health problems for children and families. There has been an inadequate number of studies focusing on family interactions vis à vis health from which to draw conclusions about the role of families in prevention. Parents and families are fairly ignorant of issues of health promotion and disease prevention, as shown by the surveys of injury hazards and prevention (e.g., Eichelberger et al., 1990; Peterson et al., 1991). Lack of knowledge and prevention behavior also have been found in surveys of knowledge about and prevention of AIDS (DiClemente, Forrest, & Mickler, 1990) and cardiovascular disease (White & Albanese, 1981). Given this ignorance, it is quite amazing that children develop so well. The linkage of knowledge, behavior, and health outcome needs to be established further.

Some external health interventions can be shown to have improved life longevity and quality of life for humans of all ages. For example, immunizations are preventive measures that have eliminated death and disability due to many diseases previously unchecked. Furthermore, fluoride in water has decreased dental caries. Historically, the most effective preventive interventions are those that rely less on the active intervention of families or individuals and more on structural, or passive, community-wide interventions. However, many remaining preventable problems are not readily amendable to these types of passive changes but will require active intervention for maximum effectiveness (Peterson & Mori, 1985; Peterson & Roberts, in press; Roberts, 1987). Active intervention will necessarily require more from families. Research and applications will need to address the following issues of conceptualization and methodology.

Better conceptualizations of families

Much of the previous research has utilized families and members as tools of convenience for preventive intervention without carefully examining the roles of the families. Family constellations and the impact of disease or injury are more complex than can be accommodated in a simplistic assertion that families should take more of a role in prevention. One important consideration is the multiple directions of influence and interaction, not just a typical framework of parent-to-child. Some work is beginning on children influencing the adults in a family or the influence of siblings on each other in adopting health promotion behaviors (e.g., Patterson et al., 1989; Roberts et al., 1988).

Questions should be resolved such as whether or not and when and how families should be involved. Should families be bypassed by going directly to children or other individual family members to take responsibility for their own health (Roberts et al., 1984; Maddux, Roberts, Sledden, & Wright, 1986)? More comprehensive conceptualization of families, including the varieties of structure, are needed as well as a more directed effort to study their involvement in prevention. A family is more than individuals composited together: It is a dynamic interactive system. This consideration should drive prevention efforts to use its potential rather than ignore the system of interacting influences. Furthermore, the diversity of family structure, interactive patterns, histories, beliefs, behaviors, economies, and other characteristics may require preventionists to develop interventions accommodating such differences. More effective prevention may result from fairly specific interventions rather than generalized, community interventions (although these, too, can be improved by enhanced knowledge of the targets of education or promotion efforts). Greater information on how families make health care decisions would benefit prevention, as would recognition of the developmental processes of the individuals (child and parent) involved in the family and the changes in the family as a unit over time.

Better conceptualizations of prevention

Successful prevention requires some (but not always total) understanding and knowledge about the etiology and development of health problems. Thus preventive conceptualizations require research into the sequences of events and behaviors preceding the occurrence of problems so that the world or specific situation might be corrected or reordered at some earlier points of the sequence. (These sequences of causes and effects are discussed further in Roberts, 1991). One of the biggest problems of prevention is that the sequence chains in problem development are not known or clearly understood (e.g., for obesity; for abuse of children, spouses, and elderly; and for substance misuse). Prevention conceptualizations need at least some empirical knowledge of various points in the chain in order to become effective.

Greater empowerment of families to do prevention

Within this context, we see a significant need for families to be given the resources and capability to make preventive decisions and behavioral and environmental changes for optimal family health. However, we emphasize that external judgments of what is good for families and children must be influenced by respect for the rights of families to make decisions and to do what the members consider appropriate. Families can fulfill their functions better when given information and ways to implement various roles. This assertion is supported by the reviewed research on hospital preparation and obesity. Families need to be empowered to assume greater and perhaps more effective preventive roles. Research should determine what and how health care decisionmaking is made when appropriate information is available. It is too simplistic and moralistic to say that families will make the right decisions and can do prevention effectively. Professionals need to determine how to convey information for changing attitudes and behavior as well as provide the means by which families can do the interventions (Peterson et al., 1991). It is not enough to scare families about hazards to health and safety. Rather, there must be corresponding actions that can be taken with some ease of implementation in the life of the family. Health professionals all too often assume an arrogant attitude of knowing better than anybody else. A family-centered empowerment would utilize family decisionmaking and ability in order to make those interventions that are deemed important to the family, with the assistance of the professionals. This type of family involvement in prevention may profit most from routinizing health behaviors into daily habit regimens so that members do not constantly need to cognitively appraise, decide, and act. That is, in health habits, the action follows from earlier active decisions with regard to acting in a particular way (e.g., toothbrushing, locking doors, buckling up, nutritional choices, sleep habits, or wearing a bicycle helmet).

More and better evaluation
of prevention programs

All too often, prevention programs are single implementations and rarely evaluated interventions. Most are well intentioned but do not consider whether the intervention has achieved the intended positive main effects or has any potential negative side effects. For example, in a survey of 90 materials designed to prevent child sexual abuse, Roberts, Alexander, and Fanurik (1990) found that rarely were even simple evaluations conducted before or after the widespread dissemination and application of program materials. As noted by Roberts, Alexander, and Fanurik (1990), "adverse effects are potentially present in the use of materials not validated or formally evaluated" (p. 783). Proper evaluation is lacking for far too many other prevention areas (e.g., swimming and firearm safety, and substance abuse prevention). More and better evaluative research is necessary.

Research designs appropriate to prevention concerns. Litman (1989) outlined several methodological issues in research into family systems in medicine. These issues are relevant and adapted here for prevention research. First, greater attention is necessary to the selection of samples on which to test an intervention. Samples from populations of convenience are often used that may be considerably different from the eventual recipients. For example, it is not appropriate to use college sophomores for more than a preliminary test of AIDS prevention messages intended for dissemination to the general population or for high-risk groups. Second, more attention should be given to the diversity of family form and type in research. Prevention research should recognize and utilize various family make-ups and constellations. Third, family medicine research projects have frequently used cross-sectional designs, but more longitudinal designs are needed. There is further need for research comparing various forms of interventions for prevention, not just reporting intervention-only or intervention-only versus a no-intervention control. Comparative efficacy for various programs can clarify etiology of the problems and outcome for different groups under various conditions.

A particular issue of prevention in family health psychology is that it should be developmentally based, with attention to changes in family members' behavior, attitudes, emotions, and cognitive properties (Roberts et al., 1984). There are interactive and reciprocal changes in other family members' attitudes and behaviors as all members in the family continue to develop over time. Prevention interventions must have a developmental foundation, therefore, research designs should utilize appropriate methodology to elucidate these developmental relationships.

Of course, a prevention program should not be considered effective only if effects are in the long-term (e.g., exercise programs for children should not just be evaluated as whether they prevent obesity or heart disease in adults). Immediate and short-term positive effects might be as worthwhile (e.g., to improve the child's current well-being or sense of self).

Better measurement of what prevention programs do. On the theme of improved evaluation of prevention programs with families, clarification of the intended outcome of the intervention program is needed. It is also important that the problem outcome measures are appropriate to the intervention itself. Most important, though, is that the measures used should be able to indicate directly that prevention of a problem occurred or did not occur; for example, are diseases that would be expected now not present? Are injuries and deaths at lower rates? Are there fewer teenage pregnancies? However, prevention researchers often need to rely on intermediate or proxy variables indicating program effects. For example, dental hygiene programs may measure plaque buildup on children's teeth after a preventive intervention with some assurance that plaque is related to dental caries and gum disease (Knapp, 1991). In a similar vein, programs to improve car passenger safety have an ultimate goal of reducing injury and death, but measures of seat belt usage are adequate intermediate measures of safety (Roberts, 1987). Thus healthier and safer behaviors may be adequate indications of program effects without having to wait for extremely long periods of time.

Knowledge or attitude change may be significant intermediate variables when a strong linkage can be established between these factors, healthier behavior, and eventual healthier outcomes. Unfortunately, evidence of the linkage between attitudes and behavior is not strong enough to make this claim conclusively, despite repeated efforts to establish it. Consequently, behaviorally based programs tend to be more able to demonstrate effects. Research is needed to establish these linkage relationships so that intermediate or substitute measures can be used to demonstrate effects.

Prioritizing of problems to be prevented. There is a multitude of problems existing in the world for preventionists to consider, especially in family health psychology. Indeed, all of us are inundated with warnings about hazards and messages to improve health such that we may begin to fear even simple and necessary acts of eating or breathing. The volume of health warnings may overload an individual's ability to cope so that each new warning becomes discounted (Etzioni, 1978). Families that are making attempts to respond preventively may become frustrated, disillusioned, or confused by too many demands for action. As a consequence, consideration should be given to prioritizing prevention goals. An example in which there have been misplaced priorities and inordinate energy given is the sexual molestation and abduction area. As noted by Reppucci and Haugaard (1989), considerable attention has been focused on prevention of abduction and molestation of children by strangers. Yet, sexual abuse and abduction problems are perpetrated more frequently by family members than by strangers. Sexual molestation is harmful regardless of who does it, but all the public outcry on strangers perhaps should have been focused on preventing sexual abuse within families. Moreover, the variables for preventing such family abuse may be considerably different from those preventing stranger abuse.

Energy and attention should become focused on the most important problems facing family health so that prevention programs do not become too numerous and diffused. The significant health reports of the last two decades noted at the beginning of this chapter can provide a beginning for decisionmaking about the most significant health problems. What are the major killers of children and adolescents? What is killing adults? What is impairing function? What are the problems most contributing to a poor quality of life in families? Once a determination is made on which problems to focus energetic prevention, then the most effective approaches can be brought to bear.

Conclusions

Obviously, many of the most significant problems are within at least nominal control or influence of families. Families can influence, but maybe not control, such health behaviors as (a) the use of safety belts and seats; (b) the personal choices of smoking, drug or alcohol consumption and driving; (c) the selection and availability of healthy or unhealthy food; (d) the psychological adaptiveness to medical events; and (e) the sexual attitudes and behavior related to adolescent pregnancy or sexually transmitted diseases. As noted, families set the environment for their members, to a large degree. Nevertheless, there will always be unavoidable interactions with other people's choices of environment and behavior. Consequently, families are *one* appropriate target and vehicle for prevention but not necessarily the *only* or the *most* appropriate. A clearer understanding of the role and functioning of family systems is needed in prevention for mental and physical health. Preventionists should be wary of overloading already overwhelmed systems. Focusing on priorities might allow more impact. A corresponding need is to give families the ability to do the prevention through empowerment. As reviewed in this chapter, some beginning work has been done, and much remains in terms of research and applications for understanding and enhancing the roles of families in prevention.

REFERENCES

Abraham, S., Collins, G., & Nordsieck, M. (1971). Relationship of child weight status to morbidity in adults. *HSMHA Health Reports, 86,* 273-284.

Alexander, D., Powell, G., Williams, P., White, M., & Conlon, M. (1991). Anxiety levels of rooming-in and non-rooming-in parents of young hospitalized children. In J. H. Johnson & S. B. Johnson (Eds.), *Advances in child health psychology* (pp. 233-248). Gainesville, FL: University of Florida Press.

Aragona, J., Cassady, J., & Drabman, R. S. (1975). Treating overweight children through parental training and contingency contracting. *Journal of Applied Behavior Analysis, 8,* 269–278.

Barone, V. J., Greene, B. F., & Lutzker, J. R. (1986). Home safety with families being treated for child abuse and neglect. *Behavior Modification, 10,* 93–114.

Beck, S., & Terry, K. (1985). A comparison of obese and normal weight families' psychological characteristics. *The American Journal of Family Therapy, 13,* 55–59.

Brazelton, T. B. (1975). Anticipatory guidance. In S. B. Friedman (Ed.), *The pediatric clinics of North America* (pp. 533–544). Philadelphia: Saunders.

Brownell, K. D., Kelman, J. H., & Stunkard, A. J. (1983). Treatment of obese children with and without their mothers: Changes in weight and blood pressure. *Pediatrics, 71,* 515–523.

Brownell, K. D., & Wadden, T. A. (1986). Behavior therapy for obesity: Modern approaches and better results. In K. D. Brownell & J. P. Foreyt (Eds.), *Handbook of eating disorders* (pp. 180–197). New York: Basic Books.

Califano, J. (Ed.). (1979). *Healthy people: The Surgeon General's report on health promotion and disease prevention.* Washington, DC: U.S. Department of Health, Education, and Welfare.

Christophersen, E. R., & Gyulay, J. E. (1981). Parental compliance with car seat usage: A positive approach with long-term follow-up. *Journal of Pediatric Psychology, 6,* 301–312.

DiClemente, R. J., Forrest, K. A., & Mickler, S. (1990). College students' knowledge and attitudes about AIDS and changes in HIV-preventive behaviors. *AIDS Education and Prevention, 2,* 201–212.

Doherty, W. J., & Campbell, T. L. (1988). *Families and health.* Newbury Park, CA: Sage.

Eichelberger, M. R., Gotschall, C. G., Feely, H. B., Harstad, P., & Bowman, L. M. (1990). Parental attitudes and knowledge of child safety: A national survey. *American Journal of Diseases of Children, 144,* 714–720.

Elkins, P. D., & Roberts, M. C. (1983). Psychological preparation for pediatric hospitalization. *Clinical Psychology Review, 3,* 275–295.

Epstein, L. H., McCurley, J., Wing, R. R., & Valoski, A. (1990). Five-year follow-up of family-based behavioral treatments for childhood obesity. *Journal of Consulting and Clinical Psychology, 58,* 661–664.

Epstein, L. H., Nudelman, S., & Wing, R. R. (1987). Long-term effects of family-based treatment for obesity on nontreated family members. *Behavior Therapy, 2,* 147–152.

Epstein, L. H., Wing, R. R., Koeske, R., Andrasik, F., & Ossip, D. J. (1981). Child and parent weight loss in family-based behavior modification programs. *Journal of Consulting and Clinical Psychology, 49,* 674–685.

Epstein, L. H., Wing, R. R., Koeske, R., & Valoski, A. (1987). Long-term effects of family-based treatment of childhood obesity. *Journal of Consulting and Clinical Psychology, 55,* 91-95.

Epstein, L. H., Wing, R. R., Valoski, A., & Gooding, W. (1987). Long-term effects of parent weight on child weight loss. *Behavior Therapy, 18,* 219-226.

Etzioni, A. (1978). Caution: Too many health warnings could be counterproductive. *Psychology Today, 12,* 20-22.

Fiese, B. H., & Sameroff, A. J. (1989). Family context in pediatric psychology: A transactional perspective. *Journal of Pediatric Psychology, 14,* 293-314.

Gallagher, S. S., Hunter, P., & Guyer, B. (1985). A home injury prevention program for children. In J. J. Alpert & B. Guyer (Eds.), *The pediatric clinics of North America: Injuries and injury prevention* (pp. 95-112). Philadelphia: Saunders.

Garn, S. M., Bailey, S. M., Solomon, M. A., & Hopkins, P. J. (1981). Effect of remaining family members on fatness prediction. *The American Journal of Clinical Nutrition, 34,* 148-153.

Graves, T., Meyers, A. W., & Clark, L. (1988). An evaluation of parental problem-solving training in the behavioral treatment of childhood obesity. *Journal of Consulting and Clinical Psychology, 56,* 246-250.

Greenberg, L. W., & Coleman, A. B. (1982). A prenatal and postpartum safety education program: Influence on parental use of infant care restraints. *Journal of Developmental and Behavioral Pediatrics, 3,* 32-34.

Gross, A. M., Stern, R. M., Levin, R. B., Dale, J., & Wojnilower, D. A. (1983). The effect of mother–child separation on the behavior of children experiencing a diagnostic medical procedure. *Journal of Consulting and Clinical Psychology, 51,* 783-785.

Harkaway, J. E. (1987). *Eating disorders.* Rockville, MD: Aspen Publications.

Harris, P. R. (1981). *Better health for our children.* Washington, DC: U.S. Government Printing Office.

Hawk, L. J., & Brook, C. G. D. (1979). Influence of body fatness in childhood on fatness in adult life. *British Medical Journal, 1,* 151-152.

Israel, A. C., Stolmaker, L., & Andrian, C. A. G. (1985). The effects of training parents in general child management skills on a behavioral weight loss program for children. *Behavior Therapy, 16,* 169-180.

Jay, S. M., & Elliott, C. H. (1990). A stress inoculation program for parents whose children are undergoing painful medical procedures. *Journal of Consulting and Clinical Psychology, 58,* 799-804.

Kirschenbaum, D. S., Harris, E. S., & Tomarken, A. J. (1984). Effects of parental involvement in behavioral weight loss therapy for preadolescents. *Behavior Therapy, 15,* 485-500.

Klesges, R. F., Coates, T. J., Brown, G., Sturgeon-Tillisch, J., Moldenhauer-Klesges, L. M., Holzer, B., Wollfry, J., & Vollmer, J. (1983). Parental influences on children's eating behavior and relative weight. *Journal of Applied Behavior Analysis, 16,* 371–378.

Knapp, L. G. (1991). The effects of persuasive communications on children's health behavior. *Journal of Pediatric Psychology, 16,* 675–686.

Litman, T. (1989). Methodological issues in family research. In C. N. Ramsey, Jr. (Ed.), *Family systems in medicine* (pp. 167–180). New York: Guilford Press.

Maddux, J. E., Roberts, M. C., Sledden, E. A., & Wright, L. (1986). Developmental issues in child health psychology. *American Psychologist, 41*(1), 25–34.

Matheny, A. (1987). Psychological characteristics of childhood accidents. *Journal of Social Issues, 43,* 45–60.

Meng, A., & Zastowny, T. (1982). Preparation for hospitalization: A stress inoculation training program for parents and children. *Maternal-Child Nursing Journal, 11* 87–94.

Miller, J. R., & Pless, I. B. (1977). Child automobile restraints: Evaluation of health education. *Pediatrics, 59,* 907–911.

Miltenberger, R. G., & Thiesse-Duffy, E. (1988). Evaluation of home-based programs for teaching personal safety skills to children. *Journal of Applied Behavior Analysis, 21,* 81–87.

Naylor, D., Coates, T., & Kan, J. (1984). Reducing distress in pediatric cardiac catheterization. *American Journal of Diseases in Children, 138,* 726–729.

Patterson, T. L., Sallis, J. F., Nader, P. R., Kaplan, R. M., Rupp, J. W., Atkins, C. J., & Senn, K. L. (1989). Familial similarities of changes in cognitive, behavioral, and physiological variables in a cardiovascular health promotion program. *Journal of Pediatric Psychology, 14,* 277–292.

Patterson, T. L., Tupp, J. W., Sallis, J. F., Atkins, C. J., & Nader, P. R. (1988). Aggregation of dietary calories, fasts, and sodium in Mexican-American and Anglo families. *American Journal of Preventive Medicine, 4,* 75–92.

Peterson, L. (1984a). The "safe-at-home" game: Training comprehensive safety skills in latch-key children. *Behavior Modification, 8,* 474–494.

Peterson, L. (1984b). Teaching home safety and survival skills to latchkey children: A comparison of two manuals and methods. *Journal of Applied Behavior Analysis, 17,* 279–292.

Peterson, L., Farmer, J., & Kashani, J. H. (1991). The role of beliefs in parental injury prevention efforts. In J. H. Johnson & S. B. Johnson (Eds.), *Advances in child health psychology* (pp. 115–126). Gainesville, FL: University of Florida Press.

Peterson, L., Farmer, J. E., & Selby, V. (1988). Unprompted between subject generalization of home safety skills. *Child and Family Behavior Therapy, 10,* 107–119.

Peterson, L., & Mori, L. (1985). Prevention of child injury: An overview of targets, methods, and tactics for psychologists. *Journal of Consulting and Clinical Psychology, 53,* 586–595.

Peterson, L., & Mori, L. (1988). Preparation for hospitalization. In D. K. Routh (Ed.), *Handbook of pediatric psychology* (pp. 460–491). New York: Guilford Press.

Peterson, L., & Mori, L., Selby, V., & Rosen, B. N. (1988). Community interventions in children's injury prevention: Differing costs and differing benefits. *Journal of Community Psychology, 16,* 188–204.

Peterson, L., & Roberts, M. C. (1986). Community intervention and prevention. In H. C. Quay & J. S. Werry (Eds.), *Psychopathological disorders of childhood* (3rd ed., pp. 622–660). New York: Wiley.

Peterson, L., & Roberts, M. C. (in press). Complacency, misdirection, and effective prevention of children's injuries. *American Psychologist.*

Peterson, L., & Shigetomi, C. (1981). The use of coping techniques to minimize anxiety in hospitalized children. *Behavior Therapy, 12,* 1–14.

Poche, C., Brouwer, R., & Swearingen, M. (1981). Teaching self-protection to young children. *Journal of Applied Behavior Analysis, 14,* 169–176.

Reisinger, K. S., & Williams, A. F. (1978). Evaluation of programs designed to increase the protection of infants in cars. *Pediatrics, 62,* 280–287.

Reppucci, N. D., & Haugaard, J. J. (1989). Prevention of child sexual abuse: Myth or reality. *American Psychologist, 44,* 1266–1275.

Roberts, M. C. (1986). Health promotion and problem prevention in pediatric psychology: An overview. *Journal of Pediatric Psychology, 11,* 147–161.

Roberts, M. C. (1987). Public health and health psychology: Two cats of Kilkenny? *Professional Psychology, 18,* 145–149.

Roberts, M. C. (1991). Overview to prevention research: Where's the cat? Where's the cradle? In J. Johnson & S. B. Johnson (Eds.), *Advances in child health psychology* (pp. 95–107). Gainesville, FL: University of Florida Press.

Roberts, M. C., Alexander, K., & Fanurik, D. (1990). Evaluation of commercially available materials to prevent child sexual abuse and abduction. *American Psychologist, 45,* 782–783.

Roberts, M. C., Alexander, K., & Knapp, L. (1990). Motivating children to use safety belts: A program combining rewards and "flash for life." *Journal of Community Psychology, 18,* 110–119.

Roberts, M. C., & Broadbent, M. H. (1989). Increasing preschoolers' use of car safety devices: An effective program for daycare staff. *Children's Health Care, 18,* 157–162.

Roberts, M. C., & Brooks, P. (1987). Children's injuries: Issues in prevention and public policy. *Journal of Social Issues, 43,* 1–12.

Roberts, M. C., Elkins, P. D., & Royal, G. P. (1984). Psychological applications to the prevention of accidents and illness. In M. C. Roberts & L. Peterson (Eds.), *Prevention of problems in childhood: Psychological research and applications* (pp. 173–199). New York: Wiley-Interscience.

Roberts, M. C., & Fanurik, D. (1986). Rewarding elementary school children for their use of safety belts. *Health Psychology, 5,* 185–196.

Roberts, M. C., Fanurik, D., & Layfield, D. (1987). Behavioral approaches to prevention of childhood injuries. *Journal of Social Issues, 43,* 105–118.

Roberts, M. C., Fanurik, D., & Wilson, D. (1988). A community program to reward children's use of seat belts. *American Journal of Community Psychology, 16,* 395–407.

Roberts, M. C., & Layfield, D. (1987). Promoting child passenger safety: A comparison of two positive methods. *Journal of Pediatric Psychology, 12,* 257–271.

Roberts, M. C., Maddux, J. E., & Wright, L. (1984). The developmental perspective in behavioral health. In J. D. Matarazzo, N. E. Miller, S. M. Weiss, J. A. Herd, & S. M. Weiss, (Eds.), *Behavioral health: A handbook of health enhancement and disease prevention* (pp. 56–68). New York: Wiley.

Roberts, M. C., & Peterson L. (1984b). Prevention models: Theoretical and practical implications. In M. C. Roberts & L. Peterson (Eds.), *Prevention of problems in childhood: Psychological research and applications* (pp. 1–39). New York: Wiley-Interscience.

Roberts, M. C., & Turner, D. (1984). Preventing death and injury in childhood: A synthesis of child safety seat efforts. *Heath Education Quarterly, 11,* 181–193.

Roberts, M. C., & Turner, D. (1986). Rewarding parents for their children's use of safety seats. *Journal of Pediatric Psychology, 11*(1), 25–36.

Roskies, E., Mongeon, M., & Gagnon-Lefebvre, B. (1978). Increasing maternal participation in the hospitalization of young children. *Medical Care, 16,* 765–777.

Sameroff, A. J., & Chandler, M. J. (1975). Reproductive risk and the continuum of caretaking casualty. In F. D. Horowitz, M. Ketherington, S. Scarr-Salapatek, & G. Sigel (Eds.), *Review of child development research* (Vol. 14, pp. 189–244). Chicago: University of Chicago Press.

Sallis, J. F., & Nader, P. R. (1988). Family determinants of health behaviors. In D. S. Gochman (Ed.), *Health behavior: Emerging research perspectives* (pp. 107–124). New York: Plenum Press.

Skipper, J., & Leonard, R. C. (1968). Children, stress, and hospitalization: A field experiment. *Journal of Health and Social Behavior, 9,* 275–287.

Stoto, M. A., Behrens, R., & Rosemont, C. (Eds.). (1990). *Healthy people 2000.* Washington, DC: National Academy Press.

Stunkard, A. J., Felix, M. R. J., & Cohen, R. Y. (1985). Mobilizing a community to promote health. In J. C. Rosen & L. J. Solomon (Eds.), *Preven-*

tion in health psychology (pp. 143–190). Hanover, NH: University Press of New England.

Sowers-Hoag, K. M., Thyer, B. A., & Bailey, J. S. (1987). Promoting automobile safety belt use by young children. *Journal of Applied Behavior Analysis, 20,* 133–138.

Tertinger, D. A., Greene, B. F., & Lutzker, J. R. (1984). Home safety: Development and validation of one component of an ecobehavioral treatment program for abused and neglected children. *Journal of Applied Behavior Analysis, 17,* 159–174.

Thomas, K. A., Hassanein, R. S., & Christophersen, E. R. (1984). Evaluation of group well-child care for improving burn prevention practices in the home. *Pediatrics, 94,* 879–882.

Turk, D. C., & Kerns, R. D. (1985). The family in health and illness. In D. C. Turk & R. D. Kerns (Eds.), *Health, illness, and families: A life-span perspective* (pp. 1–22). New York: Wiley.

Valsiner, J., & Lightfoot, C. (1987). Process structure of parent-child-environment relations and the prevention of children's injuries. *Journal of Social Issues, 43,* 61–72.

Visintainer, M. A., & Wolfer, J. A. (1975). Psychological preparation for surgical pediatric patients: Effects on children's and parents' stress responses and adjustment. *Pediatrics, 56,* 187–202.

White, C. W., & Albanese, M. A. (1981). Changes in cardiovascular health knowledge occurring from childhood to adulthood: A cross-sectional study. *Circulation, 63,* 1110–1115.

Zastowny, T. R., Kirschenbaum, D. S., & Meng, A. L. (1986). Coping skills training for children: Effects on distress before, during, and after hospitalization for surgery. *Health Psychology, 5,* 231–247.

5

PREVENTIVE INTERVENTION AND FAMILY COPING WITH A CHILD'S LIFE-THREATENING OR TERMINAL ILLNESS

Gerald P. Koocher
Bonnie L. MacDonald
Children's Hospital and Harvard Medical School, Boston, Massachusetts

Caring for a child with a life-threatening or terminal illness places tremendous stress on a family. The current state of medical diagnosis and therapeutics is such that the number of long-term survivors of life-threatening illnesses grows daily and represents a major challenge for preventive mental health care in pediatrics. As the patient's illness and treatment evolve and change over time, so do family members' reactions, coping, and adaptation. Delivery of services to the patient and family should begin at the time of initial evaluation and diagnosis and continue throughout the course of illness and its follow-up, whether this be recovery or death. This chapter describes some of the issues affecting children's and families' coping with the life-threatening or terminal illness of a child and highlight the roles of mental health practitioners in facilitating successful adaptation.

Approximately 30 to 40 years ago, acute infectious illnesses such as polio and smallpox claimed substantial numbers of children's lives. Acute lymphoblastic leukemia (ALL), the most common noninfectious cause of death of children between 5 and 15 years of age, was usually fatal within 6 months. Today immunizations have virtually eliminated polio and smallpox in the United States and children newly diagnosed with "standard risk" ALL have a better than 70% chance of surviving 5 or more years in a disease-free state. Other chronic illnesses such as cystic fibrosis and juvenile-onset diabetes have increasingly yielded to medical progress but not without some cost in terms of family stress. Indeed, the psychologic stresses associated with the uncertainties of long-term survival among children with life-threatening illness have been termed a *Damocles syndrome* (Koocher & O'Malley, 1981). The quality of life among such patients and their families is often linked to their ability to ignore the uncertainty and adopt an optimistic or hopeful attitude and use active coping strategies.

A FAMILY APPROACH TO CARE

The practitioner must be aware that the threat of death affects the whole social ecology of the patient. The costs to the patient's family are substantial in emotional and financial terms. The course of the illness is likely to sap the adaptive capacities of the parents, both as individuals and as a couple. Siblings are also likely to experience an extra burden of stress. Learning to deal with chronic stress, disruption, and uncertainty makes coping a continually trying task. One study (Koocher & O'Malley, 1981) summarizes the burdens of coping as "balancing the needs of the patient in the home with those of healthy siblings; fostering the patient's normal social and emotional development while coping with long-term uncertainty; and dealing with unresolved anticipatory grief if the child survives" (p. 30). If the patient does die, there will be a family of grief-stricken survivors. Because the illness affects the entire family, all family members must be considered part of the "patient care" locus. A family-based intervention is an absolute necessity if optimal adaptation and support of the patient and surviving family members is the goal.

THE ROLE
OF THE MENTAL HEALTH PROFESSIONAL

In formulating a service plan or clinic structure for children with terminal or life-threatening illness, teamwork is of critical importance. The most desirable strategy would be one that integrates medical and mental health care, along with home care and other ancillary services, within a single system (Koocher, Sourkes, & Keane, 1979). Such a system enables the medical and mental health personnel to know each other well. The medical staff becomes more familiar with mental health issues, and the psychosocial staff learns about the diagnostic and therapeutic events their patients encounter. Patients benefit by virtue of the fact that all caregivers interact closely and more efficiently. Families should feel they are not singled out as being crazy or in need of emotional support. If mental health services are routinely offered, no stigma accrues to those who use the service. Integrating medical and mental health services makes the use of such programs more normal for all concerned.

The mental health professional can offer important support to the patient, family, and medical staff by consulting with them on the assessment of the patient's developmental level, the meaning of psychological and psychogenic symptoms, and the care and management of the patient. Indirect consultation may lead to direct patient contact or enhanced care by medical personnel without such a referral. The mental health professional can also facilitate creation of a forum to discuss team members' emotional reactions to providing care to patients and their families.

At the outset of work with a child with a life-threatening illness, the mental health professional needs to gather information on relevant preexisting and background psychological factors, as these will affect the individual's understanding of and reaction to the diagnosis and course of treatment. These factors include in particular, developmental issues and aspects of the family environment, especially having to do with culture, communication style, openness to discussion of the illness, and cohesion or support. Age is only one developmental variable, with emotional, social, and cognitive development each playing its own role in shaping the child's reactions. Experiences with loss, separation, and illness also color the reactions of individual family members.

DEVELOPMENTAL ISSUES

Children's Developmental Tasks

Among both children and families, developmental differences pertain to stage-salient tasks that would normally be confronted and resolved at any given time. Diagnosis of a serious illness may interfere with accomplishment of these tasks and pose specific challenges to the different individuals because of their developmental levels. For children, these issues also pertain to specific concerns and fears related to their illness and treatment.

For instance, separation is a stage-salient issue for children in infancy. The infant who cannot see his or her parent cannot retain the concept that the parent still exists to provide care (Mahler, Pine, & Bergman, 1973; Piaget, 1954). The infant's reaction of acute distress to the parent's leaving is well recognized. The infant or toddler in the hospital, an unfamiliar setting with strangers as caregivers, seeks parental reassurance and comfort and finds separation even more anxiety-producing than the healthy child. Arranging for parents to sleep in the hospital room with their child and to be integrally involved in their child's care is vital at this age. This includes accompanying and comforting the child during medical procedures. At times the parents' heightened anxiety, or withdrawal due to anticipatory grief, may cause them to defer basic care of their child to the nursing staff. Clearly, parents need support and encouragement to remain in close contact with their child.

By age three, most preschoolers have established a sense of psychological autonomy and are increasingly able to tolerate parental absence (Mahler et al., 1973). The diagnosis of a life-threatening illness and the need for prolonged hospitalization, however, may lead to regressive behavior and an increased need for parental contact. Especially because preschoolers may perceive death as a type of separation from others, fears and fantasies about illness and dying may be confused with concerns about separation. Older children react most severely to perceived threats to their competence, expressing fears of falling behind in school or reacting with marked depression and anxiety to mobility losses. The parents' presence and active involvement remain essential throughout the childhood years to address and alleviate such concerns.

The adolescent is concerned about potential family withdrawal related anticipatory grief, the censoring of medical information, and social withdrawal of peers owing to their anxieties about serious illness, all of which isolate the patient. The teenager, in addition, suffers intense concerns with the loss of privacy, autonomy, peer interactions, and school activities, because these are the primary delineators of evolving self-esteem in adolescence. Separation from peer activities poses a difficulty for many adolescent patients. Overall, the issues of most concern to children are linked largely to their levels of cognitive and social functioning, including differences in time perspective, conceptual skills, and specific stage-related challenges.

Family Life Cycle

At the same time, the family itself also has a developmental life cycle. Solomon (1973) identifies five stages, based on the critical tasks to be completed. A family begins with a marriage, which includes separation from the families of origin and investment of primary commitments in the marriage. The second stage centers on the birth of the first child and involves development of new roles as parents, without neglecting the marital relationship. The third stage, individuation, begins when the first child enters school and requires accepting the child's growing independence and also encouraging socialization. In the fourth stage, departure of the children, parents must learn to let go, while the adult children separate and develop other primary relationships. In the fifth stage, integration of loss, aging parents must typically deal with losses in economic, social, and physical functioning.

Neugarten (1976) has pointed out that major life events such as those outlined by Solomon occur within a three-dimensional plane of time: historical time, life time (or chronological age), and social time. The last refers to a socially prescribed timetable for the ordering of these events. It is important to note that life cycle events are much more likely to be traumatic if they occur off-time instead of in the expected course of life. Seen from this perspective, a child's serious illness or death is extremely disruptive and difficult to accept. It is outside of not only the "natural" course of an individual's life but also the usual progression of events in the life cycle of a family.

As McCubbin and Figley (1983) note, families generally operate on a predictable, normative cycle, anticipating and accepting a sequence of events that will occur throughout the life course. Predictable transitions may themselves cause significant stress. In addition, occurrence of nonnormative events, or normative events such as illness and death at unanticipated times, may drain the family's economic and emotional resources and detract attention from other ongoing developmental demands. Responses to events that require significant change will not only be affected by but also exert an impact on developmental progress. The successful attainment of each person's developmental tasks is dependent on and contributes to the successful achievement by other family members of their appropriate tasks at the same time that the family unit is growing and changing in its own behavioral domains (Duvall & Miller, 1985).

The death or serious illness of a child may preclude the family's resolution of stage-salient tasks such as children's individuation from their parents (Herz, 1980), thereby upsetting the normative progression of life cycle transitions as described by Solomon (1973) and Duvall and Miller (1985). The death of a child is therefore particularly disruptive if the parents perceive through emotional fusion the child as an extension of themselves, their hopes, and dreams in life. The death of an adolescent is particularly disruptive from this perspective because significant stress is added to an already tumultuous period, and the family may never be truly able to complete their life cycle task of differentiating from that child (Herz, 1980).

Children's Understanding of Illness and Death

A child's understanding of and reaction to illness also vary dramatically as a function of development. These abilities and changes have implications for family members and professionals who will be explaining circumstances and events to the child. In terms of secondary prevention, an understanding of developmental progress allows adults to anticipate children's concerns over time. For example, cognitive development influences the child's ability to conceptualize the nature and consequences of his or her illness, including the possibility of death and what this means. The infant who is ill probably does not realize that circumstances could be otherwise and makes little connection of causality with respect to the disease process and the treatment program. As the toddler becomes more verbal, it is possible to communicate directly about the disease and treatment processes; however, it is difficult for a young child to differentiate between what happens to others and what happens to him- or herself. Magical thinking is also active at this age, and the perceived causes of illness-related events may differ radically from reality. Adults may want to ask a child about his or her own beliefs and to clarify when necessary.

By age six or seven, most children have many questions, although they may not always feel free to ask them. A better sense of cause and effect in the illness-treatment process is present. Death is now recognized as irreversible rather than akin to sleep or other personal experiences of the living. For a child who lost a loved one at an earlier age, new questions and fears arise along with this awareness. In adolescence, with the onset of hypothetical thinking, alternatives that might not have occurred to the younger child are prevalent (e.g.,

What will happen if the treatments do not work?). A future orientation becomes meaningful, and the long-range consequences of illness and treatment are salient for the first time.

Social and emotional development play a role in children's interpretations of and ability to adjust to their illness and the limitations that may be associated with it. Caregivers need to be aware of children's developing capacities to cope with these stressors. Emotional expression in the infant is primitive and is directly linked to impulse and sensation. As the child gets older, mood and reactivity become more stable, but fantasies and fears become important to overall emotional reactivity and adaptation. In the preadolescent years, mastery and competence-building activity helps to form adaptive mechanisms in the face of emotional stress. Intellectual problem solving becomes useful as a defense mechanism. The adolescent is thinking seriously about growing up as well as developing a sense of identity distinct from family membership.

FAMILY ENVIRONMENT ISSUES

Communication

Because development unfolds as a function of endogenous maturation in concert with experience, it is also important to assess aspects of the family environment, particularly as they pertain to openness of communication regarding the illness. Even among families who generally communicate openly, individuals may find it quite difficult to discuss their thoughts and feelings about a life-threatening illness or the realities of death. Bowen (1976) points out that first, death is a taboo subject, and second, individuals may avoid discussing illness and death honestly, for fear of producing anxiety or distress in their listener. As such, the patient, family, and medical staff may all withhold from each other their knowledge of or feelings about the threat of death.

Clinicians must be aware that it is often the caregivers' own anxiety and distress that prevents them from communicating. The classic paper by Vernick and Karon (1965) entitled "Who's Afraid of Death on a Leukemia Ward?" illustrates the discomfort effectively. Through the use of life-space interviews, they documented the fact that children clearly knew the seriousness of their illnesses and were eager to have someone to talk with about it. However, these children with leukemia sensed their caretakers' anxiety and concern, even though the adults attempted to be cheerful. The authors described the communication barriers often erected by adults to "protect the child," and they noted that children often did not ask questions because they were apprehensive about their parents' discomfort in discussing death.

Indeed, the oft-held assumption that children cannot comprehend and are upset by death has served more to justify avoiding honest discussions with dying children (Evans & Edin, 1968) than to respond to actual circumstances. Reviews of professional opinion and research data have consistently stressed that children as young as age five or six have a very real understanding of the seriousness of their illness, and still younger children show definite reactions to increased parental stress and other effects of a terminal illness on the family. Empirical data show, for example, how anxiety levels in children with leukemia increase in tandem with increases in the frequency of outpatient clinic visits (Spinetta, Rigler, & Karon, 1973). This is the opposite of what one finds in youngsters with chronic non-life-threatening illness. Other data demonstrate the increasing sense of isolation that dying children tend to experience (Spinetta, Rigler, & Karon, 1974). One cannot shield sick children from anxiety about their conditions.

Spinetta et al. (1973) also demonstrated that children as young as age six who have leukemia are aware of the meaning and possible fatal outcome of their disease. Older children are also well aware of their disease, its possible ramifications, and of the tendency of parents and physicians to withhold or distort information. The child has many fears and apprehensions about unknown possibilities, and open communication provides an opportunity to dispel them and concentrate on the adjustment required for the realities of treatment. Kellerman, Rigler, and Siegal (1977) noted an inverse relationship between a child's open discussion of his or her illness and depression. Most important, a closed communication style leads to a sense of isolation for the child. Vernick and Karon (1965) have argued that openness allows the child to feel more secure and trusting of the medical staff and parents, noting that "blows cannot always be softened, but by explanation and sharing, their impact may be made somewhat less concentrated and acute" (p. 396).

Caregivers can further help the family of a seriously ill child by paying attention to the needs and roles of siblings. A common consequence of the demands of the illness is that healthy siblings experience decreased parental attention and support. They may feel angry at both their ill sibling and their parents. They may become angry at their ill sibling for the disruption in the family, and at their parents for failing to protect the patient from the disease. School and peer relationships can also be adversely affected. School performance may decline in response to family stress. In other instances, siblings may plunge into academic pursuits as a means of escaping stresses at home, or to prove themselves competent in an effort to combat family feelings of hopelessness. Peer relationships can be interrupted for practical reasons, such as school absences or because of retreat into the family. Siblings may also feel alienated from friends who do not understand their irritability and preoccupation. Development of somatic complaints as a means of garnering parental attention or to identify with the ill sibling has also been observed. Death and mourning for a sibling may raise many issues of vulnerability, guilt, and confusion.

Open communication between the patient's physician and the siblings, including family counseling sessions, is one very beneficial approach. Siblings have many questions and fantasies that must be addressed and clarified. Par-

ents' efforts to spend special time with their healthy children and to aid them in
maintaining a normal life are also important approaches.

Cohesion and Support

Elements of the family environment such as cohesion and expressiveness may
relate to patterns of communication and styles of coping, which subsequently
affect adjustment. A balanced degree of family cohesion, without extremes on
either bonding or autonomy, is hypothesized to be the most conducive to effective family functioning and optimal individual development (e.g., Olson,
Sprenkle, & Russell, 1979). For instance, Weber and Fournier (1985) found
self-reported levels of cohesion (reflected in perceptions of support and commitment) associated with both children's decisionmaking autonomy and their
participation in death-related activities (particularly mourning rituals). Families
with higher reported levels of cohesion made decisions for their children, who
in turn had the lowest participation scores. Of further interest, children who
participated more fully in their families' death-related events had a greater
conceptual understanding of death, suggesting that participation may provide
cognitive and emotional support. However, the relationships of age and cognitive development to understanding of death were not considered. Furthermore,
the reader cannot rule out the influence of family style and communication on
the child's understanding of death; those children from highly cohesive families
who did not participate in the funeral might also have been shielded from the
facts about death.

In another study, Spinetta, Swarner, and Sheposh (1981) concluded that
openness of communication is beneficial for both the surviving family members
and the terminally ill child. Objectively scored statements from structured interviews with 23 families who had lost a child to cancer within the past 3 years
indicated that three major factors were related to the success of adaptation.
Parents who were best adjusted were those who (a) had a consistent philosophy
of life during the child's life, which helped the family accept the diagnosis and
cope with its consequences; (b) had an ongoing, supportive relationship with a
significant other, usually a spouse; and (c) gave their child the information and
emotional support he or she needed during the course of the illness at a level
consistent with the child's questions, age, and level of development. In each of
these elements, both open communication and support play an important and
beneficial part.

Families differ on distinct indicants of coping styles, and these patterns
appear to be related to both short- and long-term adjustment to loss. The majority of data indicates that open discussion of thoughts and feelings, accommodation to change, and attention to the individual needs of others are characteristics
of families who adapt most successfully.

Finally, initial assessment of the child and family should include attention to sources of support within and outside the family. Increased marital stress and financial strain are predictable phenomena. The quality of the marital relationship prior to diagnosis serves as an important predictor of the adequacy of marital coping with the crisis. Differences in parental coping styles, or being "out of synch" in the timing of emotional reactions, and differences in priorities in managing the family can also exacerbate marital tension (Sourkes, 1977). A decreased sense of parental competence can further impair coping. The survival of the marriage may be linked to survival of the patient, but professional counseling and parent support groups can play important roles in helping to manage parental and marital stress (Koocher & O'Malley, 1981).

Parents' individual ways of coping and ability to work as a team may pertain to their previous experiences with illness and loss. Concurrent stressors may heighten the risk for disturbances, whereas adaptive skills may function as a buffer. Because a family is a system of interdependent parts, actual adaptation consists of a progression of multiply determined and determining events. When a change such as the illness or death of a child occurs it will reverberate throughout the system. As individuals implement their own coping strategies such as expressing emotion or withdrawing, these will both affect and be affected by others' efforts at adaptation, which are simultaneously ongoing. The service provider needs to get a sense of family styles, strengths, and weaknesses, in order to manage predictable stress reactions and to promote communication, understanding, and mutual support.

Reactions to the Diagnosis

During the course of the illness and its treatment, the role of the mental health practitioner is certainly significant. In the initial phase, it may be especially useful to provide information to the family that normalizes their experience and clarifies that considerable difficulties are common. Normal behavior in the family of the child with terminal or life-threatening illness is different from that of the same family prior to the diagnosis. This truism is often overlooked by professionals immersed in the process of treating such families. For example, bright attentive parents talking retrospectively of the day they first learned their child's diagnosis frequently report, "After the doctor told us our child had leukemia, he said some other things too. . . . I don't remember what they were." The "other things" probably dealt with treatments that were to begin, but the parents, overwhelmed by the threat of a potentially terminal illness, were too stunned to absorb the information. Such reactions are indeed normal under the circumstances.

Children who are terminally ill, or who face an uncertain but potentially fatal outcome from some chronic illness, are at substantial risk for emotional problems as a function of stress. A host of publications has documented the core stresses and common symptoms. Depending on the course and trajectory of the disease process, even children who were quite normal prior to becoming ill may develop increased anxiety, loss of appetite, insomnia, social isolation, emotional withdrawal, depression and apathy, and marked ambivalence toward adults who are providing primary care.

These reactions are generally best regarded as responses to acute or chronic stress rather than as evidence of functional psychopathology. It is predictable, however, that children or families with preexisting emotional disorders will experience an exacerbation of preexisting problems. The primary model for conceptualizing the way in which this occurs is best described in the work of Seligman (1975) and other writers on the topic of learned helplessness. When people believe that the outcome they will confront (i.e., death) is independent of their own behavior, the helplessness syndrome and accompanying emotional stress are dramatic.

Even children who otherwise seem to be coping quite well through a prolonged illness may develop specific problems such as conditioned reflex vomiting, anxiety linked to specific medical procedures, depressive reactions to progressive loss of physical capacities, or family communication inhibitions (Koocher & O'Malley, 1981). Some children experience intense anxiety as they near the end of a long course of chemotherapy. Although this may seem a paradoxical reaction to the cessation of a noxious experience, hospitalizations and stressful treatment regimens may become imbued with some protective value, and both the patient and other family members may worry about the impact of stopping the powerful drugs that have kept the cancer away.

Maintaining a Sense of Control

In regard to learned helplessness, the loss of control implicit in the diagnosis is one of the most devastating aspects of the emotional crisis created by the diagnosis of a life-threatening illness. Parents may experience the loss of ability to protect their child from harm and to positively influence their child's future. Their own feelings of loss of control in this situation may generate intensification of their concern and caretaking behavior, thus helping regain a sense of control when they feel helpless. Often, however, this behavior can be experienced as infantilizing by the patient.

Encouraging opportunities for the patient and family to have a sense of control is another important task for caregivers. This can be done in such a way as to facilitate involvement, support, and the achievement of developmental tasks.

Preadolescent children who are seeking mastery in many new areas may experience the loss of control in terms of an inability to plan their lives. Children may displace anger onto schedules or hospitalization that interfere with such plans. Moreover, they may attempt to regain control by testing parental limits. The parents may in turn curtail discipline out of guilt or concern for their sick child. Rather than making the child feel special, however, this can make the child feel more out of control.

Although the loss of control is a salient issue for all patients, it has a heightened impact during adolescence. Adolescents strive for greater autonomy in their environment and increasing independence from parents. These gains are impeded by hospitalizations where members of the medical staff make decisions that affect the adolescent's health and daily life. Patients often feel bombarded by intrusive medical practices. The hospital experience can foster passivity and regressive dependence that inhibits adolescents' sense of mastery over their environment. The ability to experience competence through school, social experiences, and planning for the future is also seriously disrupted when treatments or medical conditions make it difficult for the patient to keep up.

Another adolescent task is developing mastery over one's changing body. Body image issues are directly challenged by the physical changes often accompanying illness. For instance, alopecia (baldness), a frequent side effect of chemotherapy, is a visible, inescapable reminder to the patient of his or her disease as well as a possible source of embarrassment and diminution of self-esteem. Comfort and confidence in sexual attractiveness also are challenged severely by the effects of both the disease and its treatment.

Just as with younger children, the loss of control accompanying a hospitalization is also stressful for adolescents. The daily schedule is disrupted, familiar people and activities are missing, and the result is loss of control. Some adolescent patients may be especially uncomfortable at some particular time of day, often coinciding with a missed special activity or lonely late evening hours. Increasing patients' perception of control can improve their ability to cope with disease (Langer & Rodin, 1976; Seligman, 1975). This can be accomplished by permitting patients to wear their own clothes in the hospital or engage in other such normalizing activities.

PLANNING PSYCHOLOGICAL CARE
FOR THE DYING CHILD

The dying child requires the support, care, and love of his or her family and friends. One of the interdisciplinary team's key roles is to encourage and facilitate the family's ability to offer such care. The patient's feelings of being surrounded by a network of understanding people and not being isolated is vital to successful coping with end-stage disease. The knowledge that he or she can openly discuss fears and thoughts about death without being censored is equally important. Knowing that people important to them are available to conduct "unfinished business," such as telling rival siblings that they are loved or asking a parent to carry out a request about belongings or the funeral, can be very comforting to patients.

Modeling of Responses

Much of children's reactions to stress is learned through their observation of caregivers. Kübler-Ross (1981, cited in Bowlby-West, 1983) said that dying children showed little fear of their own death and were more concerned for what would happen to their parents afterward. She concluded that children are not afraid of death unless shown otherwise. In a similar vein, Bowen (1976) reported that he had never seen a child hurt by exposure to death, but rather only affected by the anxiety of survivors. The health care professionals affiliated with a family also serve as powerful role models, and their portraying a stance toward the illness that emphasizes honesty, openness, and trust will help the family to feel comfortable with such communication.

Terminal Care at Home

Another way for the family to be involved and to have a sense of control is through terminal care at home or in an alternative center such as a hospice. An important study of terminal care of pediatric patients at home provided useful information about this alternative (Martinson et al., 1978). Martinson and her colleagues studied children who died of cancer while participating in a home care program and noted four essential requirements for the success of such programs: the availability of (a) a family member to provide daily care, (b) a nurse on 24-hour call for telephone consultation and home visits, (c) necessary equipment such as oxygen or air mattresses, and (d) a physician for direct consultation with the family and primary nurse and for prescribing medication, particularly analgesics. The nurse and physician must work together closely for home care to be successful. The nurse has the pivotal role in providing medical, emotional, and practical support to the patient and family.

Martinson reported that children under 4 years of age did not have a strong awareness that they were dying. School-age children reported feeling secure in being home with their family and were relieved that they could avoid medical procedures associated with the hospital. Adolescents were reported to be frustrated and angry at their need to be dependent, often depressed, but in some cases accepting of imminent death. Martinson concluded that there is insufficient demand for pediatric hospices but that home care directed by a hospital staff is a desirable alternative for families and patients who prefer the home setting. She believes that the security of the home is preferable to the hospital for the dying child. Finally, she underscored the need for postmortem follow-up and supportive services.

Family environment measures of cohesion, independence, and moral and religious emphasis have been found to differ between families who had a child die of cancer either at home or in the hospital (Mulhern, Lauer, & Hoffman, 1983). Families who participated in the home care program reported significantly more commitment, support, and ethical and religious values, and significantly less assertiveness and self-sufficiency. Between 3 and 29 months after the death, siblings in home care families were rated by their mothers as exhibiting behaviors well within normal limits on a standardized checklist, whereas the siblings of patients who were not provided home care showed fears and neurotic behavior in the clinical range. These children also showed more social isolation, sensitivity, fear, and somatic behaviors than their home care counterparts, and fewer socially valued qualities.

The parents who did not provide home care scored higher on seven clinical scales of the Minnesota Multiphasic Personality Inventory, assessing somatic complaints, depression, denial of problems, anxiety and self-doubt, expression of anger and social maladjustment, alienation and self-dissatisfaction, and social withdrawal. It is important to note that several of these characteristics are typically stable over time (e.g., anxiety and alienation) and so may have influenced parents' decisions to participate in the home care program in the first place, which was voluntary.

In a similar manner, family environment variables may have contributed to parents' assessment of their ability to care adequately for their child at home, although these early data are not directly available here. That is, both parental adjustment and family environment may be related to decisions about caring for a terminally ill child at home, which in turn influences family cohesion and the adjustment of both parents and siblings following the patient's death.

Follow-up Visits

Continued follow-up care is valuable for both bereaved families and those whose children become long-term survivors of life-threatening illness. This should be a routine part of treatment and liaison services. Inviting the family to return to the hospital or to meet with professionals who helped to care for the deceased often can be helpful weeks or months after death. Some families feel that they cannot ask for this because the patient is dead and their own needs do not seem a satisfactory basis for "imposing" on the staff.

Sometimes an invitation by the staff to discuss autopsy results provides an opportunity for surviving family members to discuss residual emotional issues. A similar opportunity is also frequently welcomed by families who are told that follow-up discussions are "routine." The family members do not want to feel "crazy," "emotionally disturbed," or different from other families, and establishing a return visit as "normal" helps them to make use of it.

Often, friends, neighbors, and relatives do not understand why the immediate family has not "gotten over" the loss after several weeks or months. People outside the family may overtly or subtly give messages that they no longer wish to hear about the deceased. In such circumstances, those who helped to care for the deceased child may offer the only emotional outlet available.

The ever-increasing numbers of children who survive, and their families also, have ongoing needs. The patients may live with diseases such as cancer or cystic fibrosis only to experience relapses after prolonged periods of relatively good health. These children require special consideration and psychological care as they struggle with the uncertainties of survival beneath a Damoclean sword (Koocher, 1984; Koocher & O'Malley, 1981).

The families of such children experience similar stresses, with occasional conflicting messages about whether to prepare for a death or hold realistic hope for the future of these children. Encouraging such families to make use of psychological services, while offering them appropriate medical information and sensitive follow-up care, is the best intervention strategy. The key issue is not to assume that because the disease is under control, the emotions about the threat of loss are also under control.

AFTERCARE ISSUES

Stage Theories of Emotional Response to Terminal Illness

In cases in which children die, health care workers need to understand the parameters of grief reactions among parents and surviving children and be able to recommend or provide additional services when necessary.

The notion that people progress through predictable stages of emotional responses to life events has been widely discussed in recent years. Kübler-Ross's (1969) stage theory of adjustment to terminal illness is well known. Silver and Wortman (1980; Wortman & Silver, 1989) have questioned whether such theories with intuitive appeal are indeed borne out by empirical research. They note the relative paucity of controlled studies applying stage theories to responses to adverse circumstances. Moreover, none of these studies has included pediatric patients. In reviewing the relevant primate and human studies, the authors concluded:

> The limited data [do] not appear to cleanly fit a stage model of emotional response following life crises. In addition, the extreme pattern of variability that exists in response to [adverse] life events also does not support the notion of stages of response. . . . It must also be recognized that some theorists contend that people may experience more than one stage simultaneously, may move back and forth among the stages, and may skip certain stages completely. (1980, pp. 304–305)

The crucial point here is that we must recognize the great variability in human response, and the nonlinear progression of emotional responsivity, and conceptualize in terms of reactions rather than lock-step stages. Wortman and Silver (1989) provide a provocative stance on such variability that exists in response to loss and comment that "recognition of this variability is crucial in order that those who experience loss are treated non-judgementally and with the respect, sensitivity and compassion they deserve" (p. 355). These concerns may be especially salient in work with pediatric patients. In thinking about adolescents with cancer, for example, one is likely to see a significant, direct, and continuing expression of anger beyond what Kübler-Ross has predicted. The adolescent is also much less likely to reach a stage of acceptance of death. Case management must therefore be focused on individual patient responses and needs. The clinician should not fall into the conceptual trap of pondering why a patient has not yet reached a certain stage at an expected juncture.

Assessing Grief Reactions

When the patient dies, the pediatrician must consider the needs of surviving family members, and even when the patient is a long-term survivor, the doctor must focus special attention on the grief reactions that normally occur. Although most articles on this topic have focused chiefly on adults, it is important to note that grief reactions have at least three phases that may apply to people of all ages: acute, chronic, and anticipatory grief. The acute sadness and tearfulness that may follow immediately after a loss is probably the best recognized manifestation of grief. However, it is the long-term reactions leading up to a death from chronic illness or following the loss by several months that create the more subtle management problems.

Symptoms associated with grief reactions in childhood often include tearfulness, social and emotional withdrawal, loss of interest in favorite toys or pastimes, a decreased attention span, the development of tics, loss of appetite, persistent insomnia or nightmares, decreased ineffectiveness in school, increases in the unfocused activity level, and expressions of guilt over past activities, especially in relation to the deceased (Bowlby, 1973; Lindemann, 1944). The natural dependency of children, along with their potential for animistic and magical thinking, makes them particularly vulnerable to prolonged adverse psychological sequelae following an important loss (Lonetto, 1980). At the same time, the absence of symptoms of acute grief or a sharply truncated reaction may herald premature application of denial or avoidance defenses, with the potential for emergence of symptoms much later.

One key to the diagnostic assessment of childhood grief reactions is the presence or absence of anxiety. The child or adolescent who is in the process of adapting to a loss should be able to verbalize some sadness and related feelings in the course of an interview. Inability to discuss the loss, denial of affect, or anxiety and guilt related to the deceased or surviving family members are all indicators that additional evaluation or psychotherapeutic intervention may be warranted.

Time can also be an important factor in assessing adaptation to loss, but there are no uniform guidelines to apply. Although the intensity of the depressive symptoms often abates substantially over a period of several weeks, so-called "anniversary phenomena" may trigger their return. Arrival of a birthday, holiday, or other family event may induce a return of sadness, tension, or stress, along with thoughts of the deceased person. Usually, these recurrences are much less intense than the acute mourning experience. If they persist more than several days following the stimulus events or evoke a heretofore unseen intensity, a psychological evaluation is warranted.

Consideration of Grief Reactions
Within the Family Context

The clinician must also be especially sensitive to the fact that the bereaved child cannot accurately be evaluated outside the family context. Grief reactions in children are subject to both amelioration and exacerbation based on the presence or absence of emotional support within the surviving family. Behavioral contagion and social learning also play roles in determining children's response. Religious rituals and family behavior patterns provide opportunities for observational learning and imitation that may be either facilitative or inhibitory with respect to children's adaptation. Children may also react to mourning, depression, or anxiety in their parents or caretakers, even though they have had no personal contact with the deceased. It is therefore important for the pediatrician confronted with a patient's grief reaction to consider the parents' emotional status as well.

In one of the few studies that provided an intervention program to bereaved families, Black and Urbanowitz (1987) showed that not only communication within the family but also adjustment of other individuals affect children's responses to loss. One year after the death of a parent, children who had cried and talked about the deceased in the first month post-loss had fewer and less serious behavioral and emotional problems. This emotional expression in the family therapy setting functions as a process variable that dovetails with other familial support factors.

In their discussion, the authors point out that the higher level of adjustment among the treatment-group families in comparison with controls may have been primarily due to the improvement of surviving mothers' mood state. Indeed, voluminous literature exists demonstrating the relationship of maternal depression to a variety of child behavioral and emotional problems. From a family systems perspective, the significance of this factor lies in its contributions to numerous, ongoing exchanges between the parent and the child that are characterized by lack of responsiveness, inability to please the parent, rejections, and emotional unavailability (e.g., Weintraub, Winters, & Neale, 1986). This is also consistent with a transactional, developmental view of depression and other psychopathologies in childhood (e.g., Cicchetti & Schneider-Rosen, 1984; Emde, Harmon, & Good, 1986; Rutter, 1986).

When the death or serious illness of a sibling occurs, children need considerable support, but unfortunately the people who would usually provide it are the parents, who also have been affected traumatically. Under such circumstances, parents may feel impatient or irritated with the demands of their bereaved children. Patterns of discipline and other life-style factors may change, adding to the stress and likelihood of disturbance in both parents and children. Rather than the atmosphere of stability and consistency recommended for a better outcome, the common situation following a death in the nuclear family may be considerable disorganization, confusion, and uncertainty (Osterweis, Solomon, & Green, 1984).

Management of Grief Reactions

The emotional care of the bereaved child, whether a surviving sibling or another patient, should have two focal points. First is the need to help children differentiate their fate from that of the deceased. Second is the need of children to arrive at a sense of closure with regard to the loss. This may involve expressing feelings of guilt or responsibility for the death, as well as magical fears about what actually transpired. Both foci are important issues for any child who experiences a loss, although the need is more acute when considerable anxiety persists.

When another patient known to the child dies, the stress may be particularly intense. The need to differentiate between the recently deceased and the living is a common cognitive adaptive response among children and adults. Adults are not immune to magical thinking, especially in times of emotional stress, but children have a particular need to distinguish between real and imaginal causes of death. Investigators of cognitive development have long documented the difficulties that children of different ages may have in coping with abstractions and, because death is a one-time-only, final experience for each of us, it qualifies as an abstract experience of individual mastery.

The questions a child may be presumed to worry about in the aftermath of a death include the following: How (i.e., by what means) did the person die? Will that happen to me (or someone else I care about)? Did I have anything to do with it? Who will take care of me now (if the deceased was one of the child's caretakers)? Although these questions may not be specifically articulated by the child, they are almost always a part of the underlying anxiety that accompanies a prolonged grief reaction. Addressing them must involve both informational and emotional components.

In a family context, involvement of surviving siblings in funerary rituals may also be quite helpful and supportive if such involvement is well explained and consistent with the child's wishes. Vicarious satisfaction of adults' needs is not a proper basis for making the decision whether to involve a child in a funeral. Introduction of philosophic or religious concepts may tend to confuse and frighten young children, especially in the absence of close family support.

A CLOSING NOTE

Many professionals are fearful of working with families of terminally ill children. Most often, they cite their own helplessness or sense of inadequacy in the face of death as a basis for this fear. The patients and their families are also afraid but want and need the support of professionals who can provide some encouragement and advice about how to cope with stress and uncertainty. The emotional rewards of working with families during this difficult time are substantial.

REFERENCES

Black, D., & Urbanowitz, M. A. (1987). Family intervention with bereaved children. *Journal of Child Psychology and Psychiatry, 28,* 467–476.

Bowen, M. (1976). Family reaction to death. In P. J. Guerin (Ed.), *Family therapy: Theory and practice.* New York: Wiley.

Bowlby, J. (1973). *Separation: Anxiety and anger.* New York: Basic Books.

Bowlby-West, L. (1983). The impact of death on the family system. *Journal of Family Therapy, 5,* 279–294.

Cicchetti, D., & Schneider-Rosen, K. (1984). Toward a transactional model of childhood depression. In D. Cicchetti & K. Schneider-Rosen (Eds.), *Childhood depression.* San Francisco: Jossey-Bass.

Duvall, E. M., & Miller, B. C. (1985). *Marriage and family development* (6th ed.). Philadelphia: Harper & Row.

Emde, R. N., Harmon, R. J., & Good, W. V. (1986). Depressive feelings in children: A transactional model for research. In M. Rutter, C. E. Izard, & P. B. Read (Eds.), *Depression in young people: Developmental and clinical perspectives.* New York: Guilford Press.

Evans, A. E., & Edin, S. (1968). If a child must die . . . *New England Journal of Medicine, 278,* 138–142.

Herz, F. (1980). The impact of death and serious illness on the family life cycle. In E. A. Carter & M. McGoldrick (Eds.), *The family life cycle: A framework for family therapy* (pp. 223–240). New York: Gardner.

Kellerman, J., Rigler, D., & Siegal, S. E. (1977). Psychological effects of isolation in protected environments. *American Journal of Psychiatry, 134,* 563–567.

Koocher, G. P. (1984). Terminal care and survivorship in pediatric chronic illness. *Clinical Psychology Review, 4,* 571–583.

Koocher, G. P., & O'Malley, J. E. (1981). *The Damocles syndrome: Psychosocial consequences of surviving childhood cancer.* New York: McGraw-Hill.

Koocher, G. P., Sourkes, B. M., & Keane, W. M. (1979). Pediatric oncology consultations: A generalizable model for medical settings. *Professional Psychology, 10,* 467–474.

Kübler-Rose, E. (1969). *On death and dying.* New York: Macmillan.

Langer, E., & Rodin, J. (1976). The effects of choice and enhanced personal responsibility for the aged: A field experiment in an institutional setting. *Journal of Personality and Social Psychology, 32,* 951.

Lindemann, E. (1944). Symptomatology and management of acute grief. *American Journal of Psychiatry, 101,* 141–148.

Lonetto, R. (1980). *Children's conceptions of death.* New York: Springer-Verlag.

Mahler, M., Pine, F., & Bergman, A. (1973). *The psychological birth of the human infant.* New York: Basic Books.

Martinson, I. M., Armstrong, G. D., Geis, D. P., Anglin, M. A., Gronseth, E. C., MacInnis, M., Nesbit, M. E., & Kersey, J. H. (1978). Facilitating home care for children dying of cancer. *Cancer Nursing, 1,* 41–50.

McCubbin, H. I., & Figley, C. R. (1983). Bridging normative and catastrophic family stress. In H. I. McCubbin & C. R. Figley (Eds.), *Stress and the family: Vol. 1. Coping with normative transition* (pp. 218–228). New York: Brunner/Mazel.

Mulhern, R. K., Lauer, M. E., & Hoffman, R. G. (1983). Death of a child at home or in the hospital: Subsequent psychological adjustment of the family. *Pediatrics, 71,* 743–747.

Neugarten, B. (1976). Adaptation and the life cycle. *The Counseling Psychologist, 6,* 12–20.

Olson, D. H., Sprenkle, D. H., & Russell, C. S. (1979). Circumplex model of marital and family systems: Cohesion and adaptability dimensions, family types, and clinical applications. *Family Process, 18,* 3–27.

Osterweis, M., Solomon, F., & Green, M. (Eds.). (1984). *Bereavement: Reactions, consequences, and care.* Washington, DC: National Academy Press.

Piaget, J. (1954). *The construction of reality in the child.* New York: Basic Books.

Rutter, M. (1986). The developmental psychopathology of depression: Issues and perspectives. In M. Rutter, C. E. Izard, & P. B. Read (Eds.), *Depression in young people: Developmental and clinical perspectives* (pp. 3–32). New York: Guilford Press.

Seligman, M. E. P. (1975). *Helplessness.* San Francisco: W. H. Freeman.

Silver, R. L. & Wortman, C. B. (1980). Coping with undesirable life events. In J. Garber & M. E. P. Seligman (Eds.), *Human helplessness: Theory and applications* (pp. 279–340). New York: Academic Press.

Solomon, M. A. (1973). A developmental conceptual premise for family therapy. *Family Process, 12,* 179–188.

Sourkes, B. M. (1977). Facilitating family coping with childhood cancer. *Journal of Pediatric Psychology, 2,* 65–67.

Spinetta, J. J., Rigler, D., & Karon, M. (1973). Anxiety in the dying child. *Pediatrics, 52,* 841–845.

Spinetta, J. J., Rigler, D., & Karon, M. (1974). Personal space as a measure of a dying child's sense of isolation. *Journal of Consulting and Clinical Psychology, 42,* 751–756.

Spinetta, J. J., Swarner, J. A., & Sheposh, J. P. (1981). Effective parental coping following the death of a child from cancer. *Journal of Pediatric Psychology, 6,* 251–264.

Vernick, J., & Karon, M. (1965). Who's afraid of death on a leukemia ward? *American Journal of Diseases of Children, 109,* 393–397.

Weber, J. A., & Fournier, D. G. (1985). Family support and a child's adjustment to death. *Family Relations, 34,* 43–49.

Weintraub, S., Winters, K. C., & Neale, J. M. (1986). Competence and vulnerability in children with an affectively disordered parent. In M. Rutter, C. E. Izard, & P. B. Read (Eds.), *Depression in young people: Developmental and clinical perspectives* (pp. 205–222). New York: Guilford Press.

Wortman, C. B., & Silver, R. C. (1989). The myths of coping with loss. *Journal of Consulting and Clinical Psychology, 57,* 349–357.

II

FAMILIES AND ILLNESS

6

OVERVIEW

Mary Jean Petron
Sarah L. Clark
Kent State University

Section I of this volume was devoted to a discussion of the prevention of children's health and emotional problems, with an underlying theme of the development of children's health beliefs and cognitions. Although more research is needed, it is clear that families play an important role in the prevention of illness and maintenance of healthy behaviors among children, in part because families are the system in which children's cognitions and behaviors develop. Section II is devoted to a discussion of the interaction of families and illness. Within this general area, several important themes are developed regarding the role of families in health and illness and the nature of the family itself.

As was true in Section I evident throughout Section II is the issue of the definition of the family unit. The traditional definition of a family no longer applies to a large proportion of today's households, however, no alternative definition has been agreed upon widely. Kazak (Chapter 7) defines the family from a social ecological perspective that encompasses systems far beyond the nuclear family level. Jacobs (Chapter 8) focuses on the regulation of boundaries within the family and between it and the outside world. Coyne and Fiske (Chapter 9) and Jones (Chapter 10) recognize the couple as the core definitional unit of the family without losing sight of the family as a system. Although each of the authors in this section approaches families from a systems perspective, they differ in their level of analysis, thus providing a variety of viewpoints from which to examine the family as it copes with illness.

Regardless of the perspective taken, a second theme that emerges is that the family is inherently dynamic. This is especially evident when viewing the impact of chronic and acute illnesses on families. The authors within this section address the dynamic nature of the family in different ways. Kazak identifies pediatric illness as a significant factor that has an impact on the development of the family, relationships within the family, and between the family and other social systems. Jacobs focuses on the impact of chronic illnesses on the norms and boundaries that exist within the family. The regulation of these norms and boundaries is critical in helping families cope with chronic illness. Coyne and Fiske, examine the repercussions of myocardial infarction on the married couple and their relationship. Jones views physical and psychological illness as the sequelae of marital conflict.

A third theme implicit throughout this section is the need to expand the role of the health care system in the lives of families coping with illness. Kazak clearly suggests this in her application of social ecological theory to chronic pediatric illness in which she examines families with chronically ill children at a number of levels. She uses social ecological concepts to provide a more precise as well as expanded understanding of the family in relation to the numerous environments within which it functions and with which it interacts. Jacobs discusses the role that health professionals have in psychoeducational interactions with families with an ill member. Coyne and Fiske place strong emphasis on the need to understand families and couples within the context of the medical system (e.g., to recognize the constraints placed on the couples' adaptive efforts at coping) and the need to alter the system to address such factors.

In addition to the above themes, each author makes a unique contribution to the discussion of families and illness. First, although she focuses on families with young children, Kazak's use of the social ecological perspective is applicable across the life span. Bronfenbrenner's theory proposes that there are several levels at which an individual functions. Each level encompasses an increasingly larger portion of the individual's universe. The theory defines the family as the microsystem and, as such, it is of primary importance to the child. Within the family, the impact of a child's illness is bidirectional. The child's illness influences each parent as an individual; the illness also affects their marital relationship. On the other hand, the ill child is affected by the parents' responses to the illness and the parents' relationship with one another. In a similar manner, there is a bidirectional influence between siblings and the ill child. Sibling influences often go unnoticed but their importance should not be underestimated. The next level is the mesosystem, which includes peers, schools, hospitals, and local communities. Little is known about how this level affects a child and his or her family when dealing with chronic illness. The exosystem includes parental social networks and siblings' schools and influences the family without involving the ill child directly. The outermost layer of this social ecological model is the macrosystem, which is composed of the family's cultural and political environments. Consideration of each level of the ecological system and the interfaces among them are important in fully understanding the situation. Kazak argues that both structural (e.g., size and density) and qualitative aspects (e.g., types of network members, perceived helpfulness, and reciprocity) are important to understanding fully the social ecological perspective of families coping with pediatric illness. The importance of viewing the family from a social systems perspective continues in Jacob's consideration of the impact of chronic illness on the traditional family. She proposes that families have "internal working models of the ways in which they relate to the outside world," which she labels the family paradigm. This construct is relevant to functioning at the social ecological mesosystem level discussed by Kazak. Families also have unique identities that are the "shared beliefs, values, and traditions that make a family feel uniquely itself." These identities are relevant to functioning at the social ecological microsystem level. Jacobs uses her concepts of family paradigm and family identity to facilitate her clinical work with families coping with illness. Initially, this clinical intervention focuses on making the demands of the illness explicit. Next, the clinician works to mobilize the family's ability to cope with those demands that are the most threatening to the family's integrity. Finally, the clinician may strengthen family rituals or modify them to meet the demands of the illness. Although Kazak and Jacobs share their focus on the family unit, they differ in the level at which they intervene.

In contrast with Kazak and Jacobs, Coyne and Fiske focus on the marital couple as the most essential portion of the family. They argue that understanding the couple is the first step in delineating family processes. Coyne and Fiske have identified several themes in their study of marital couples coping with chronic and catastrophic illness. First, couples are interdependent. That is, when one member of the couple is physically or emotionally ill, both are at risk for psychological distress. In addition, when they look to their spouses for support, they may find the spouse less able to provide it. Second, the illness itself imposes parameters on coping processes. Third, gender differences have been found in spouses' abilities to cope with their partner's illness. Fourth, the life stage of the couple may affect their coping (e.g., younger couples may have more difficulty coping with spousal illness). Finally, couples' interactions with the health care system may have a profound impact on their coping efficacy.

Consistent with Coyne and Fiske's discussion, Jones proposes that not only is the state of being married important in determining susceptibility to illness but also the quality of the marriage. She reviews the literature on marriage and illness in the context of the selection and protection/support hypotheses, then describes her own work in treating troubled marriages. In her clinical work she has found a significant linear trend such that people who divorce experience the most illness whereas those who resolve their conflicts experience the least illness. Those who remained in a conflictual marriage fell between these extremes. These findings lend clinical evidence to empirical research that suggests that conflict can have profound deleterious effects on health, whereas conflict resolution may maintain health.

Each author discusses methodological concerns in the study of families and illness. It is clear that there exists no consensus regarding the composition of the family. Problems in the definition of the family unit have resulted in inconsistencies in the unit of analysis throughout the literature. Kazak points to the need to broadly define the family unit in such a way that allows for diversity in family constellation, cultural and ethnic background, and religious beliefs. A second concern is the lack of longitudinal data, which has prevented assessment of the developmental nature of the family. Third, there is considerate disagreement about the development and composition of outcome measures reflecting the impact of illness on family systems. A fourth problem with the existing literature is the lack of culturally and ethnically diverse samples, which results in a seriously biased view of the family. Finally, the deficit model of physical and psychological illness underlies most of the studies in this area. The authors highlight the fact that this model seriously restricts our view of the family and keeps us from recognizing its adaptive capabilities.

Within this discussion of methodological concerns, the authors identify directions for future research. For example, a broader definition of the family unit will allow researchers to more accurately reflect families as they exist in today's society. Data based on such a definition will allow clinicians to develop more effective interventions. More consistent operational definitions also are needed to facilitate comparison across the literature. This second goal may be difficult to achieve in light of the first; however, it would add the dimensions of replicability and theoretical soundness to the literature. Future research should attempt to view the family from the competency model, which would promote a more positive outlook on families coping with illness. In addition, research should address the dynamic nature of the family through the use of longitudinal designs. Any efforts to address these methodological concerns will serve only to improve our understanding and treatment of families coping with illness.

7

FAMILY SYSTEMS, SOCIAL ECOLOGY, AND CHRONIC PEDIATRIC ILLNESS: CONCEPTUAL, METHODOLOGICAL, AND INTERVENTION ISSUES

Anne E. Kazak
University of Pennsylvania and The Children's Hospital of Philadelphia

The emergence of family health as a field that integrates psychological, sociological, family, and health care perspectives in understanding the impact of illness on family systems is an exciting development. The confluence that results from these contributions promises to exceed that which any one perspective can offer. However, a major challenge facing family health is the integration of disparate theoretical orientations and research methodologies and the development of a model that is conceptually valid and testable. Rather than simply applying existing family methodologies to families with an ill member, medical conditions, treatments, and health care systems must be conceptualized as unique and powerful situations that interact with family (and other) systems.

In the present chapter, the focus is on childhood chronic conditions, including physical disabilities and serious long-term medical conditions. Bronfrenbrenner's (1979) social ecological theory is presented as a model that may be useful in understanding childhood chronic illness and in guiding research. The present chapter builds on other articles integrating social ecology and childhood illness (Kazak, 1986, 1989a; Kazak & Nachman, 1991). This chapter addresses three broad issues of major concern to family health researchers and practitioners: (a) *conceptual difficulties* in the field of families and health that relate to family systems and social ecological models; (b) *methodological concerns* that must be considered in family, social support, and systems research; and (c) *intervention and mental health services* that can be designed and evaluated and are consistent with a family systems/social ecological approach.

SOCIAL ECOLOGY
AND CHILDHOOD CHRONIC ILLNESS

In this section of the chapter, social ecological theory is reviewed. Selected research consistent with the theory is presented. Social ecology is the study of the relation between the developing human being and the settings and contexts in which the person is actively involved (Bronfrenbrenner, 1979). The best known concept of social ecology is that the child may be considered at the center of a model of concentric rings, with nested circles representing increasingly larger environments with which the child interacts.

Of primary emphasis in families with ill children has been the ring (*microsystem*) that represents the child's most immediate setting, the family. The growing literature on family adaptation to a disabled child rests within the microsystem of the family, examining, for example, family resources, interactions, and adaptations in coping with stressful life events around illness. The next ring out from the child is the *mesosystem*, which encompasses the interactive relationships of smaller settings in which the child participates, including schools, hospitals, neighborhoods, and agencies. Research on children with handicaps and chronic illnesses has tended to focus on individual settings in isolation rather than explore the interface between systems and the implications of these interfaces for ongoing care (Kazak & Rostain, 1989; Power & Bartholomew, 1987; Schwartzman & Kniefel, 1985).

The next ring peripheral to the child is the *exosystem*, defined as settings that do not involve the child directly but that affect him or her indirectly, as in parents' work environments, parental networks, and schools attended by other siblings. Cochran and Brassard (1979) provide insightful examples of ways in which research could address exosystems, although this work has remained at a theoretical level. Most peripheral to the child is the *macrosystem*, the largest environments that have an impact on the child, including the impact of culture and policy on children. Some macrosystemic issues affect ill children and their families directly, and quickly, such as the enactment of Public Law 99-457, providing access to educational services for preschool handicapped children. Others, such as societal beliefs and stigmas (Stern & Arenson, 1989), ethnic and racial diversity in families (Pfefferbaum, Adams, & Aceves, 1990), and insurability of once-ill persons (Monaco, 1987), remain complex issues that are more difficult to assess and integrate into clinical interventions.

As a developmental psychologist, Bronfrenbrenner's (1979) work ultimately addresses the development of the individual child. In contrast, the focus of this chapter is the family system and the stressors and coping responses of significant adults and siblings (and patients) over the course of illness. There are several tenets of social ecology that are important in terms of bridging social ecology and family functioning. From a social ecological perspective, interactions among people are characterized by their *nonlinear* character and by their *reciprocity*. The chronically ill or handicapped child is not a passive recipient of unidirectional actions of other people and environments but rather an active contributor in multidimensional interactions. Direct parallels exist between social ecology and family systems with respect to the importance of *dyads* and other subsystems within families and the fact that a change experienced by one member of a system will affect others. As a developmental theory, social ecology focuses on the importance of *transition* and the natural processes of change and transition inherent in growth. In this area, family theory has far to go to approximate notions of growth and development in systems containing more than one individual.

Microsystems: Coping and Distress in Families with Chronic Childhood Illness

The diagnosis of a disabling or chronic health problem in a child is understandably a time of emotional distress, upheaval, and uncertainty for parents, and the beginning of a long-term process of reorganization and accommodation. Research on adjustment has looked at the ill child, parents, siblings, and family variables. The results are somewhat contradictory and are complicated by methodological concerns.

Higher incidences of psychiatric problems have been reported in children with chronic diseases (Cadman, Boyle, Szatmari, & Offord, 1987), indicating that although psychological distress is not inevitably associated with chronic illness, these children are indeed "at risk," and that they may show a generally higher level of emotional behaviors, both negative and positive. Research that addresses this risk status and examines ways in which family distress and resources can have an impact on child outcome suggests the importance of evaluating parental mental health, family processes, and social support (Daniels, Moos, Billings, & Miller, 1987; Kupst & Schulman, 1988).

Although stressful for marital relationships, the research points quite clearly to levels of marital satisfaction and distress in this population that conform to normative values (Sabbeth & Leventhal, 1984). Less research has looked at the effects of childhood illness and disability on other children in the family. Results on the effects of illness on siblings have been mixed, with little integration of sibling data with that of other members of the system.

Three studies described below focus on understanding differences in family subsystems (affected child, parents, siblings, marriage, families, and social networks) between families with a child with a physical handicap or chronic illness and those without such a child. The samples were composed of families of children with spina bifida ($N = 66$), ages 1–16 (Study I; Kazak & Clark, 1986; Kazak & Marvin, 1984; Kazak & Wilcox, 1984); early treated phenylketonuria (PKU; $N = 43$), ages 1–8 (Study II; Kazak, Reber, & Carter, 1988; Kazak, Reber, & Snitzer, 1988; Reber, Kazak, & Himmelberg, 1987); and mental retardation ($N = 36$), ages 9–30 (Study III; Kazak, 1988, 1989b). In each, families with disabled children are compared with matched comparison group families with respect to measures of distress within the family and in terms of social support network characteristics. Fathers and mothers are included in all studies. Results of the multivariate and univariate analyses (MANOVAs and ANOVAs) for the family stress variables for these three studies are summarized below (Kazak, 1987b).

Overall, the data have helped to dismantle the notion of pervasive levels of distress in families with handicapped children and to identify specific areas of concern. In Study I, mothers and fathers of spina bifida children were found to have higher levels of anxiety and depression than the comparison families. This difference was most striking for mothers. Marital satisfaction differences between the groups provided some evidence that the families of handicapped children actually perceived themselves to have somewhat higher levels of marital cohesion. Parenting stress levels were significantly higher for the spina bifida group. With respect to the spina bifida children, lower self-concepts were seen in this group, with no differences found for siblings.

In contrast, in Studies II and III, parents of affected children did not differ from comparison parents in parental distress, marital satisfaction, or parenting stress. Parents of children with PKU perceived their families to be less cohesive and less adaptable than the comparison families, and PKU children were found to have lower levels of social competence than matched comparison children. The families with retarded offspring were more cohesive than the comparison families, and there was evidence that family adaptability is linked to parental coping. These results not only underscore the lack of group differences but also suggest that the areas of difference between the two groups of families are those that seem very understandable given the demands of the medical condition. When the three groups were combined, MANOVAs indicated that maternal distress and marital satisfaction, in combination, differentiated the combined group from the controls and that the strongest group difference was in terms of maternal distress.

In general, the data from these three studies show relatively few differences between families with disabled/ill children and matched comparison families. One compelling interpretation of this is that these families are not deviant or deficient, but rather functioning adaptively and competently, particularly in light of the increased demands related to caring for ill children. However, the vulnerability of mothers is significant and merits further investigation. Presumably, mothers assume a very large caretaking burden and become more vulnerable to anxiety and depression. The generally normative levels of marital satisfaction and higher levels of parenting stress suggest that much of the distress stems from the demands of parenting. More information is needed on how families cope and adjust and how they can be helped to provide needed support for all members of the system. It is also important to consider extra-familial variables such as mothers' employment outside the home, which has been found to be related to general satisfaction and child behavior problems in families with handicapped and ill children (Walker, Ortiz-Valdes, & Newbrough, 1989).

The family systems social ecological approach has been utilized with families of children with cancer. In these studies, a more developmentally focused approach has been taken. One project followed seventy 10–15-year-old long-term survivors of childhood cancer and their families over 3 years during the transition to adolescence. With respect to overall functioning, data are consistent with other studies supporting normative levels of adjustment (Greenberg, Kazak, & Meadows, 1989). Some of the most interesting results focus on social support variables and the finding that learning problems (those related to cranial irradiation and requiring educational intervention) predict family distress (Kazak & Meadows, 1989).

Another study focused on a sample of twenty-five 3–5-year-old siblings of children who were in active cancer treatment. It examined differences between these children and a comparison group on developmentally relevant variables for this age group, including specific measures of prosocial behavior and behavior problems (Horwitz & Kazak, 1990). As a link among siblings as individuals, the sibling subsystem, and family functioning, data were collected on parental perceptions of similarities and differences between the siblings, and on family adaptability and cohesion. The results indicate that siblings of this age do engage in positive prosocial behaviors. The results also support the notion that particular family configurations that differ from the norm are seen in these families. These families are more extreme in terms of adaptability, falling at one end of the continuum or the other.

To assess social support in our sample of teenage long-term cancer survivors, we used an adaptation of the Social Support Rating Scale (Cauce, 1986), which allows for determination of support from family, friends, and school/ other adults. Relative to a comparison group, the cancer survivors reported somewhat less support from friends and, over the course of a prospective study, showed declines in perceived social support from family, friends, and teachers. Those long-term survivors with learning problems who received special services in school reported higher levels of social support across the three domains (Kazak & Meadows, 1989). These data support the need to look closely at different types of network members and to consider the role that social support plays over time and under particular circumstances (such as learning problems).

Mesosystems: Peers, Schools, Hospitals, and Communities

How children with chronic illnesses or physical handicaps interact with peers is an important, and often neglected, area of concern. In a study comparing children with cancer with a matched sample of healthy peers, teacher ratings indicated that children with cancer were found to be more isolated and were perceived as having less leadership potential than their peers (Noll, Bukowski, Rogosch, LeRoy, & Kulkarni, 1990). The peer group parallels the family system as an environment in which children learn about interpersonal relationships and social strengths and weaknesses, establishing templates for personal and work relationships.

The school is an environment in which children spend much time and in which participation and success are important; it is a critical system in which chronically ill and disabled children must be understood. A vast pool of knowledge exists regarding the educational needs of these children, with information contributed in particular from the fields of special education and school psychology. Less well understood are the ways in which schools become part of children's social environment and the implications of this for coping and adaptation. At a theoretical level, Power and Bartholomew (1987) describe five types of interaction styles between schools and families (avoidant, competitive, merged, one-way, and collaborative), and Schwartzman and Kniefel (1985) discuss ways in which families and other systems replicate or complement one another in their interrelationships. In discussing reasons for a lower than expected utilization of mental health services by chronically ill children and their families, Sabbeth and Stein (1990) identify attitudes and behaviors from families, hospital staff, and mental health providers. These theoretical articles provide useful and provocative areas for research, which unfortunately remain unexplored to date.

Exosystems: Parental Social Support and Social Support Networks

One of the ways in which social support can be measured is by analysis of social support networks. In Study I (spina bifida), mothers and fathers of children with spina bifida had significantly smaller social networks than comparison parents, although the difference was accounted for by size of the friendship network not number of family members (Kazak & Wilcox, 1984). These differences were not demonstrated in Studies II and III (Kazak, 1988; Kazak et al., 1988). In Studies I and III, higher density networks (characterized by members of one's social network knowing and interacting with one another, independently of the focal person) were found in the families with disabled children. Density was associated with higher levels of maternal distress in Study I. In Study II, the interaction between distress and social network characteristics were examined; main effects for distress were found for network size and density, with an interaction between group and distress for mothers' friendship network density (Kazak et al., 1988). Interestingly, analysis of the qualitative data in the PKU and comparison samples indicated that PKU parents perceived less support from immediate family members than did the comparison parents.

MANOVAs combining data from the three samples supported overall differences with respect to network size and density. However, the differences in network structure among the three groups are also intriguing. Analyses of covariance (ANCOVAs), controlling for age, indicated significant differences among the groups with respect to mothers' and fathers' total network size, family network size, and density and size of fathers' friendship network. These data suggest that differences in medical condition or other untested parameters of the disease, its treatment, or the family may be interacting with network structure. Different network structures may also be equally adaptive under different family and health circumstances.

With respect to the question of whether families with handicapped or ill children are socially isolated, the analysis of network size suggests that they are not. Of concern are the subset of families who are more isolated and hence at greater risk. A comprehensive social ecological approach must also include consideration of aspects of individuals that may influence perceptions of networks and inclinations to seek help. Hobfoll and Lerman (1988) investigated mothers of well, acutely ill, and chronically ill children and provide data that indicate that emotional distress and mastery affect perceptions of social networks. They also present intriguing data that show that the timing of social support and the balance of support received from spouse and others at different times in the course of the illness have a differential impact on adjustment.

Our social network data suggest the importance of close examination of the type of memberships in the network. In a study of families of young hearing-impaired children, smaller networks were found than in a comparison group, and it was noted that networks had a large membership of professionals in them (Quitner, Glueckauf, & Jackson, 1990). We also found that professionals were often considered to be integral members of the network. The benefits and difficulties of this network composition have not been explored. It provides, however, a natural link between studying the family, the network, and the larger systems to which the professionals belong (Kazak, 1987a).

The results with respect to network density indicate a tendency for the networks of parents of disabled children to be more dense than those of comparison children and show consistency with previous research in terms of linking higher levels of density with distress. Highly dense networks may be likened to family systems characterized by "enmeshment," a well-known family construct usually associated with less adaptive functioning in families with ill children. This may help explain the higher levels of distress associated with dense networks. These highly dense networks lack what Granovetter (1973) termed "weak links," or openings to people outside the more immediate, highly connected network. Such networks may reduce individuals' ability to act independently and could contribute to conflict avoidance. Some of the potentially negative implications of social support reported by others (Brenner, Norvell, & Limacher, 1989) may actually be related to high density, an association that has not been tested in other work. Within the professional network, high density may approximate the type of coordinated care among providers that is usually considered ideal. Investigations of the density of the professional network could be explored in more detail with regard to their reciprocal impact on families and on accomplishing treatment goals.

A related point is the need to determine the meaning of levels of density. Density is obviously a relative concept, and specification of levels of involvement of network members with one another that are associated with levels of distress will be important. In an interesting study of "successful" families with young disabled children, using comparable measures, Trute and Hauch (1988) found that high-density networks were characteristic of their well-functioning families. The general picture is one of a small, interconnected, but rich network that involves social support from both sides of the children's extended families.

CONCEPTUAL DIFFICULTIES IN FAMILY HEALTH RESEARCH

In the following section, important conceptual issues that are often unacknowledged in family health research—developmental issues, normality, competency, and illness characteristics—are reviewed.

Developmental Concerns

Understanding families and health can be facilitated through the identification of important dimensions of the experience of illness. Prime among these dimensions is concern for the age of the patient and the concomitant developmental stage of the family. There has been surprisingly little overlap and collaboration between adult and child health researchers. Age is often ignored or treated as a silent variable, obvious but unexplained. Ways that child and adult illness differ in terms of their psychosocial impact include the following:

(1) *Cognitive Development*. Cognitive development affects the child's understanding of the illness. Specific ways in which development interacts with understanding of illness and death are addressed in recent articles (cf. Burbach & Peterson, 1986; Cotton & Range, 1990). Within a systems model, the child's cognitive abilities also interact with parental and family beliefs, values, and behaviors in response to illness and death.

(2) *Rapid Developmental Changes*. Children grow and develop rapidly, with these changes marking different interests, issues, and understanding. Thus, a child who was told at age 4 that leukemia involves "good cells and bad cells" merits a more sophisticated explanation later. In a similar vein, a child who becomes ill as a preschooler later must (along with the family)

face different issues as school attendance and peer relationships become more salient.

(3) *Importance of the Family.* The prominence of the family for children is accepted readily. Nonetheless, much remains to be understood in terms of the reciprocal interactions of child and family.

(4) *Impact on Family Members, Including Siblings.* The child's illness clearly affects others in the nuclear and extended family, including siblings (who are themselves usually children) and grandparents, whose roles in the family often become intensified in order to promote family stability.

(5) *Parenting.* A major difference between adult and child illness concerns the child's need to be cared for and parented, despite a medical condition. Within the family, the ways in which parenting must change, and how it can remain constant, are major issues, with evidence that this differs for mothers and fathers.

(6) *Locus of Responsibility.* Whereas adults are presumed to be responsible for their own care unless illness precludes responsible decisionmaking, the issue of who is responsible for procedure and treatment decisions for children is more ambiguous and changes developmentally.

(7) *School Systems.* Children spend much of their day in school, necessitating inclusion of that setting in conceptualizing the impact of illness on children and families.

(8) *Long-term Impacts.* Children's treatment, daily life-style, and ultimate prognosis have long-term consequences that reverberate throughout present and future families. For example, siblings of children with muscular dystrophy may experience feelings of guilt and responsibility that could alter their plans as young adults. Whereas adult disability may necessitate a restructuring of the family, it is different from that necessitated by the long-term demands of disabled children.

Child age is only one developmental variable of concern. The developmental stage of the family may also affect the meaning of illness and the ways in which coping unfolds. For example, families with infants or preschool children must meet different needs from those of families with adolescents. Although family development has often been characterized by the age of the oldest child, this formulation appears oversimplified given the diversity in family structures and ages of family members seen today.

Bronfrenbrenner (1986) expands the notion of developmental research to involve changes over time in the environment and in the interactions between individuals and settings. These chronosystem models can be focused on periods of transition (entering school, divorce, or retirement) or can examine development over the life course. Despite the obvious complexities of conducting chronosystemic research, it will help provide an understanding of processes of change and accommodation, which are critical aspects of the process of coping with illness.

Illness and Normality

Chronic childhood illness, as has been illustrated in this chapter, is sometimes associated with psychological difficulties, although positive adaptation is being increasingly recognized. Assuming continuity of development and relative stability in the family's social ecology, functioning prior to the onset of an illness should be related to functioning afterward. In understanding coping and adaptation, appreciation of positive ("normal") functioning across life domains and family members is important. At a conceptual level this translates into articulating underlying beliefs about the normality of individual and family functioning during illness and treatment.

Unlike individual development, there are few standards for family normality. Normal families have been conceptualized as asymptomatic, statistically average, ideal, and able to cope with changes (Walsh, 1982). These concepts of normal have been found to be affected by one's own experiences and life stage and differ developmentally and ethnically (Kazak, McCannell, Adkins, Himmelberg, & Grace, 1989). It is accepted widely that illness is a stressor to which individuals and families must adapt and that families with ill or disabled children are generally "normal" families coping with a demanding and distressing situation. Clarification of what is normal coping with abnormal life events is much needed, particularly at the level of the family.

Competence Versus Deficit Orientations

Although having chronically ill children is unquestionably stressful in ways that can be both chronic and acute, families can and must survive and endure the difficulties associated with childhood chronic illness. There are relatively little data available in terms of understanding strengths and competencies of these families. A large portion of the literature prior to 1980 was directed toward identifying psychopathology and addressed areas of weakness and deficit in families. This literature left little doubt that having a child with medical needs would result in family disorganization and divorce, with similarly negative outcomes expected for siblings. Although we understand more clearly now that the birth of a disabled child, or the diagnosis of a serious illness, undeniably alters the preexisting family, we also appreciate more fully the ways in which the family can cope and creatively adapt to these demands (Kazak & Marvin, 1984).

Although children and families with chronic illness are strong and successful in many ways, concern for the psychological vulnerability of the children and families cannot be neglected. That is, we must not naively assume that successful family adaptation is to be expected uniformly. The mental health status of chronically ill and disabled children as they grow older is mixed (Pless, Cripps, Davies, & Wadsworth, 1989). The high level of distress noted in mothers is of similar concern. Although recent epidemiological evidence suggests that abuse of disabled children is less likely that suspected earlier (Benedict, White, Wulff, & Hall, 1990), the association between domestic violence and depleted social resources is a strong one, not to be ignored in this population (Garbarino & Sherman, 1980).

Characterizing Diseases and Handicapping Conditions

The question of whether phenomena seen in families with medical problems are specific to one disease or if a noncategorical approach is more appropriate (Stein & Jessop, 1982) has been raised, with ambiguous conclusions. At more global levels of outcome (stress and general coping styles), there are many commonalities across diseases (i.e., general distress, caretaking, and family reorganization). However, when looking at more specific outcomes and family patterns, there are data that support differences among related diseases. In two gastrointestinal conditions (ulcerative colitis and Crohn's disease), distinct patterns of marital adjustment, divorce rates, and sibling response were found (Zimand & Wood, 1986).

Rolland (1984, 1987) has outlined four dimensions of illness (onset, course, outcome, and degree of incapacitation) that are presumed to have an impact on the family differentially. This model is a theoretically solid and creative approach to families and health that has not yet been tested empirically. In general, there is relatively little methodologically rigorous research comparing and contrasting illnesses. In conducting such research, it will be important to carefully articulate the types of differences expected related to parameters of Rolland's (or others') models. For example, how does the uncertainty of a childhood illness with a fluctuating course relate to particular family coping strategies? There are many complexities to consider, including subtypes of illness and degrees of severity within each condition, and the course of the illness within an individual. Ultimately, it seems as if a model that identifies a core group of variables related to adjustment and coping across illnesses, with specific factors that would contribute positively or negatively to coping with specific types of conditions, is necessary.

The Role of Individuals in the System

Although the model presented emphasizes interpersonal, family, social, and ecological factors influencing chronically ill children, individuals are also systems themselves and can be considered as such in a systems model. As Garmezy (1985) indicates, resilience in childhood can be thought of as related to individual dispositional characteristics of the child, and family and social support variables. Similar to the biopsychosocial approach, consideration of individual variables in childhood chronic illness might include studying the relationship between disease variables and family functioning, or increased attention to individual psychological variables and how they interact with family functioning. For example, relatively high levels of episodic anxiety are not unusual in children in treatment for cancer. Yet, there has been little effort to understand how the frequency and intensity of children's or parents' anxiety relates to psychological reactions in other members of the system.

METHODOLOGICAL CONCERNS
IN FAMILY HEALTH RESEARCH
Design and the Deficit Orientation

When comparing groups of families, with and without illness, the expectation (hypothesis) usually is that the affected group will differ from the other in the direction of more problems, less positive coping, and so on. Stated another way, the null hypothesis of "no difference" will be rejected. This design conceptually promotes a deficit view and can fail to provide insight into more adaptive functioning. It also contributes to a broader support of the deficit orientation in that studies that fail to find group differences are less likely to be submitted and published (Greenwald, 1975). Thus there may be many studies that indicate fewer differences between families with and without an ill child than the published literature reflects. Alternatives to the null hypothesis model allow for testing theoretical models such as that of Rolland and can promote research that may help understand what differentiates more and less well-functioning families with chronically ill children, rather than emphasizing how they may differ from unaffected families.

Measuring Outcome in Family Health Studies

An important design issue concerns the choice of outcome measures to be used in family health research. The questions that must be addressed in selecting an outcome measure are many, and probably cannot all be answered satisfactorily in any one study. The questions include: (a) Is the outcome physical or psychological health, or a combination? (b) Will emphasis be on identification of problems (e.g., psychopathology) or strengths (e.g., coping)? (c) How can family outcomes be determined with many individuals comprising the family and a broad array of measures and methods available? (d) How can outcome be determined when different systems are assessed? (e) At what point in time is the outcome important? (f) What are the values inherent in any choice of outcome? and (g) What are the political issues and implications for choices of outcome? A difficulty in conducting systems research is that in the course of answering very large questions, the researcher can tend to become overwhelmed by the enormity of the issue. It may be best to pick small questions and pinpoint more specific outcome measures, retaining awareness of the limitations of the study in light of the larger systemic concerns.

Diversity

Heterogeneity has been discussed thus far in terms of developmental issues, disease dimensions, and ranges in adaptive and maladaptive responses. A social ecological/systemic model also necessitates acknowledgment of the social diversity of our society and commitment to meaningful, creative, and rigorous ways in which diversity can be appreciated. In particular, ethnic and racial variability in families needs to be considered an integral part of the illness and coping experience, rather than as a variable "to be controlled." Data indicate that non-Caucasian children and families respond in ways that are different (but not necessarily deviant) from white families with respect to pain and illness (de Parra, Cortazar, & Covarrubias-Espinoza, 1983; Pfefferbaum et al., 1990). Because most children and families may be considered "normal" prior to illness, the ways in which these families and children cope are important to understand (Pfefferbaum et al., 1990). Differences with respect to how families of different ethnic backgrounds view behavior and mental health services have been described (McGoldrick, Pearce, & Giordano, 1982). More attention is needed on how ethnic values and beliefs may affect family interactions with medical and educational systems, and how this can affect compliance with treatment (Kazak & Rostain, 1989). Furthermore, although families without two parents are still often referred to as "alternative families," we have the opportunity to expand our notions of "family" and ensure that our research and treatments are not based on assumptions of Caucasian, two-parent, self-contained heterosexual family units.

Alternative Research Methodologies

The issues and recommendations raised throughout this chapter are ones that challenge existing family health research methods. Given the wide array of disease and family variables that warrant inclusion, it is close to impossible to conduct research at only one site. Thus creative, interinstitutional research efforts are needed. Building on interdisciplinary approaches to research, longitudinal, ethnographic, interview, and observational methodologies need to be considered in any study. The issues raised in this chapter will hopefully generate research questions that are exploratory and can be approached through creative hypothesis-generating research. This is particularly important with respect to developing models for interactions among systems.

INTERVENTION
AND MENTAL HEALTH SERVICES

The higher rates of psychopathology identified in chronically ill children indicate the need for increased mental health services for these children. The need is likely to be even greater given that the overall adjustment of families of these children has not been the focus of investigation. Furthermore, most of these children are treated in pediatric (not mental health) settings and may not be screened or referred for mental health services. Sabbeth and Stein (1990) clearly document the multiple tangible barriers to mental health care for these children.

A systems/social ecological approach to intervention necessitates involvement at multiple levels, including systems-oriented therapy with individual patients, parents, or siblings, and group therapy. The multiple-family discussion group format is an example of a creative intervention utilizing groups of families (Gonzalez, Steinglass, & Reiss, 1989). A systems approach also highlights the need for intervention at the level of the social network, school system, and at a policy level. A review of all the issues and methodologies for such intervention is beyond the scope of this chapter. However, the approach suggests the need to consider preventive interventions at levels beyond that of the individual child.

Interventions can be implemented at more than one level as well. In any particular family or setting, there may be several equally important needs that can be addressed and that may necessitate multiple interventions. Within a social ecological approach it is clear that interventions also must occur in a variety of settings, at school and in the hospital and clinic, for example. This requires knowledge of the settings and realistic appraisal of the best type of intervention for each. In a pediatric hospital, for example, some level of psychosocial support is generally provided for children and families. Yet, even with a relatively high level of resources, families' needs will exceed staff availability. The focus is usually on the patient and family, without due attention to the individual and systemic characteristics of the health care team and hospital. An interesting social ecological question focuses on how we can predict psychosocial outcome for children and families over time, including nonfamily settings in our assessment.

From the issues outlined in this chapter, it can be seen that a broad array of variables might predict outcome (i.e., child resiliency, disease course, network density, family adaptability, and school environment) and that the process of untangling which factors influence which patients and families when will involve many years of research. This research can be linked actively to intervention, and the design of services can, in turn, help refine the questions and help verify the types of intervention needed.

REFERENCES

Benedict, M., White, R., Wulff, L., & Hall, B. (1990). Reported maltreatment in children with multiple disabilities. *Child Abuse and Neglect, 14,* 207–217.

Brenner, G., Norvell, N., & Limacher, M. (1989). Supportive and problematic social interactions: A social network analysis. *American Journal of Community Psychology, 17,* 831–836.

Bronfrenbrenner, U. (1979). *The ecology of human development.* Cambridge, MA: Harvard University Press.

Bronfrenbrenner, U. (1986). Ecology of the family as a context for human development: Research perspectives. *Developmental Psychology, 22,* 723–742.

Burbach, D., & Peterson, L. (1986). Children's concepts of physical illness: A review and critique of the cognitive-developmental literature. *Health Psychology, 5,* 307–325.

Cadman, D., Boyle, M., Szatmari, P., & Offord, D. (1987). Chronic illness, disabilities and mental and social well-being: Findings of the Ontario Child Health Study. *Pediatrics, 79,* 805–813.

Cauce, A. (1986). Social networks and social competence: Exploring the effects of early adolescent friendships. *American Journal of Community Psychology, 14,* 607–628.

Cochran, M., & Brassard, J. (1979). Child development and personal social networks. *Child Development, 50,* 601–616.

Cotton, C., & Range, L. (1990). Children's death concepts: Relationship to cognitive functioning, age, experience with death, fear of death, and hopelessness. *Journal of Clinical Child Psychology, 19,* 123–127.

Daniels, D., Moos, R., Billings, A., & Miller, J. (1987). Psychosocial risk and resilience factors among children with chronic illness, healthy siblings, and healthy controls. *Journal of Abnormal Child Psychology, 15,* 295–308.

de Parra, M., Cortazar, S., & Covarrubias-Espinoza, G. (1983). The adaptive pattern of families with a leukemic child. *Family Systems Medicine, 1,* 30–35.

Garbarino, J., & Sherman, D. (1980). High risk neighborhoods and high risk families: The human ecology of child maltreatment. *Child Development, 51,* 182–198.

Garmezy, N. (1985). Stress-resilient children: The search for protective factors. In J. E. Stevenson (Ed.), *Recent Research in Developmental Psychopathology* (pp. 213–333). Oxford: Pergamon Press.

Gonzalez, S., Steinglass, P., & Reiss, D. (1989). Putting the illness in its place: Discussion groups for families with chronic medical illnesses. *Family Process, 28,* 69–87.

Granovetter, M. (1973). The strength of weak ties. *American Journal of Sociology, 78,* 1360–1380.

Greenberg, H., Kazak, A., & Meadows, A. (1989). Psychological adjustment in 8 to 16 year old cancer survivors and their parents. *Journal of Pediatrics, 114,* 488–493.

Greenwald, A. (1975). Consequences of prejudice against the null hypothesis. *Psychological Bulletin, 82,* 1–20.

Hobfoll, S., & Lerman, M. (1988). Personal relationships, personal attributes, and stress resilience: Mothers' reactions to their child's illness. *American Journal of Community Psychology, 16,* 565–589.

Horwitz, W., & Kazak, A. (1990). Family adaptation to childhood cancer: Sibling and family system variables. *Journal of Clinical Child Psychology, 19,* 221–228.

Kazak, A. (1986). Families with physically handicapped children: Social ecology and family systems. *Family Process, 25,* 265–281.

Kazak, A. (1987a). Professional helpers and families with disabled children: A social network perspective. *Marriage and Family Review, 11,* 177–191.

Kazak, A. (1987b). Families with disabled children: Stress and social networks in three samples. *Journal of Abnormal Child Psychology, 15,* 137–146.

Kazak, A. (1988). Stress and social networks in families with older institutionalized retarded children. *Journal of Social and Clinical Psychology, 6,* 448–461.

Kazak, A. (1989a). Families of chronically ill children: A systems and social ecological model of adaptation and challenge. *Journal of Consulting and Clinical Psychology, 57,* 25–30.

Kazak, A. (1989b). Family functioning in families with older institutionalized retarded offspring. *Journal of Autism and Developmental Disabilities, 19,* 501–509.

Kazak, A., & Clark, H. (1986). Stress in families of children with myelomeningocele. *Developmental Medicine and Child Neurology, 28,* 220–228.

Kazak, A., & Marvin, R. (1984). Differences, difficulties, and adaptation: Stress and social networks in families with a handicapped child. *Family Relations, 33,* 67–77.

Kazak, A., McCannell, K., Adkins, E., Himmelberg, P., & Grace, J. (1989). Perceptions of normality in families: Four groups. *Journal of Family Psychology, 2,* 277–291.

Kazak, A., & Meadows, A. (1989). Families of young adolescents who have survived cancer: Social-emotional adjustment, adaptability, and social support. *Journal of Pediatric Psychology, 14,* 175–191.

Kazak, A., & Nachman, G. (1991). Family research on childhood chronic illness: Pediatric oncology as an example. *Journal of Family Psychology, 4,* 462–483.

Kazak, A., Reber, M., & Carter, A. (1988). Structural and qualitative aspects of social networks in families with young chronically ill children. *Journal of Pediatric Psychology, 13*, 171–182.

Kazak, A., Reber, M., & Snitzer, L. (1988). Childhood chronic disease and family functioning: A study of phenylketonuria. *Pediatrics, 81*, 224–230.

Kazak, A., & Rostain, A. (1989). Systemic aspects of family noncompliance. *Newsletter of the Society of Pediatric Psychology, 13*, 12–17.

Kazak, A., & Wilcox, B. (1984). The structure and function of social networks in families with handicapped children. *American Journal of Community Psychology, 12*, 645–661.

Kupst, M., & Schulman, J. (1988). Longterm coping with pediatric leukemia: A six year followup study. *Journal of Pediatric Psychology, 13*, 7–22.

McGoldrick, M., Pearce, J., & Giordano, J. (Eds.). (1982). *Ethnicity and family therapy.* New York: Guilford Press.

Monaco, G. (1987). Socioeconomic considerations in childhood cancer survival. *The American Journal of Pediatric Hematology/Oncology, 9*, 92–98.

Noll, R., Bukowski, W., Rogosch, F., LeRoy, S., & Kulkarni, R. (1990). Social interactions between children and their peers: Teacher ratings. *Journal of Pediatric Psychology, 15*, 43–56.

Pfefferbaum, B., Adams, J., & Aceves, J. (1990). The influence of culture on pain in Anglo and Hispanic children with cancer. *Journal of the American Academy of Child and Adolescent Psychiatry, 29*, 642–647.

Pless, I., Cripps, H., Davies, J., & Wadsworth, M. (1989). Chronic physical illness in childhood: Psychological and social effects in adolescent and adult life. *Developmental Medicine and Child Neurology, 31*, 746–755.

Power, T., & Bartholomew, K. (1987). Family-school relationship patterns: An ecological assessment. *School Psychology Review, 16*, 498–512.

Quitner, A., Glueckauf, R., & Jackson, D. (1990). Chronic parenting stress: Moderating versus mediating effects of social support. *Journal of Personality and Social Psychology, 59*, 1266–1273.

Reber, M., Kazak, A., & Himmelberg, P. (1987). Outcome in early treated phenylketonuria: Family psychosocial and metabolic variables. *Journal of Developmental and Behavioral Pediatrics, 8*, 311–317.

Rolland, J. (1984). Towards a psychosocial typology of chronic and life threatening illness. *Family Systems Medicine, 2*, 245–262.

Rolland, J. (1987). Chronic illness and the life cycle: A conceptual framework. *Family Process, 26*, 203–221.

Sabbeth, B., & Leventhal, J. (1984). Marital adjustment to chronic childhood illness. *Pediatrics, 73*, 762–768.

Sabbeth, B., & Stein, R. (1990). Mental health referral: A weak link in comprehensive care of children with chronic physical illness. *Developmental and Behavioral Pediatrics, 11*, 73–78.

Schwartzman, H., & Kniefel, A. (1985). Familiar institutions: How the child-care system replicates family patterns. In J. Schwartzman (Ed.), *Families and other systems* (pp. 87–107). New York: Guilford Press.

Stein, R., & Jessop, D. (1982). A noncategorical approach to childhood chronic illness. *Public Health Reports, 97,* 354–362.

Stern, M., & Arenson, E. (1989). Childhood cancer stereotype: Impact on adult perceptions of children. *Journal of Pediatric Psychology, 14,* 593–605.

Trute, B., & Hauch, C. (1988). Social network attributes of families with positive adaptation to the birth of a developmentally disabled child. *Canadian Journal of Community Mental Health, 7,* 5–16.

Walker, L., Ortiz-Valdes, J., & Newbrough, J. (1989). The role of maternal employment and depression in the psychological adjustment of chronically ill, mentally retarded, and well children. *Journal of Pediatric Psychology, 14,* 357–370.

Walsh, F. (1982). *Normal family processes.* New York: Guilford Press.

Zimand, E., & Wood, B. (1986). Implications of contrasting patterns of divorce in families of children with gastrointestinal disorders. *Family Systems Medicine, 4,* 385–397.

8

UNDERSTANDING FAMILY FACTORS THAT SHAPE THE IMPACT OF CHRONIC ILLNESS

Jane Jacobs
George Washington University School of Medicine

Dramatic medical advances in recent years have resulted in the survival of thousands of victims of trauma and severe illness who previously would have died. One of the consequences of this revolution in medical technology is a large increase in the number of families who are now responsible for the long-term care of seriously disabled relatives. It is critical for family researchers to learn as much as possible about the impact of chronic illness on family life so that realistic and effective methods can be developed to alleviate the burdens these families must face.

This chapter presents a brief summary of the prevailing views of families and chronic illness in the empirical literature over the past 30 years and then suggests a model that clinicians and researchers can use to help families assess the impact of the illness on their lives and to mobilize inherent strengths within the family's repertoire to manage the illness demands more effectively.

HISTORICAL VIEWS OF FAMILIES AND CHRONIC ILLNESS

Views of the relationship between families and medical illness have gone through a series of transformations in the last 30 years, emphasizing positive and negative family influences and later reflecting a more complex view of the reciprocal influences between chronic disorders and family dynamics. There have been four perspectives in the literature describing these relationships.

Family Pathology Model

In the 1960s and 1970s, family research on medical disorders, following the psychosomatic model developed in the previous decade (Alexander, 1950), focused on the impact of dysfunctional family patterns on chronic disorders (Minuchin et al., 1975; Minuchin, Rosman, & Baker, 1978; Purcell et al., 1969). Poor conflict resolution, weak interpersonal boundaries, overprotection of family members, and rigid transactional patterns were believed to be central contributors to the development of many chronic medical disorders. A popular concept among intervention researchers at the time was the "parentectomy," or the removal of the chronically ill child from the family in order to provide a healthier environment for the child's recovery.

In recent years, many family therapists have concluded that family dynamics cannot singlehandedly *cause* such diseases as asthma, diabetes, and schizophrenia in the absence of a predisposing biological vulnerability. However, several family factors similar to those mentioned in the psychosomatic literature have been shown to influence the *course* of illness after its onset.

Two studies exemplify the effect of family factors on illness course. Among a sample of patients with end-stage renal disease, families whose members operated more as a single unit than as separate individuals were associated with earlier patient deaths, even after the severity of the patients' illness was controlled (Reiss, Gonzalez, & Kramer, 1986). Among stroke survivors the degree of effective family behavior control and effective responsiveness predicted the number of rehospitalization days. The degree of successful problem solving, family communication skills, and patient self-care ability predicted family-rated patient adjustment (Evans et al., 1987).

Family Coping Model

Groundbreaking family research in the schizophrenia field, first in England (Brown, Birley, & Wing, 1972; Vaughn & Leff, 1976) and later in the United States (Anderson, Reiss, & Hogarty, 1986; Falloon, Boyd, & McGill, 1984), has also made a clear distinction between the family's influence on the *etiology* and the *course* of a chronic disorder. Without challenging the data supporting the biological underpinnings of schizophrenia, this research demonstrated that certain family attitudes and behaviors (critical comments, emotional overinvolvement, and hostility) could adversely affect the course of the disease, resulting in more frequent relapses.

It was rare in the family research field to have a series of such carefully replicated studies documenting the relationship between specific family behaviors and particular illness outcome. Excitement over this rich body of research strengthened interest in the *stress and coping* model of families and chronic illness. In this approach, the illness was seen as an independent biological entity that afflicts a family; however, the family can affect the course of the illness through its efficacy in dealing with the disease.

From this data base emerged the *psychoeducational* approach (Anderson et al., 1986), a behavioral intervention model in which families are taught specific information about illness course and specific coping strategies that would minimize exacerbations of the disease. This model is organized around the identification of coping strategies aimed at managing a specific disease.

Impact of the Illness on the Family

Although the family coping model has constituted a major advance over the more restrictive family pathology approach, it, too, has its limitations. Focusing on constructive coping strategies has been of enormous practical value to families facing chronic diseases, but the model focuses largely on strategies the family can use to improve the patient's condition, sometimes neglecting the considerable toll the illness takes on the family.

Several important studies have demonstrated the importance of looking at family members as potential casualties of the illness process, not merely as sources of social support (Bloom, 1982; Ell, Nishimoto, Mantell, & Hamovitch, 1988; Magni, Carli, Leo, Tshilolo, & Zanesco, 1986; Rabins, Fitting, Eastham, & Fetting, 1990). A useful construct that has emerged in relation to this issue is that of *family burden* (Gallagher et al., 1989; Montgomery, Gonyea, & Hooyman, 1985; Zarit, Todd, & Zarit, 1986). The concept of family burden refers to the subjective and objective difficulties experienced by family members in the course of caring for a chronic disorder over a period of years. Researchers in this area assess the emotional distress and reallocation of roles in the family that characterize the presence of serious chronic illness.

Several groups have developed interventions that address the difficulties of individuals with a chronically ill family member. Exemplars of these interventions include a discussion group for family caregivers of dementia patients that offers information about dementia, problem-solving strategies, and a potential support network (Zarit, Anthony, & Boutselis, 1987). Another psychoeducational intervention for family members helps families balance illness needs and family needs (Gonzalez, Steinglass, and Reiss, 1986, 1989). This model is based on the notion that chronic illness has a reorganizing effect on family life and that families must work to protect valued family practices.

Categorical Approach to Illness Impact

A promising development of recent years is a consideration of the *types of illness characteristics*, rather than specific illnesses, that are most likely to threaten family functioning. Stein and Jessop (1989) provided an empirical rationale for this approach when they demonstrated that there is more variance in psychological impact on family members within traditional diagnostic categories than between categories. In other words, the fact that an individual has multiple sclerosis is not as predictive of his or her family's level of functioning as other factors, such as the extent of social support the family has. Drotar (1981) has also suggested that traditional indices of illness severity are not related to levels of family stress. These researchers make a cogent case for abandoning individual diagnoses and looking for commonalities among disease categories in considering illness impact on families.

Rolland (1984) and Jacobs (1991b) also have proposed grouping illnesses by risk factors that are meaningful to the families who must cope with them. This method makes it possible to classify disorders in terms of the *type of challenge* they pose to family life. For example, because of differences in their respective histories and values, one family would have more problems dealing with a relative's extensive disability than with frequent unpredictable crises, whereas for another family the opposite would be true.

This chapter presents a model that builds on the contributions of three of the areas discussed above—the coping paradigm, the construct of family burden, and the notion that certain illness characteristics that cross diagnostic lines pose a particular threat to family equilibrium. This model can be used to guide the practitioner through a systematic assessment of the illness and the family and leads ultimately to the formulation of a family-based intervention that can help family members achieve greater control over the impact of the illness on their lives.

CURRENT MODEL

In this chapter, a model is proposed for understanding the experience of families that must cope with chronic illness. This model proposes a systematic approach to assessing both the challenges to family functioning posed by the illness and the availability of skills in the family for coping with the illness. It is aimed primarily at helping the family to shape its own view of the illness and to design a management strategy that fits best with its own preexisting value system. The model provides a method for addressing three important issues facing families: (a) What are the specific challenges posed by the illness? (b) How effective is the family functioning in those areas most critical to illness management? What core features of this particular family are most threatened by the illness? and (c) How can the family reorganize its view of the illness within the context of its core identity?

The model rests on three underlying principles:

(1) *Invasion.* Chronic disorders pose a generic risk of invading the priorities, traditional practices, and affective rules that typically give a family a sense of coherence and continuity. When a loved family member is ill, the natural instinct of family members is to mobilize themselves in the service of giv-

ing their relative the most comprehensive care possible. They usually do not realize that by shifting the customary practices that have worked over the years, they are disrupting familiar rhythms that make the family uniquely identifiable to itself. Researchers investigating chronic medical and psychiatric disorders have described the risks to families inherent in these disruptions (Gonzalez et al., 1989; Gubman & Tessler, 1987; Wolin, Bennett, & Jacobs, 1988).

(2) *Fit*. A family's experience of chronic illness is a combination of the particular risk factors associated with that illness and the particular set of values, convictions, and vulnerabilities that characterize that family. One family, because of its history and traditions, may be able to handle an illness with a deadly but certain prognosis more easily than an illness with an uncertain prognosis. One family may deal aggressively with a stigmatizing disease, whereas another will be devastated by its inability to avoid shame and isolation. A comprehensive assessment process must take into account the fit between the salient risk factors of the disorder and the culture of that particular family (Jacobs, 1989).

(3) *Reshaping the meaning of the illness*. Most families have a set of organizing values growing from their family history, religious convictions, moral precepts, or individualistic beliefs. These values, often an implicit basis for the marriage, are reshaped in an increasingly collective vein over time and are expressed in the family's important stories, rituals, and decisions. In moments of crisis, these beliefs can provide the family with an immediate rationale for a particular coping strategy. At times, however, the very nature of the crisis can challenge the underlying tenets of the family's belief system. Their belief in a particular moral order or in the efficacy of certain forms of behavior may be violated profoundly by a cataclysmic event such as a severe chronic illness.

When a family cannot reconcile the adversity it must face with the values that have sustained the family, a profound crisis ensues. At these times it is critical to help the family utilize its sustaining belief system to understand the illness experience so that the family can incorporate the new illness-related demands within the workable tenets of the core family values.

In the following three sections, each of the steps in the model is discussed. They are composed of (a) understanding the impact of the illness, (b) understanding the family's response to the illness, and (c) helping the family to shape the meaning of the illness experience. Table 1 summarizes the three steps in the model.

Understanding the Impact of the Illness

A group of illness characteristics has emerged in the empirical literature that appears to contain those risk factors that are most challenging to family life.

Table 1   Helping Families Shape Their Experience of Chronic Illness

---

A. Understanding the impact of the illness
  1. Degree of unpredictability in illness course
  2. Degree of disability
  3. Degree of stigma
  4. Degree of monitoring
  5. Degree of uncertainty in prognosis
B. Understanding family response
  1. Family identity
  2. Boundary regulation
  3. Role allocation
  4. Problem solving
  5. Communication
C. Helping families shape the meaning of the illness experience
  1. Making the family identity explicit
  2. Identifying the challenge of the illness to the family's core identity
  3. Helping the family to incorporate the illness experience within the context of its shared identity

---

These are the factors that families themselves describe as the most disruptive (Gonzalez et al., 1989) as well as those that appear most successfully to predict family functioning in the context of serious illness (Evans et al., 1987). A specific illness may contain two or more of these risk factors. The following five characteristics are recommended for use with families in assessing the *nature* of the illness challenge.

Degree of predictability

The degree to which family members can anticipate acute episodes of the illness has a significant impact on the extent to which they can plan short- and long-term activities. Much of family coherence is grounded in the *planning and carrying out of meaningful events* such as vacations, attendance at children's school or sports events, and bedtime storytelling (Wolin et al., 1988). The loss of predictability triggers an unusual degree of vulnerability in some families because of a trauma in an earlier generation that exposed family members to intolerable disruptions (Jacobs, 1991b). Examples of illnesses that present high levels of unpredictability include lupus, bipolar disorders, chronic fatigue syndrome, and sickle cell anemia.

Degree of disability

The extent of a patient's disability has major implications for *role allocations* in the family. To care for a seriously disabled person, the family must either purchase service or provide it themselves. The wife or mother in the family is often the individual singled out for the lion's share of this task (Hobbs, Perrin,

& Ireys, 1985). This may mean that she must relinquish her full- or part-time paid employment, thus depleting other forms of family resources. Individuals who act as the primary caregiver report significant levels of burden (Gallagher et al., 1989), although it is believed widely that women are reluctant to admit to negative feelings in relation to the care of a loved one (Rabins et al., 1990). Parents who share the responsibility for the care of a child with a demanding disorder, such as spina bifida, relate their stress specifically to the everyday demands of the illness as opposed to other possible sources of stress (Goldberg, Morris, Simmons, Fowler, & Levison, 1990). Other examples of disorders with pervasive disability include multiple sclerosis, stroke, and trauma.

Stigma

Disorders carrying significant social stigma primarily affect *boundary regulation* in the family. Family members are reluctant to share information about the condition with friends, neighbors, extended family, school personnel, or clergy members. Both children and adults are hesitant to invite friends to their home. Opportunities for concrete financial assistance (e.g., from insurance companies) may be lost. Infrequent access to the outside world resulting from collective shame has a tendency to exacerbate boundary problems within the family or self-defeating family myths. Restrictive coalitions and distortions in family perceptions of its capacities are further reinforced by the family's self-imposed isolation (Jacobs, 1991b; Walker, 1991). Examples of illnesses with considerable stigma include AIDS, psychiatric disorders, alcoholism, physical anomalies, and mental retardation.

Degree of monitoring

The extent to which blood levels, sugar levels, physical activity levels, or medication must be supervised has profound effects on *autonomous functioning* in the family. This becomes particularly important when the patient is an adolescent or noncompliant. The family must struggle with the degree of regulation it should provide and the patient with the degree he or she should accept. Families that think of themselves as functioning as highly differentiated or highly coordinated members may find this new dilemma particularly challenging (Hauser et al., 1986; Reiss, 1983). Examples of disabilities that may require extensive monitoring include renal disease, diabetes, psychoses, and Alzheimer's disease.

Certainty of prognosis

Ambiguity about the ultimate fate of the patient, particularly when the stakes are very high, has a major impact on *risk-taking behavior* and *long-term planning* in the family. Studies of parents with children with a variety of chronic illnesses (Jessop & Stein, 1985) as well as those specifically dealing with cancer

(Koocher & O'Malley, 1981) or a congenital heart defect (Goldberg, Morris, Simmons, Fowler, & Levison, 1990) demonstrated that uncertainty was a major cause of stress. Healthy family fights and the necessary airing of controversial subjects are truncated as family members live in fear of triggering a relapse or sudden death (Gonzalez et al., 1989). Family members are hesitant to express fears of their relative's demise and to discuss future phases of the family when the patient may be institutionalized or deceased (Walker, 1991). Examples of disorders with uncertain prognoses include cancer, cardiac disease, and renal disease.

Understanding Family Response

It is both interesting and hopeful that researchers report such a wide variation in the capacity of families to deal with serious chronic illness. In evaluating the psychological status of caregivers of cancer and Alzheimer's disease patients, for example, investigators found that despite a considerable degree of anxiety, depression, anger, and somatic complaints among a minority of caregivers, 61% were in the healthy range of functioning (Rabins et al., 1990). A large literature suggests that family attributions about the illness and preexisting behavioral patterns have a strong bearing on the family's ability to cope successfully with the disorder (Jacobs, 1991a; Patterson & McCubbin, 1983; Venters, 1981).

In the following section, attributes that heavily influence the family's ability to deal with the illness challenge are discussed. Each of these areas of functioning has been empirically linked with family adaptation in the context of chronic disorder.

Family identity

Many families can describe the qualities that make them distinct from other families—the characteristics that make them feel most like themselves. These characteristics include core values that give the family (a) a moral identity, (b) a sense of purpose that guides the family's priorities, and (c) perception of style that provides the family with its own unique flavor. The family's rituals and traditions symbolically reflect this identity. The family's identity usually grows from key events in the parents' (or parent, in the case of a single-parent family) histories that shape the current family's definitions of its most distinctive qualities as well as its aspirations. The family, for example, may define itself as highly purposeful, relaxed and flexible, consistently honest with each other, or resourceful.

The family's subjective view of itself has been shown repeatedly to be a critical resource in the management of a major crisis, and specifically useful in coping with chronic illness. Venters (1981) demonstrated that families who endowed the arrival of a child's illness with special meaning of a scientific, philosophical, or religious nature, particularly when they relied on a preexisting family belief system, were more successful in coping with the disorder (in this case, cystic fibrosis). Reiss (1983) documented the influence of families' views of their members' relationships to each other on the development of several chronic illnesses.

Boundary regulation

Boundary regulation involves the appropriate management of space and privacy among individuals in the family, between generations, and between the family and the outside world. Although this aspect of family functioning is always important, it becomes especially critical as the family develops coping strategies to deal with the illness.

All three boundaries described above are particularly vulnerable in the presence of a chronic disorder. Individual family members may feel they have no right to private time or recreational activities when the patient requires care or other family members need emotional support. Boyfriends, school activities, or private time in one's room may appear selfish under the circumstances. Generational boundaries may suddenly become more fluid; the partner of the ill parent, for example, may feel justified in confiding his frustration and fear to his children. Single parents who are chronically ill may feel particularly overwhelmed and rely more on their children to take care of their physical and emotional needs. Familial boundaries may become more rigid, particularly if the illness carries some stigma with it.

By contrast, boundary regulation may be a source of resilience in the family. Some families who have extensive social networks in the community rely on these friendship networks creatively to take pressure off family members by spreading caretaking responsibilities around a wider sphere. In a study of caregivers' psychological status in the context of managing relatives with both cancer and Alzheimer's, a greater number of social contacts named by caregivers was associated with more positive mood among these family members (Rabins et al., 1990). The family members' perception of the quality of their social support may be as important as the objective number of extrafamilial social contacts (Ell et al., 1988). In families in which individual boundaries are valued, parents often make sure that the children and other family members have a chance to leave the family periodically to pursue their own interests.

Role allocation

Familiar family roles must change substantially in the face of a chronic disorder. Families organized around a particular role structure, for example, a traditional gender division, may have difficulties adapting their preexisting values to the requirements of the illness. In a case in which the wife becomes ill, neither the husband nor the wife may be able to accept an increased domestic role for the husband. A wife, who in a traditional family may consider herself an active mother until her children are self-sufficient, may never, by her own definition, be able to leave the central caretaking role for her disabled child. A single parent who takes pride in handling household and child-care responsibilities themselves may suddenly be forced to rely on extended family members.

Children may realistically be needed to assist in the care of a disabled relative. Families must learn to strike a delicate balance between overburdening children and giving them appropriate caretaking tasks that will heighten their sense of self-esteem. In the case of episodic illnesses, families must learn to shift back and forth between "ill phase" and "well phase" role arrangements. This flexibility requires that family members not define themselves exclusively in terms of the primary role they play. Finally, the patients themselves must take on a meaningful role in their own care to the fullest possible extent.

The family's management of roles can be a source of family strength. Explicit discussion of the family's usual role arrangements and negotiation of new assignments has been found to alleviate family burden (Gonzalez et al., 1989). Families that systematically shared the illness care with one another and with someone outside the family were more successful in coping with cystic fibrosis (Venters, 1981). The successful establishment of patient self-care also predicted positive outcomes in the case of stroke (Evans et al., 1987).

Problem solving

Problem-solving strategies that work adequately with no adverse condition often are badly strained in the presence of a chronic illness. Family members must be able to assess accurately the nature and severity of the disorder. They must overcome the tendency to deny its presence, yet they must also absorb the shock of the news so that they may determine realistic measures that can be taken to minimize the illness impact. The central role of initial appraisal has been documented by Waltz, Badura, Pfaff, and Schott (1988) in their discussion of the mediating effect of "primary health appraisal" of cardiac patients on outcome.

A family with an effective problem-solving approach is able to identify the need for a problem-solving session without having to have a crisis. They are able to identify the problem areas, open the discussion to entirely novel ideas, come up with a concrete new strategy, and subsequently evaluate it (Falloon et al., 1984). Effective problem-solving formats are not dependent on the leadership of one family member.

Empirical evidence supports the importance of effective problem solving. In dealing with breast cancer, diabetes, or fibrocystic breast disease, families who engaged in "familial introspection," which included coping behavior characterized by frequent feedback, reflection, and goal adjustments, had better parent–child relationships, child psychosocial functioning, and family functioning (Lewis, Woods, Hough, & Bensley, 1989). The Evans group (1987) cited earlier also found successful problem solving to be predictive of positive patient and family outcomes.

Communication

Because the illness is a source of anxiety for family members, it is particularly important for them to be able to communicate their fears as well as other feelings and needs. The most common occurrence in a family with a chronic illness is the gradual restriction of affect among family members in the interest of protecting the person with the illness. Particularly in cases in which the illness is life threatening, family members fear that strong expressions of feelings may exacerbate the medical condition and perhaps even cause the person's death (Koocher & O'Malley, 1981).

The rules that govern the family's expression of affect may shift in important ways. If one family member was responsible for the expression of feelings in the family, that individual may now abdicate the role if she or he is the patient or the primary caretaker. If no new rule supersedes this arrangement, there will be an impasse.

The importance of a confiding marital relationship as a buffering effect on depression has been demonstrated in a classic study by Brown et al. (1972). Depression is a frequent presence in the homes of families with a chronically ill relative. For example, a supportive marital relationship has been shown to mediate the level of depression experienced by post-myocardial infarction patients (Waltz et al., 1988). The importance of marital communication was documented again in a study of family coping mechanisms with breast cancer, diabetes, and fibrocystic breast disease. Only in the context of good marital adjustment did higher illness demands result in the implementation of constructive family problem-solving methods initiated by the husband (Lewis et al., 1989).

Helping Families to Shape the Meaning of the Illness Experience

One of the most promising avenues in the understanding of the family's experience of chronic illness involves the examination of *fit* between a particular family and the illness with which it must cope. This area is not well researched and deserves the close attention of family-oriented investigators. A particularly fruitful arena is the examination of the mechanisms through which families incorporate an illness crisis successfully into their existing value system so that their natural coping strategies can be maximized and their creative problem-solving abilities strengthened.

A family intervention, aimed at maximizing the family's preexisting successes, is described in this section of this chapter. This brief educational intervention is composed of three steps. The family first systematically reviews the illness features to determine the most important illness challenges *as the family experiences them* (impact of illness). Second, the family considers the five areas of functioning outlined above (family response) and evaluates its level of adaptation. A considerable amount of time is spent during which family members reflect on the core family identity, particularly in articulating the family's positive views of itself. The family is then invited to think about the ways in which the illness has *challenged* the core identity. Family members are asked about the *meaning* of concrete changes, such as the loss of their father's mobility or the family's decision not to move to a new community as planned.

Finally, in the most creative part of the intervention, the family receives help in mobilizing its own most powerful shared beliefs in reaching a new understanding of the illness (helping families shape the impact of the illness). The family concentrates on the area of its core identity that seems most challenged by the illness. Family members search for additional ways of understanding their core values that will facilitate their acceptance of the profound changes associated with the illness. Summaries of two family interviews conducted by the author are provided to demonstrate the sequence of the intervention.

Shaping the impact of the illness: Example 1

A family with a strong commitment to traditional gender roles was coping with the mother's rather advanced case of multiple sclerosis. The role divisions were embedded in a rich and highly valued family history in which the men provided for their families through labors outside the house and the women made their contributions inside.

Family members' appraisal of the illness was realistic, their extrafamilial supports were strong, and communications were effective and intimate in this close-knit family. However, the mother's extensive disability—and specifically her inability to cook, shop, do laundry, and clean the house—had come to represent an intolerable loss of her proper role and a profound violation of the contract holding the family together. When they tried to grapple with a reallocation of roles, the family's ordinarily effective problem-solving approach foundered in the face of the threatened loss of their collective identity.

It would not be appropriate to challenge this family's value system. Instead, it would be more useful to question them about the underlying values that had produced the role divisions that had worked well for their family for generations. In reflecting on this over some time, the husband and wife each stated that the underlying tradition in both families was to "do what was necessary" to provide nurturance for the family. Both men and women in earlier generations had at times reshaped their priorities to support family needs. It was suggested to the family that they use the broader definition of role—that of "doing what is necessary"—to guide them in dealing with the illness circumstances.

Using this more flexible definition, family members began to generate two new ways of thinking about the illness on their own. First, the family members began to accept the absolute necessity of delegating the household tasks to others (which involved an additional step of grieving for the mother as she had been); they could then accept their taking on these roles as fulfilling the moral legacy of the family. Second, the family began to help the mother redefine her concept of nurturance by reminding her of the substantial nurturance involved in many activities she could still continue, such as advising family members about important issues, organizing activities, and influencing long-range family plans. Once the family was able to make this shift, they were able to develop and follow through on new role arrangements as the illness progressed.

In this example, the key step was for the family to reexamine the underlying tenets of its value system. Initially, the role changes inherent in the illness seemed to violate a cherished set of values. By exploring the most basic beliefs behind their traditions, however, they were able to maintain the integrity of their beliefs at the same time that they made necessary changes in their routines. The illness was no longer a disruptive invader, but rather a stimulus for the recapitulation of their traditional values. By engaging in some shared reflection, the family had found a fit between the illness and their identity that supported healthy adaptation.

Shaping the impact of the illness: Example 2

A family with the tradition of "talking everything out" was dealing with the mother's ovarian cancer. The mother's mother had died of a stroke at age 40 following what the daughter perceived as an authoritarian marriage in which her mother "swallowed everything." She swore to herself that neither she nor her children would suffer this fate. From the beginning of the marriage she instituted a rule whereby first the couple, and later their two daughters, had a weekly family meeting in which anything could be discussed. Anyone could challenge the status quo and their ideas would be listened to, as long as they treated each other with respect.

When the mother developed cancer she became depressed and withdrawn. Everyone was worried about her uncertain prognosis, but no one spoke about it. Because the mother had been the main organizer of the family meetings, they became irregular and then stopped. The tasks in the house were successfully carried out, but the hallmark of the family's identity—emotional expressiveness—was suddenly gone. Both the father and the two teenage girls were too frightened about their own feelings about the illness to push for the meetings. The meetings had been so special that they had been the main context for venting feelings, and none of the family had particularly strong confidants outside the family.

In this case, the affective rules in the household had been organized largely by one person. When she was not able to play that role, the family was not able to carry on the practices that made things feel so familiar. The intervention here again involved helping the family to become more explicit about its own values. Several important ideas emerged. All family members valued the free expression of feelings, but some found the weekly meetings constricting. They inadvertently had limited emotional sharing to that time and to the whole family context rather than through dyads or through persons outside the family. The daughters wanted the family to change what had become a rigid format. They had felt guilty about confiding in others outside the family. Second, the husband was very angry at his wife for being sick and possibly dying. Even with the tradition of openness, he could not discuss this anger with his daughters without his wife's active help. He realized spontaneously that this was something he had to discuss with her privately. This represented a change in the previous rules.

The family negotiated major changes in the methods they used to express their feelings without giving up the underlying value of emotional honesty. The changes made possible particular intimacies between family members and opened up the family boundaries as well, a development that was appropriate to the daughters' ages. Although the mother's illness had exposed problems in an important family practice, the family eventually realized that the illness had allowed the family to improve and update the practice while preserving an important element of their identity.

In the first example, the illness had invaded the organizational structure of the family, whereas in the second it had invaded the implicit affective rules in the household. Each of these arenas tapped into the particular values that gave each respective family their most enduring sense of coherence. Adapting to the illness demands would have constituted a violation of these sustaining beliefs. With some guidance, the families came to view the illness circumstances as a life event for which the family could mobilize. Their core beliefs were left intact, but the means of expressing them had been partially transformed to respond appropriately to the illness context.

Demonstrating the efficacy of this brief intervention depends on the successful resolution of several questions. Among the most important are the following: Is the construct of family identity a recognizable one to most families and can it be operationalized and measured? Is the disruption of the family belief system a frequent consequence of chronic illness? Does the disruption of a family's shared belief system affect its ability to implement changes in its day-to-day operations? These and other questions are currently being addressed by the author through a series of family interviews.

SUMMARY

This chapter has suggested a model for assisting the practitioner to help families to understand and manage the experience of chronic illness. Building on empirical studies that identify (a) those aspects of illness that most challenge family life and (b) those aspects of family life that are most affected by chronic disorders, a three-step approach is proposed in which the practitioner reviews the impact of the illness on the family and helps the family to mobilize its preexisting resources. The approach maximizes the capacity of the family's underlying family belief system to adapt to illness demands while protecting the integrity of its most enduring values.

REFERENCES

Alexander, F. (1950). *Psychosomatic medicine: Its principles and applications.* New York: Norton.

Anderson, C., Reiss, D., & Hogarty, G. (1986). *Schizophrenia and the family: A practitioner's guide to education and management.* New York: Guilford Press.

Bloom, J. (1982). Social support, accommodation to stress, and adjustment to breast cancer. *Social Science and Medicine, 16*, 1329–1338.

Brown, G., Birley, J., & Wing, J. (1972). Influence of family life on the course of schizophrenic disorders: A replication. *British Journal of Psychiatry, 121*, 241–258.

Drotar, D. (1981). Psychological perspectives in childhood chronic illness. *Journal of Pediatric Psychology, 6*, 211–228.

Ell, K., Nishimoto, R., Mantell, J., & Hamovitch, M. (1988). Longitudinal analysis of psychological adaptation among family members of patients with cancer. *Journal of Psychosomatic Research, 32*, 429–438.

Evans, R., Bishop, D., Matlock, A., Stranaman, B., Halar, E., & Noonan, W. (1987). Prestroke family interaction as a predictor of stroke outcome. *Archives of Physical Medicine and Rehabilitation, 68*, 508–512.

Falloon, I., Boyd, J., & McGill, C. (1984). *Family care of schizophrenia.* New York: Guilford Press.

Gallagher, D., Rose, J., Rivera, P., Lovett, S., & Thompson, L. (1989). Prevalence of depression in family caregivers. *The Gerontologist, 29*, 449–456.

Goldberg, S., Morris, P., Simmons, R., Fowler, R., & Levison, H. (1990). Chronic illness in infancy and parenting stress: A comparison of three groups of parents. *Journal of Pediatric Psychology, 15*, 347–358.

Gonzalez, S., Steinglass, P., & Reiss, D. (1986). *Family-centered interventions for chronically disabled: The eight-session multiple family discussion group program* (treatment manual). Washington, DC: George Washington University Rehabilitation and Research Center, Center for Family Research.

Gonzalez, S., Steinglass, P., & Reiss, D. (1989). Putting the illness in its place. *Family Process, 28*, 69–87.

Gubman, G., & Tessler, R. (1987). The impact of mental illness on families: Concepts and priorities. *Journal of Family Issues, 8*, 226–245.

Hauser, S., Jacobson, A., Wertlieb, D., Weiss-Perry, B., Follansbee, D., Wols-
dorf, J., Herskowitz, R., Houlihan, J., & Rajapark, D. (1986). Children
with recently diagnosed diabetes: Interacting with their families. *Health
Psychology, 5,* 273-296.
Hobbs, N., Perrin, J., & Ireys, H. (1985). *Chronically ill children and their
families: Problems, prospects, and proposals from the Vanderbilt Study.*
New York: Jossey-Bass.
Jacobs, J. (1989, June). "Family resilience in the context of chronic medical
illness." Plenary paper presented at the annual meeting of the American
Family Therapy Association, Colorado Springs, Colorado.
Jacobs, J. (1991a). Family therapy in the context of childhood medical illness.
In A. Stoudemire and B. Fogel (Eds.), *Advances in medical-psychiatric
practice,* Vol. 1, pp. 483-506. Washington, DC: American Psychiatric
Press.
Jacobs, J. (1991b). Family therapy with families with a chronically ill member.
In F. Herz-Brown (Ed.), *Reweaving the family tapestry* (pp. 242-261).
New York: Norton.
Jessop, D., & Stein, R. (1985). Uncertainty and its relation to the psychological
and social correlates of chronic disease in children. *Social Science and
Medicine, 10,* 993-999.
Koocher, G., & O'Malley, J. (1981). *The Damocles Syndrome: Psychosocial
consequences of surviving childhood cancer.* New York: McGraw-Hill.
Lewis, F., Woods, N., Hough, E., & Bensley, L. (1989). The family's functioning with chronic illness in the mother: The spouses's perspective. *Social Science and Medicine, 11,* 1261-1269.
Magni, G., Carli, M., Leo, D., Tshilolo, M., & Zanesco, L. (1986). Longitudinal evaluations of psychological distress in parents of children with ma-
lignancies. *Acta Paediatrixca Scandinavia, 75,* 283-288.
Minuchin, S., Baker, L., Rosman, B., Liebman, R., Milman, L., & Todd, T.
(1975). A conceptual model of psychosomatic illness in children: Family
organization and family therapy. *Archives of General Psychiatry, 32,* 1031-
1038.
Minuchin, S., Rosman, B., & Baker, L. (1978). *Psychosomatic families.* Cambridge, MA: Harvard University Press.
Montgomery, J., Gonyea, J., & Hooyman, N. (1985). Caregiving and the experience of objective and subjective burden. *Family Relations, 34,* 19-26.
Patterson, J., & McCubbin, H. (1983). Chronic illness: Family stress and coping. In C. Figley and H. McCubbin (Eds.), *Stress and the family: Volume
II. Coping with catastrophe* (pp. 21-36). New York: Brunner-Mazel.
Purcell, K., Brady, K., Chai, H., Muser, J., Molk, L., Gordon, N., & Means,
J. (1969). The effects of asthma in children of experimental separation
from the family. *Psychosomatic Medicine, 31,* 144-163.

Rabins, P., Fitting, M., Eastham, J., & Fetting, J. (1990). The emotional impact of caring for the chronically ill. *Psychosomatics, 31*, 331-335.

Reiss, D. (1983). *The family's construction of reality*. Cambridge, MA: Harvard University Press.

Reiss, D., Gonzalez, S., & Kramer, N. (1986). Family process, chronic illness, and death: On the weakness of strong bonds. *Archives of General Psychiatry, 43*, 795-804.

Rolland, J. (1984). Toward a psychosocial typology of chronic illness. *Family Systems Medicine, 2*, 245-262.

Stein, R., & Jessop, D. (1989). What diagnosis does not tell: The case for a noncategorical approach to chronic illness in childhood. *Social Science and Medicine, 29*, 769-778.

Vaughn, C., & Leff, J. (1976). The influence of family and social factors on the course of psychiatric illness: A comparison of schizophrenics and depressed neurotic patients. *British Journal of Psychiatry, 129*, 125-137.

Venters, M. (1981). Familial coping with chronic and severe childhood illness: The case of cystic fibrosis. *Social Science and Medicine, 15A*, 289-297.

Walker, G. (1991). *In the midst of winter: Systemic therapy with individuals, couples and families with AIDS infection*. New York: Norton.

Waltz, M., Badura, B., Pfaff, H., & Schott, T. (1988). Marriage and the psychological consequences of a heart attack: A longitudinal study of adaptation to chronic illness after 3 years. *Social Science and Medicine, 27*, 149-158.

Wolin, S., Bennett, L., & Jacobs, J. (1988). Assessing family rituals. In E. Imber-Black, J. Roberts, and R. Whiting (Eds.), *Rituals in families and family therapy* (pp. 230-256). New York: Norton.

Zarit, S. H., Anthony, C., & Boutselis, M. (1987). Interventions with caregivers of dementia patients: Comparison of two approaches. *Psychology and Aging, 2*, 225-232.

Zarit, S. H., Todd, P. A., & Zarit, J. M. (1986). Subjective burden of husbands and wives as caregivers: A longitudinal study. *The Gerontologist, 26*, 260-266.

9

COUPLES COPING WITH CHRONIC AND CATASTROPHIC ILLNESS

James C. Coyne
Veronica Fiske
University of Michigan Medical Center

Dramatic changes in the patterns of morbidity and mortality in the United States over the past century have resulted in longer life expectancy and longer periods of time during which people must live with chronic illness. Coping with chronic and catastrophic illness has become a normative task of married and family life, even if the timing and scope of the task varies greatly across different couples and families.

Progress in medicine and public health has led to a marked decrease in the number of deaths during infancy and childhood, as well as for women during the childbearing years (National Center for Health Statistics [NCHS], 1983, 1984). The average life expectancy has increased from 49 years in 1900 to over 75 years today, and the proportion of the population 55 years and older has more than doubled (NCHS, 1983, 1984). People are living longer, but they are also living longer with chronic health conditions (Satariano & Syme, 1981). Cardiovascular disease, cancer, and stroke have replaced infectious diseases as the leading causes of death. Most people age 65 and older have at least one chronic condition and, in the older age ranges, most will have multiple chronic problems, the most common being arthritis, hypertension, heart disease, and vision and hearing impairment. Furthermore, life expectancy has been increasing even for people with diagnosed chronic conditions that are likely to become their primary causes of death (Manton, 1990).

The need for long-term management and treatment of chronic conditions can place substantial demands and limitations on the life-style of patients and their families above and beyond the actual symptoms of the illness. For instance, as a result of fewer deaths from hypertension, greater survival of heart

129

attacks, and a general aging of the population, millions of people are now living with congestive heart failure. Management involves multi-drug regimens with considerable side effects, the need for regular exercise but avoidance of excessive demands on cardiac workload, sodium restriction, and careful monitoring of weight and drug toxicity. Lapses in adherence may result in exacerbation, hospitalization, or even death of the patient. In addition, patients and their families must also contend with the patients' deaths being imminent despite their best efforts to prevent them. Across a variety of chronic conditions, accepted patterns of medical care now emphasize reduced utilization of hospitalization and earlier discharge and resumption of normal activities in order to avoid invalidism. Such trends have increased the responsibility of the patients and families for coping with chronic illness.

There is a considerable literature concerning how individuals cope with chronic and catastrophic illness and, although it is smaller, there is also a growing literature concerning families and illness (Campbell, 1986). In this chapter, we make the case for considering the married couple as an intermediate level of analysis. How couples cope can be a crucial determinant of both biomedical and psychosocial outcomes for the patient, and chronic illness in a spouse can have profound implications for married life. A focus on the couple may highlight some key issues that might be distorted or ignored in focusing on either the individual patient or the larger family unit. Moreover, even when theoretical or practical concerns dictate a focus on the individual or the family, our attending to the implications of the marriage and spouse for the individual as well as to the differences between marriage and other family relationships can be important.

WHY FOCUS ON THE COUPLE?

Despite increases in nonmarital cohabitation, the majority of all American families is organized around the married couple, and over 90% of all adults marry at some point in their lives (U.S. Bureau of the Census, 1989). Our focus on the marriage should not be interpreted as a slighting of the experience of adults living alone or with kin, those in single-parent families, or those having alternative life-styles such as gay and lesbian relationships. We simply cannot ignore the importance of marriage and the spouse for the many people who are married. Indeed, the distinctiveness of the marital relationship should deter theorists and researchers from making broad generalizations about families and illness without considering whether the families are organized around a marital unit.

Marriage is associated with psychological well-being, good physical health, and lower mortality (Ross, Mirowsky, & Goldstein, 1990), although the benefits of marriage may be limited to those in satisfactory marriages (Reene,

1971). Among the married, marital happiness is the largest single source of variance in general happiness and quality of life (Glenn & Weaver, 1988). There is now a large literature on the effects of social support on health and well-being, and it seems that marriage may be the most important determinant of these effects. Furthermore, it is possible that support from other relationships may not readily compensate for what is lacking in a marriage (Coyne & DeLongis, 1986).

It has been suggested that marriage is the most important relationship in late middle and old age, and it is a key determinant of global well-being among older men and women (Glenn, 1975; Lee, 1978). Being a husband or wife is a "master" role, central to identity and self-concept, which becomes even more important when other roles are lost. Marriage is distinct from other family relationships. It is more intense, more equal although gender-differentiated, voluntary but enduring, interdependent (Kelley, 1981; Wish, Deutsch, & Kaplan, 1976), and it is also sexual.

Married couples are now living longer and bearing fewer children, which extends the couple-alone period of the family life-cycle. In middle and old age, when chronic and catastrophic illnesses have their greatest impact, there is less change in the couple than in parent–child relationships. Children grow up and move out, they pursue independent education and career goals, and they get married and have children of their own. Whereas most married people over age 64 have offspring, only a minority lives with their children (Smith, 1981).

Marriage is not only a more primary relationship, but how the spouse, and particularly the wife, function may influence the type of involvement that children and other family members have with the couple. As long as she can perform basic, everyday tasks of living, these tasks tend to be left to the wife; the intervention of children and other kin may depend both on her functional capabilities and her negotiation of their involvement.

Taken together, one might speculate that marriage and the spouse have a crucial role in a patient's convalescence from catastrophic illness and are important determinants of the rate and extent of the patient's recovery. For married couples, coping with chronic and catastrophic illness can be expected to be largely a dyadic affair, and the effects of illness and treatment on the spouse and the marriage should be considered as well as patient adaptational outcomes. One might also anticipate that because changes in patterns of medical care transfer greater responsibility to the spouse and the couple, it would be important to deal with the couple directly and as a unit involve the spouse in medical care. Nothing in the existing literature would seriously contradict these speculations, but the literature is quite limited and lacks an overarching theoretical framework. Medical educators and practitioners can find little systematic guidance as to how to work with spouses and couples. For the purpose of understanding how couples cope with illness, one can start by drawing on the individual and family literatures, but one needs to be appreciative of their limitations as well as their contributions. Ultimately, a better understanding of how couples cope with chronic illness will have implications for the reformulation of both individual and family perspectives.

The Individual Perspective and the Couple

Two major frameworks for understanding how individuals cope with illness are stress and coping theory and Bandura's social learning theory (Bandura, 1986). According to one widely accepted model of stress and coping, a person facing a health problem makes an appraisal of the threat, loss, or challenge posed by the problem (primary appraisal), as well as the resources available to deal with it (secondary appraisal); engages in problem- and emotion-focused coping; and experiences positive and negative emotions and other adaptational outcomes as a result (Coyne & Lazarus, 1980; Lazarus & Folkman, 1984). This model represents an improvement over conceptualizations of stress simply as the occurrence of environmental events or as an individual response. However, it is focused narrowly on the efforts of the individual. The concept of social support is the main acknowledgement that adaptation to stress occurs in the context of interpersonal relationships, but even this is generally reduced to a matter of the individual's *perception* of social support (Coyne & DeLongis, 1986).

Individual stress and coping theory does a poor job of accounting for processes occurring in couples in which one partner has a health problem. The shortcomings of this approach were apparent from the outset in pilot work for the Michigan Family Heart Study, which focused on couples coping with a husband's myocardial infarction (Coyne, Ellard, & Smith, 1990). In our focus group discussions with post-infarction couples, it was obvious that wives were not simply support persons. Their husbands' health problems had direct implications for their own well-being and they were faced with their own coping tasks. What needed to be done in coping with the infarction—the tasks or issues that it entailed—was shaped by the marital relationship, what each partner did, and how that affected the other. To a large degree, this give-and-take determined how the event unfolded and reverberated in these people's lives and not just their perception of it (Coyne et al., 1990). Both the patient and spouse had the crucial and sometimes preemptive task of coming to terms with the presence of the other partner who shared some responsibility for the situation, who also had opinions about what should be done and some influence on the situation, and who had to some degree a shared fate. In that sense, coping with a myocardial infarction could be seen as having three potentially competing functions: managing one's own distress (emotion-focused), attending to various instrumental tasks (problem-focused), and grappling with each other's presence and emotional needs (relationship-focused).

Once one appreciates that coping has a relationship-focused function, one can see that a special set of competencies may be involved when coping occurs in the context of a significant relationship: How does one contribute to the partner's well-being, avoid unnecessary conflict, and yet look after oneself and balance concern for the partner with one's own needs? There is potential source of conflict for the person confronting a health problem in that what is efficacious in reducing one's own distress or dealing with an instrumental task may be counter to what is needed to deal with a relationship, and vice versa. We found evidence to support this assertion in the Michigan Family Health Study. Wives' protective buffering of their husbands—their readily conceding in disagreements and hiding of negative affect—was associated with greater distress for them and greater self-efficacy for the patients (Coyne & Smith, 1991a, 1991b). Coping with chronic illness may involve such tradeoffs between protecting one's own well-being and contributing to a partner's recovery.

Bandura's social learning theory gives a central role to peoples' beliefs about their capabilities to execute the behaviors needed to pursue their desired ends. Our *perceived self-efficacy* is an important determinant of how much effort a person will exert and how long he or she will persevere in the face of significant challenges. Consistent with Bandura's theory, self-ratings of efficacy have been shown to predict short- and long-term success in initiating and maintaining health-promoting behaviors and adherence to medical regimens (see O'Leary, 1985, and Bandura, 1986, for reviews). For instance, among men recovering from an uncomplicated myocardial infarction, changes in self-efficacy following a treadmill test predicted home activity better than their actual performance on the treadmill did (Ewart, Taylor, Reese, & DeBusk, 1983)

Although Bandura's (1986) theory may adequately explain tasks that are largely a matter of individual initiative such as increasing aerobic capacity, it does not elucidate tasks directly involving other people, such as changing lifestyle or increasing tolerance for stress and anger. The main role this theory gives to significant others in patients' attainment of self-efficacy is as sources of encouragement and support for enactment of new behaviors or the resumption of old activities—yet, spouses do more than that. For instance, reports from our focus groups with post-infarction couples suggest that in many cases it was the wives who implemented needed changes in their husbands' diets and daily routines. Much less depended on patients' own self-confidence and initiative. On the other hand, wives in some couples took a more passive role, and still other couples became bogged down in disputes over who should decide what needed to be done and how to proceed (Coyne et al., 1990). Given that interpersonal conflict is perhaps the major source of everyday stress (Bolger, Delongis, Kessler, & Schilling, 1989), patients' ratings of their efficacy in dealing with stress and anger might reflect the quality of the marital relationship rather than just the individual patients' characteristics. High ratings of self-efficacy might be a function of how little is required of patients who have the benefit of more active and efficacious wives or wives who effectively buffer them from overwhelming stress. Patients' ratings of their self-efficacy in confronting complex tasks in their everyday social environments may be inexorably confounded by what other people in these environments are doing. Although patients' ratings may indeed predict the success with which tasks are met, the processes determining self-ratings and their relationship to outcome may be quite different than those emphasized in Bandura's individualistic accounts of self-efficacy.

Although patients' ratings of their self-efficacy in meeting specific tasks remain a useful indicator of progress in coping with a health problem, we needed to examine a broader range of patient, spouse, and relationship variables that influence self-efficacy. For example, again focusing on results of the Michigan Family Heart Study, we found that characteristics of the wives added significantly to the prediction of the patients' self-efficacy beyond what could be predicted from patient characteristics alone (Coyne & Smith, 1991a). Wives' own functional capabilities, their own self-efficacy in dealing with the changes imposed on them by the heart attack, and their protective buffering of the patients all made independent contributions to patient self-efficacy.

Guidance and Misguidance
from the Family Literature

Family perspectives on coping with illness involve a conceptual shift from viewing the family and other relationships from the perspective of patients to viewing patients in terms of their involvement in these relationships (Ransom, 1989). Drawing on the traditions of both family therapy and family sociology, some family approaches tend to focus on family conditions that are generally dysfunctional or pathological and how these conditions may influence and be influenced by physical illness (Beavers, 1989; Minuchin, Rosman, & Baker, 1978). Other approaches deemphasize definitions of what is pathological and concentrate on the fit between families' style, organization, and values and the tasks that that illness presents, as well as the form their dysfunction would take if their adaptative style were to fail (Reiss, 1989).

Family perspectives underscore that coping with chronic illness in not simply a matter of individual appraisal and response but of the organization of relationships. Yet, in highlighting the importance of social relationships, they have sometimes exaggerated the role of marriage and the family in precipitating and determining the outcome of health crises. (For an influential example of this, see Minuchin et al. 1978.) There has been a tendency for these theorists to *decontextualize* the marital and the family unit, ignoring the constraints imposed by health problems and the influence of the health care system (Coyne &

Anderson, 1988, 1989). However important the family or couple's coping may be, it is not the only, or even the most crucial determinant of the outcomes that patients achieve.

In chronic and catastrophic illness, patients' medical conditions may largely determine both the range of possible outcomes and how well everyone adapts. Furthermore, the appropriateness of the family's efforts and the outcomes they achieve are also shaped by their involvement with the medical system. A lack of information and support from medical personnel after husbands' myocardial infarctions may hamper the couple's adaptation and create unnecessary distress. If one fails to take these influences into account, one may misattribute negative effects of the medical condition, or couples' lack of guidance from the medical system, to inadequacies in the couples' efforts at adaptation (Coyne & Anderson, 1989; Gillis, 1984). In an important sense, therefore, couples coping with health problems can be viewed as *open* interpersonal systems, in which the patients' and spouses' efforts are influenced and even constrained by a number of factors, including the patients' medical condition and the couples' contact with medical personnel. (For an excellent discussion of couples and families as open systems in contact with the larger medical system, see Reiss & Kaplan De-Nour, 1989.)

By focusing on the family's adaptation rather than the efforts of individual family members, family perspectives have maintained a high degree of gender-blindness. Namely, they ignore the extent to which women absorb the larger part of the burden of families' and couples' adaptation to illness, whether these women be the patients or spouses. When men return from the hospital after a myocardial infarction, they withdraw from household responsibilities and are nurtured by their wives. When women return after suffering a myocardial infarction, they are likely to resume light household responsibilities more quickly, attend to family members' needs, and feel guilty about changes in their household responsibilities imposed by their functional limitations. Men do not report such guilt (Hamilton, 1990).

Furthermore, in contrast to the "Pollyanna-ish" view of social relationships that the social support literature has provided, family theorists have been biased toward viewing family members with suspicion and as probable negative influences on patient adaptation. In the absence of data, they have presumed both a high prevalence of wives' and mothers' overprotectiveness and conceptualized it as a cover for hostility. Yet, some degree of protectiveness is both normative and necessary to assist vulnerable and dependent patients and forestall catastrophic outcomes (Gillis, 1984). There is also little acknowledgment in the family literature that when helping efforts become miscarried or overprotectiveness occurs, it may reflect either misinformation or family members' efforts to manage their own anxieties and sense of responsibility, rather than hostility toward the patient or more fundamental family dysfunction

(Coyne, Wortman, & Lehman, 1988). In our research, we have found little evidence that wives' overprotectiveness undermines their husbands' self-efficacy (Fiske, Coyne, & Smith, 1991b). We found that overprotectiveness was related to wives distress and the couple having become closer following the heart attack. It did not predict low self-efficacy in patients. Another study found that wives' overprotectiveness was predicted by patients' complaints of angina pectoris, suggesting that overprotectiveness may represent wives' attempt to manage their husbands' physical distress (Wicklund, Sanne, Vedin, & Wilhelmsson, 1984). In our study, we found it was wives' hostile-critical attitude that had a negative impact on patient efficacy and psychological distress, and this attitude was unrelated to overprotectiveness (Fiske et al., 1991). Unlike overprotectiveness, a hostile-critical attitude among wives was predictive of the couple being *less* close after the heart attack, and the wife feeling that the couple did not have frequent enough discussions about how to cope with the heart attack.

Family theorists have shown a distinct preference for pursuing elusive direct links between family functioning and physiological processes. At the same time, they have often ignored more readily demonstrable, even if mundane, links between family functioning and the implementing of medical regimens or the maintenance of quality of life of patients and family members in the face of serious illness and complicated medical regimens. Apparent associations between family functioning and physiological measures (Minuchin et al., 1978) and mortality (Reiss, Gonzalez, & Kramer, 1986) have been accepted uncritically and given causal interpretation without attention to the serious methodological limitations of the studies that produced them or the availability of more plausible alternative interpretations.

The study of literatures concerning individual and family adaptation to illness can help to develop an approach to understanding how couples cope with chronic and catastrophic illness. The individual literature needs a greater consideration of the centrality of a close, intimate relationship to adaptational outcomes. How the marital relationship shapes the tasks, the coping efforts, and the outcomes that are achieved are important areas of study. Individual patients are not alone in their predicaments, and spouses are more than sources of perceived support. Analysis of the determinants of patients' efficacy and outcomes needs to encompass the burden and benefits afforded by involvement in relationships. Yet, in shifting to the more contextual and systemic family perspective as an alternative, one should not overlook the fact that families are composed of individuals and that women may assume a disproportionate share of the responsibility for the burden and efforts that are typically attributed to the family as a whole. What these women and their families are able to accomplish may be constrained by the features of chronic illness and the nature of their involvement with the medical system.

THEMES IN UNDERSTANDING COUPLES COPING WITH ILLNESS

Our understanding of couples coping with chronic illness is decidedly prepara-digmatic. There is much we need to discover about the particulars of how couples cope with chronic illness before we can offer an adequate explanation of what they do. At this stage, rather than attempting to construct an elaborate theoretical model in the absence of basic data, our first priority should be to extend what we know in a theory-informed but phenomena-driven fashion. We can, however, identify at the outset some crucial themes that must be addressed as we proceed, which can guide both our integration of the data that are avail-able and our efforts to obtain further data. These themes include interdepen-dency in the marriage, the character of the illness with which the couple must cope, gender and gender roles, issues relevant to phase of life course, and the couples' involvement with the health care system.

Interdependency

The interdependency of patients and spouses emerges as a theme in a number of different, but related, ways (Kelley, 1981). First, across a variety of chronic medical conditions, spouses' distress is correlated with the patients' distress and is of the same magnitude. This could be interpreted as evidence of these couples reacting as units or systems (Baider & Kaplan De-Nour, 1988; Coyne & Smith, 1991b; Shanfield, Heiman, Cope, & Jones, 1979; Soskoline & Kaplan De-Nour, 1989). Patient efficacy in meeting the challenges of a chronic illness is also correlated with spouses' efficacy in meeting their own challenges (Coyne & Smith, 1991a). Furthermore, distress and demoralization in spouses may have a negative impact on patient rehabilitation (Carnwath & Johnson, 1987; Mayou, Foster, & Williamson, 1978).

Furthermore, although there can be tremendous benefits to being able to depend on a relationship, coping with health problems in close relationships also poses some predictable dilemmas (Coyne et al., 1990). At crucial times, doing what is ultimately most beneficial for the patients' and couples' well-being may seemingly conflict with being a loving, caring spouse. For example, it may sometimes be most advantageous to allow a diabetic patient to suffer the consequences of nonadherence to diet to encourage greater self-responsibility but difficult for the spouse to remain uninvolved as the patient becomes ill.

There may be predictable differences in patient and spouse perspectives on the risks and benefits of patient exertion (Taylor, Bandura, Ewart, Miller, & DeBusk, 1985) and the necessity of strict adherence of regimen (Speedling, 1982). Patients are more confident in their physical capabilities and are less concerned about failing to adhere to the regimen than are their spouses. These differences may complicate each partner's efforts to manage his or her own feelings and balance these efforts with consideration for the other partner. Empathic responses to spouses' distress may disrupt patients' focus on what they need to do for themselves (DeLongis & O'Brien, 1990). They may defer to spouses' expressions of concern and not take needed initiatives, or they may overexert themselves in defiance of their spouses. Decisions about taking initiatives, accepting or giving help, expressing one's distress, or letting a partner struggle without one's help can all pose complex issues as to the priority of one partner's well-being over the other's. As suggested earlier, there may be trade-offs, such as those between wives' distress and patients' self-efficacy (Coyne & Smith, 1991b).

In contrast, spouses seem to routinely and effectively invoke their interdependency as a basis for motivating patients (Coyne et al., 1990). In our study, spouses seemed to feel that they could cite the patients' responsibility to them in conflict situations. There was a recognition that there are certain things that only the patients could do and that the welfare of both people depended on the patients doing them. Responsibility to a spouse could be an impetus for appropriate behavior such as undertaking and maintaining life-style changes, even when patients' morale flagged or sense of self-responsibility failed. Thus some of the benefits of close relationships come from the constraint or social control that they provide, rather than their supportiveness per se.

Influence of Parameters of the Illness on the Couple's Functioning

In attempting to understand how couples cope with illness, it is important to start with an appreciation of the character of the illness and how it may shape and constrain stress and coping processes. Even when illness involves a discrete event, such as an unanticipated first myocardial infarction, its influence on stress and coping may unfold over time. Furthermore, patients do not just confront an illness, they *are* ill. The associated impairment may profoundly affect how they can cope, the kind of relationship that can be had with them, and the range of adaptational outcomes that the couple can achieve. Sometimes it can be exceedingly difficult or even impossible to separate biomedical concomitants of illness (such as depression following stroke or the fatigue experienced by end-stage renal patients undergoing dialysis) from the morale problems or distress arising from ineffective coping. It is therefore important that researchers start with a full appreciation of biomedical aspects of the conditions they study and how fluctuations in patients' medical condition might be misattributed to psychological processes.

It is important to see how the biomedical aspects of the illness affect the experience of coping more directly. Rolland (1984) has cogently argued for the use of a typology in which certain dimensions classify illness rather than traditional biological diagnoses. We would add at least two other dimensions of treatment and rehabilitation to his classification system: the degree to which the patient's health or functional capabilities depend on the effectiveness and persistence of the couple's coping efforts, and the degree to which the couple can affect ultimate outcomes. Some conditions such as an incapacitating stroke or certain cancers may impose serious burdens on the spouses but fail to provide the prospect of spouses making a positive difference in outcomes other than for their own and the patients' morale. In other conditions, such as recovery from an uncomplicated myocardial infarction, there may be good prospects of resumption of normal activities, and progress may be more contingent on the couple's efforts. However, in other conditions such as congestive heart failure or the later stages of insulin-dependent diabetes, patients and spouses must work together to maintain a complicated medical regimen. They are faced with the risk that nonadherence will have immediate dire consequences such as complications or even death, even though the patients' further deterioration and impending death may be unavoidable.

Reiss and Kaplan De-Nour (1989) argue that there may be different kinds of challenges associated with different stages of illness, from the acute phase, through chronicity, and in many illnesses, to the terminal phase. Characteristics of the coping of the individual and couple that are adaptive in one phase may not be adaptive in another. What is most adaptive is a matter of fit, in that optimal coping may vary depending on the nature of the illness and its stage.

In the acute phase, when the patient is being hospitalized with chronic illness, the role of the spouse may be a limited and passive one, mainly consisting of reinforcing the doctor and supporting the patient with only an occasional assumption of a more active role as patient advocate. As Reiss and Kaplan De-Nour (1989) point out, the boundary between the acute and chronic phase of an illness will vary with the illness. However, it generally involves a shift away from the anxious uncertainties of diagnosis and immediate survival to the maintenance of morale, and away from the intensity of critical care to the routinization of medical care in the context of everyday life. Typically, this entails the patient and spouse abruptly going from passive to active roles and developing the capabilities to interpret vague signs and symptoms. They also make crucial decisions and skillfully implement complex regimens in the absence of much guidance from medical personnel. The relief associated with the patient having survived a mortal threat and the daunting set of demands facing the couple may give rise to a "honeymoon period" for them (Speedling, 1982). They may have a heightened sense of closeness and cooperation. Each partner may feel a renewed sense of being needed and appreciated by the other, and conflict may be suppressed. Yet, with passage of time, the challenges and tasks that brought them closer together may become sources of conflict, and any preexisting tension and dissatisfaction may resurface and intensify.

In the terminal phase of the illness, there may be another honeymoon period, whether it be brought about by a sense of impending loss or guilt feelings. The couple may also be reconnected with medical personnel. Although some medical personnel will maintain their composure by assuming a position of emotionally distant, authoritarian leadership, other personnel will close some of the role distance and more actively comfort the couple and share in the impending loss. A variety of configurations are possible in the physician-patient–spouse system. In some instances, the patient may assume the role of specialist in the system by conveying the subtle information needed by the physician and spouse in interpreting the patient's state. In other instances, the physician and spouse may assume a protective stance and cut the patient out of the flow of medical information as the end comes near.

Issues of Gender Role and Gender

One can readily fall into a pattern of discussing the couple in terms of patients and spouses. Yet, one must be careful not to obscure processes that depend on gender roles, and one must be sensitive to both how our statements must be qualified according to the gender of the patient and when gender role supersedes patient status as a consideration.

As Gilligan (1982) noted, women tend to be socialized into caretaking roles in close relationships. Much of their functioning when a husband is ill may be seen as an extension of their existing caretaking role. The existing allotment of family responsibilities may be such that women will absorb a disproportionate share of the burden of adjustment to the illness and implementation of the regimen. This may be particularly true when their husbands become functionally impaired, dependent, or demoralized. Such changes impose fundamental limits on the kinds of relationships that they can have with their husbands and the kinds of life-styles that are possible for the wives. Demands on wives may also sharply curtail their freedom to engage in outside activities, including employment, and their reasonable expectations for the future may be drastically changed.

Catastrophic health events such as a husband's myocardial infarction may lead to a negotiation of a more egalitarian marital relationship even when the changes are not necessitated by the husband's impairment (Croog & Levine, 1982). However, there may be cohort effects such that in couples that are currently late middle-aged and aged, the gender differentiation of roles may be so well established that they are relatively immune to both recent societal change and to the pressures for renegotiation arising from functional impairments associated with wives' chronic illness. Zarit, Todd, and Zarit (1986) have made some interesting observations about the persistent influence of gender roles in the face of partial incapacitation of a spouse. Whereas a husband may hire a housekeeper to come in and take over his wife's instrumental chores around the house, a wife is more likely to assume her husband's previous duties herself. When she does hire someone to come into the home to help, that person is likely to serve as a "sitter" who does not decrease the wife's workload but may allow her to go out to perform other chores.

Men and women may differ in the importance that they attach to the quality of the marital relationship, their strategies for resolving conflict, and the value they ascribe to ventilating negative feelings as a means of coping with stress (Gilligan, 1982; Gottleib, in press; Gottman, 1991; Raush, 1974). Wives are more likely than husbands to base their feelings of well-being on the quality of their marriage and therefore have a greater need to deal with any marital short-comings (Gottman, 1991). Coping with chronic illness in the face of preexisting marital difficulties may pose particular problems. Under these circumstances, coping may be a matter of *antagonistic cooperation* (i.e., persons who are dissatisfied with each other and prone to conflict or disagreement must nonetheless collaborate in facing a threat to the well-being of both of them). What the couple does together may be a matter of obligation and necessity rather than caring, and it may be done with tension rather than appreciation (Coyne & Smith, 1991b). Given differences in both relationship orientation and instrumental roles, women may assume more of this burden.

In discussing gender differences, it is important to be sensitive to how roles can be confounded with biomedical differences between men and women. For instance, although there may be readily describable differences in couples in which the wife rather than the husband has had a heart attack, the sources of these differences may be difficult to disentangle. For instance, women tend to have heart attacks later than men and their heart attacks are more likely to be associated with complications. Women are more likely than a man the same age to have an older spouse and one who has health limitations. It is in light of such differences that one must interpret findings that indicate that post-infarction women resume household responsibilities more quickly than post-infarction men, or that they are less likely than post-infarction men to resume employment or sexual activity (Hamilton, 1990).

Life Course Issues

The challenge of coping with chronic illness must be understood in the context of other challenges and developmental tasks facing couples, and these vary as a function of stage of life. Younger couples may be more distressed by catastrophic health events (Coyne & Smith, 1991b), in part because they are off schedule. When such events occur earlier in life and are therefore more unexpected, they require more of a readjustment of long-term plans (Neugarten & Hagestad, 1976). For instance, an earlier heart attack is more disruptive of child rearing and employment. Yet, to the extent that functional recovery depends on the involvement of others, it may be linked to patients' and spouses' ages in more complex ways. Older spouses may themselves have more functional limitations and therefore be less able to assist. Teenage offspring may be more able than young children to assume instrumental responsibilities. As they get older, offspring may be more inclined to decrease their involvement in the family as they go away to college, seek employment, and get married and have families of their own.

Middle-aged and aged couples who have long histories together may be better able to draw on their well-established shared understandings and routines in coping with chronic illness than couples without such histories together. So long as they are congruent with the demands of the illness and its regimen, well-defined patterns in their relationship may provide structure, efficiency, and predictability that make adaptation to a medical regimen more manageable. For patients and spouses to be self-efficacious in the context of effective relevant routines requires less personal initiative. On the other hand, such routines can become a source of inflexibility and a source of problems when they were incompatible with meeting the demands posed by the illness.

Expressive aspects of routines are also important. They can provide regular opportunities to demonstrate concern, appreciation, and confidence. To the extent that routines are successful, explicit displays of support may prove superfluous and negotiating skills may be less crucial. A wife from a seemingly well-functioning couple remarked in one of our focus groups, "We don't talk much about what we need to do. Luckily we don't need to, because we would probably disagree and wouldn't get anything done" (Coyne et al., 1990, p. 134). This is consistent with research that suggests that the advantage of married couples over pairs of strangers in problem solving is not that the married couples display better problem-solving skills in working together but that they have the benefits of shared understandings that make the use of negotiating skills less crucial (Winter, Ferreira, & Bowers, 1973).

Discussions of couples' adaptational outcomes need to take life-course issues into account. For instance, changes in employment status are ambiguous. Depending on their circumstances, older persons may not necessarily view work as a desirable and valuable part of their lives. "After years of heavy and perhaps unpleasant work, when nearing retirement or having enjoyable family or other leisure pursuits, a return to one's old job is likely to appear as an actual decline in life quality" (Radley, 1988, p. 7).

The Couple as an Open System: Involvement with the Health Care System

Although the medical system and the adequacy of care received obviously affect the disease outcome directly, they may also affect the couple's ability to cope. The medical system generally is not prepared to accommodate the spouse as an active participant in the treatment of the patient. In the acute phase of chronic illness at the hospital, medical staff may view the spouse as an intruder in the physician–patient relationship, and a spouse who assertively seeks a more active role may be seen as a nuisance. Furthermore, efforts to communicate with spouses often do not take into account their emotional states at the hospital or the responsibilities that they must abruptly assume on the patients' discharge.

Inadequate contact between medical personnel and spouses before patient discharge may set a trajectory for the couples' later adjustment. Even after controlling for the severity of husbands' functional limitations and the quality of the marriage before a myocardial infarction, the adequacy of wives' contact with medical personnel before husbands' discharge is a significant predictor of wives' psychological distress 6 months later (Coyne & Smith, 1991b). Wives frequently complain of a lack of information and support from medical personnel after husbands' myocardial infarctions (Thompson & Meddis, 1990), and most feel that they did not have adequate opportunity to ask questions of medical personnel at the hospital (Thompson & Cordle, 1988). They may be least informed about matters that directly involve them, such as permissible sexual activity and changes in diet.

One reason that spouses' contact with medical personnel at the hospital may be so crucial for later adjustment is that there is so little opportunity for consultation later (Speedling, 1982). It is only on the patients' return home that the couple may appreciate the vagueness and incompleteness of the information that they have been given, but by then spouses may feel cut off from access to the medical system. Wishnie, Hackett, and Cassem (1971) noted that controversy over specific meaning of physician's instructions can be a source of a "steady, eroding conflict" in couples:

> Vague terms such as 'use in moderation,' 'a few times daily,' and 'use your own discretion' were seized upon by the family and patient and interpreted in an entirely personal way. Arguments resulted, the manifest content of which centered about the patient's activity, diet, and 'nervousness.' (p. 1294)

Simple interventions by medical personnel could serve to decrease spouses' distress and increase their efficacy in dealing with their partners' condition. Yet, such efforts must take into account that a sizable proportion of these spouses may be experiencing psychological distress, which may interfere with their ability to benefit from whatever the hospital personnel offer. It may be crucial that such interventions give ample opportunities for spouses to be active participants in learning by asking questions, and be assured that they are negotiating a continuing relationship with the medical system and are not being abandoned on patients' discharge from the hospital.

Routinely involving spouses in medical care and making the couple the unit of care would involve some complex challenges. Although there have been a few noteworthy demonstrations of the efficacy of spouse involvement in programs for weight loss, smoking cessation, and life-style changes (Brownell,

Heckerman, Westlake, Hayes, & Monti, 1978; Morisky et al., 1983), the literature is best characterized as dominated by mixed and negative results (Brownell & Stunkard, 1981; Lichtenstein, Glasgow, & Abrams, 1986; O'Neil, 1979). Brownell and Stunkard (1981) have aptly summarized the problems of such programs:

> *The interactions between patients and spouses are complex. Attempts have often been made to alter these interactions and the associated patterns of behavior before these interactions and patterns are clearly understood. Couples training is a potentially powerful approach to treatment, but careful assessment is needed of attitudes, shared eating patterns, and marital coping skills. (p. 1228)*

CONCLUSION

We have made a case for focusing on the married couple coping with chronic and catastrophic illness as an intermediate level of analysis between the individual and the family, and we have suggested a number of themes that must be addressed. We wish to close with a note on methodology.

The study of individual stress and coping processes and, to a lesser extent, the study of families is characterized by a plethora of widely used instruments to assess key variables such as stress, social support, and coping. Yet, once some basic relationships are established, the availability of such instruments can prove to be a drawback, in that it reduces the burden on investigators to develop a more "intimate familiarity" (Lofland, 1976) with the phenomena of interest. Indeed, the study of individual stress and coping processes in particular is settling into an unfortunate state of affairs such that investigators can feel comfortable mindlessly applying previously used instruments with yet another population, and yet again discovering that stress is bad, social support is good, and coping should make more of a difference than they are able to demonstrate. There is little critical reflection on the inadequacy of such instruments or on the paucity of insight they yield into the lives of the people who are being studied. The family literature is less well developed than the stress and coping literature, but it gives every indication of quickly falling into the same pattern. It is hoped that something can be learned and that the study of couples coping with chronic illness will be able to proceed differently.

We need to start with an active effort to appreciate the circumstances of the people we study and the complexity of the processes that connect them to each other and to the illness and the medical system (Coyne et al., 1990; Gottlieb, in press). Getting a sense of the experiences of patients and their families can be important, but there may be systematic shortcomings in peoples' ability to reflect on their lives, recall what their lives were like before a catastrophic health event, judge how much it has affected them, or explain why they behave as they do (Davis, 1991; Mechanic, 1991). Furthermore, impressionistic qualitative research may only compound the biases and limitations of respondents with those of investigators. On the other hand, we know all too well, from the individual stress and coping literature, the limitations of simple checklists and other standardized measures that do not map well the key features of individuals' lives or the unfolding of crucial events in them (Coyne & Downey, 1991). One part of a solution to this dilemma is to develop more contextual methods (Brown & Harris, 1978) that utilize semistructured interviews to obtain rich information from respondents and then to apply investigator-based categories to systematize and quantify it. With respondents actively engaged, criteria well specified, and raters well trained, we can have more confidence in the validity of the resulting data than in investigators' summary impressions of qualitative data or blind inferences about what life circumstances are reflected in respondents' endorsements of items on questionnaires and checklists.

REFERENCES

Baider, L., & Kaplan De-Nour, A. (1988). Adjustment to cancer: Who is the patient: The husband or the wife? *Israel Journal of Medical Science, 24,* 631–636.

Bandura, A. (1986). *Social foundations of thought and action: A social cognitive theory.* Englewood Cliffs, NJ: Prentice-Hall.

Beavers, W. R. (1989). Beavers systems model. In Ramsey, C. N. (Ed.), *Family systems in medicine* (pp. 62–74). New York: Guilford Press.

Bolger, N., DeLongis, A., Kessler, R. C., & Schilling, E. A. (1989). Effects of daily stress on negative mood. *Journal of Personality & Social Psychology, 57,* 808–818.

Brown, G. W., & Harris, T. (1978). *Social origins of depression: A study of psychiatric disorder in women.* New York: Free Press.

Brownell, K. D., Heckerman, C. L., Westlake, R. J., Hayes, S. C., & Monti, P. M. (1978). The effect of couples training and partner cooperativeness in the behavioral treatment of obesity. *Behavior Research and Therapy, 16,* 323–333.

Brownell, K. D., & Stunkard, A. J. (1981). Couples training, pharmacotherapy, and behavior therapy in the treatment of obesity. *Archives of General Psychiatry, 38,* 1224–1229.

Campbell, T. (1986). Family's impact on health: A critical review. *Family Systems Medicine, 4,* 135–328.

Carnwath, T. C., & Johnson, D. A. (1987). Psychiatric morbidity among spouses of patients with stroke. *British Medical Journal, 294,* 409–411.

Coyne, J. C., & Anderson, B. J. (1988). The "psychosomatic family" reconsidered: Diabetes in context. *Journal of Marital and Family Therapy, 14,* 112–123.

Coyne, J. C., & Anderson, B. J. (1989). The "psychosomatic family" reconsidered II: Recalling a defective model and looking ahead. *Journal of Marital and Family Therapy, 15*, 139–148.

Coyne, J. C., & DeLongis, A. (1986). Going beyond social support: The role of social relationships in adaptation. *Journal of Consulting and Clinical Psychology, 5*, 454–460.

Coyne, J. C., & Downey, G. (1991). Social factors in psychopathology: Stress, social support, and coping processes. *Annual Review of Psychology, 42*, 401–425.

Coyne, J. C., Ellard, J. H., & Smith, D. A. (1990). Unsupportive relationships, interdependence, and unhelpful exchanges. In I. G. Sarason, B. R. Sarason, & G. Pierce (Eds.), *Social support: An interactional view* (pp. 129–149). New York: Wiley.

Coyne, J. C., & Lazarus, R. S. (1980). Cognitive style, stress perception and coping. In I. L. Kutash & L. B. Schlesinger (Eds.), *Handbook on stress and anxiety* (pp. 144–158). San Francisco: Jossey-Bass.

Coyne, J. C., & Smith, D. A. (1991a). Coping with a myocardial infarction: II. Determinants of patient self-efficacy. Manuscript under review.

Coyne, J. C., & Smith, D. A. (199b). Couples coping with myocardial infarction: A contextual perspective on wives' distress. *Journal of Personality and Social Psychology, 61*, 404–412.

Coyne, J. C., Wortman, C., & Lehman, D. (1988). The other side of support: Emotional overinvolvement and miscarried helping. In B. Gottlieb (Ed.), *Social support: Formats, processes, and effects* (pp. 305–330). New York: Sage.

Croog, S. H., & Levine, S. (1982). *Life after a heart attack: Social and psychological factors eight years later*. New York: Human Sciences.

Davis, F. (1991). *Passage through crisis: Polio victims and their families*. New Brunswick, NJ: Transaction Press.

DeLongis, A., & O'Brien, T. (1990). An interpersonal framework for stress and coping: An application to the families of Alzheimer's patients. In M. A. P. Stephens, J. H. Crowther, S. E. Hobfoll, & D. L. Tennenbaum (Eds.), *Stress and coping in later-life families* (pp. 221–239). New York: Hemisphere.

Ewart, C. K., Taylor, C. B., Reese, L. B., & DeBusk, R. F. (1983). The effects of early post myocardial infarction exercise testing on self perception and subsequent physical activity. *American Journal of Cardiology, 51*, 1076–1080.

Fiske, V., Coyne, J. C., & Smith, D. A. (1991). Couples coping with myocardial infarction: An empirical reconsideration of the role of overprotectiveness. *Journal of Family Psychology, 5*, 4–20.

Gilligan, C. (1982). *In a different voice: Psychological theory and women's development*. Cambridge, MA: Harvard University Press.

Gillis, C. (1984). Reducing family stress during and after coronary artery by-
pass surgery. *Nursing Clinics of North America, 19,* 1103–1111.

Glenn, N. D. (1975). Psychological well-being in the post-parental stage: Some
evidence from national surveys. *Journal of Marriage and the Family, 35,*
105–110.

Glenn, N. D., & Weaver, C. N. (1988). The changing relationship of marital
status to reported happiness. *Journal of Marriage and Family, 50,* 317–
324.

Gottlieb, B. H. (in press). Stress and coping processes in close relationships.
In J. Eckenrode (Ed.), *The social context of stress.* New York: Plenum
Press.

Gottman, J. M. (1991). Predicting the longitudinal course of marriages. *Journal of Marital and Family Therapy, 17,* 3–7.

Hamilton, G. A. (1990). Recovery from myocardial infarction in women. *Cardiology, 77* (Suppl 2), 58–70.

Kelley, H. H. (1981). Marriage relationships and aging. In J. G. March (Ed.),
Aging: Stability and change in the family (pp. 275–300). New York:
Academic Press.

Lazarus, R. S., & Folkman, S. (1984). *Stress, appraisal, and coping.* New
York: Springer.

Lee, G. R. (1978). Marriage and morale in later life. *Journal of Marriage and
the Family, 40,* 131–139.

Lichtenstein, E., Glasgow, R. E., & Abrams, D. B. (1986). Social support in
smoking cessation: In search of effective interventions. *Behavior Therapy,
17,* 605–619.

Lofland, J. (1976). *Doing social life.* New York: Wiley.

Manton, K. G. (1990). Mortality and morbidity. In R. H. Binstock, & L. K.
George (Eds.), *Handbook of aging and the social sciences* (3rd ed., pp.
64–90). San Diego: Academic Press.

Mayou, R., Foster, A., & Williamson, B. (1978). The psychological and social
effects of myocardial infarction on wives. *British Medical Journal, 1,* 699–
701.

Mechanic, D. (1991). Medical sociology: Some tensions among theory,
method, and substance. *Journal of Health and Social Behavior, 30,* 147–
160.

Minuchin, S., Rosman, B. L., & Baker, L. (1978). *Psychosomatic families:
Anorexia nervosa in context.* Cambridge, MA: Harvard University Press.

Morisky, D. E., Levine, D. M., Green, L. W., Shapiro, J., Russel, R. P., &
Smith, C. R. (1983). Five year blood pressure control and mortality fol-
lowing health education for hypertensive patients. *American Journal of
Public Health, 73,* 153–162.

National Center for Health Statistics. (1983). Americans assess their health:

148   FAMILIES AND ILLNESS

United States, 1978. (DHHS Publication No. PHS 83-1570). *Vital and Health Statistics,* Series 10, No. 142. Washington, DC: U. S. Government Printing Office.

National Center for Health Statistics. (1984). *Health, United States, 1984* (DHHS Publication No. PHS 85-1232). Washington, DC: U. S. Government Printing Office.

Neugarten, B. L., & Hagestad, G. O. (1976). Age and the life course. In R. E. Binstock & E. Shanas (Eds.), *Handbook of aging and the social sciences* (pp. 35–55). New York: Van Nostrand Reinhold.

O'Leary, A. (1985). Self efficacy and health. *Behavioral Research and Therapy, 23,* 437–451.

O'Neil, P. M. (1979). Effects of sex on subject and spouse involvement on weight loss in a behavioral treatment program: A retrospective investigation. *Addictive Behaviors, 4,* 167–178.

Radley, A. (1988). *Prospects of heart surgery.* New York: Springer-Verlag.

Ransom, D. C. (1989). Development of family therapy and family theory. In C. N. Ramsey (Ed.), *Family systems in medicine* (pp. 18–35). New York: Guilford Press.

Rausch, H. (1974). *Communication, conflict, and marriage.* San Francisco: Jossey-Bass.

Reiss, D. (1989). Families and their paradigms: An ecologic approach to understanding the family in its social world. In C. N. Ramsey (Ed.), *Family systems in medicine* (pp. 119–134). New York: Guilford Press.

Reiss, D., & Kaplan De-Nour, A. (1989). The family and medical team in chronic illness: A transactional and developmental perspective. In C. N. Ramsey (Ed.), *Family systems in medicine* (pp. 435–444). New York: Guilford Press.

Reiss, D., Gonzalez, S., & Kramer, N. (1986). Family process, chronic illness, and death. *Archives of General Psychiatry, 43,* 795–804.

Renne, K. S. (1971). Health and marital experience in an urban population. *Journal of Marriage and the Family, 32,* 54–67.

Rolland, J. S. (1984). Toward a psychosocial typology of chronic and life-threatening illness. *Family systems in medicine, 2,* 245–262.

Ross, C. E., Mirowsky, J., & Goldstein, K. (1990). The impact of the family on health: The decade in review. *Journal of Marriage and the Family, 52,* 1059–1078.

Satariano, W. A., & Syme, S. L. (1981). Life changes and disease in elderly populations: Coping with change. In J. G. March (Ed.), *Aging: Biology and behavior* (pp. 311–328). New York: Academic Press.

Shanfield, S. B., Heiman, E. M., Cope, N. D., & Jones, J. R. (1979). Pain and the marital relationship: Psychiatric distress. *Pain, 7,* 343–351.

Smith, D. S. (1981). Historical change in the household structure of the elderly in economically developed societies. In J. G. March (Ed.), *Aging: Stability and change in the family* (pp. 91-114). New York: Academic Press.

Soskoline, V., & Kaplan De-Nour, A. (1989). The psychosocial adjustment of patients and spouses to dialysis treatment. *Social Science and Medicine, 29*, 497-502.

Speedling, E. J. (1982). *Heart attack: The family response at home and in the hospital.* New York: Tavistock.

Taylor, C. B., Bandura, A., Ewart, C. K., Miller, N. H., & DeBusk, R. F. (1985). Exercise testing to enhance wives' confidence in their husband's cardiac capacity soon after clinically uncomplicated acute myocardial infarction. *American Journal of Cardiology, 55*, 635-638.

Thompson, D. R., & Cordle, C. J. (1988). Support of wives of myocardial infarction patients. *Journal of Advanced Nursing, 13*, 233-228.

Thompson, D. R., & Meddis, R. (1990). Wives' responses to counseling early after myocardial infarction. *Journal of Psychosomatic Research, 34*, 248-258.

U. S. Bureau of the Census. (1989). Household and family characteristics: March 1988. *Current Population Reports*, Series P-20, No. 437 (May 7). Washington, DC: U. S. Government Printing Office.

Wiklund, I., Sanne, H., Vedin, A., & Wilhelmsson, C. (1984). Psychosocial outcome one year after a first myocardial infarction. *Journal of Psychosomatic Research, 28*, 309-321.

Winter, W. D., Ferreira, A. J., & Bowers, N. (1973). Decision-making in married and unrelated couples. *Family Process, 12*, 83-94.

Wish, M., Deutsch, M., & Kaplan, S. J. (1976). Perceived dimensions of interpersonal relations. *Journal of Personality and Social Psychology, 33*, 409-420.

Wishnie, H. A., Hackett, T. P., & Cassem, N. H. (1971). Psychological hazards of convalescence following a myocardial infarction. *Journal of the American Medical Association, 215*, 1292-1296.

Zarit, S. H., Todd, P. A., & Zarit, J. M. (1986). Subjective burden of husbands and wives as caregivers: A longitudinal study. *The Gerontologist, 26*, 260-266.

10

PHYSICAL AND PSYCHOLOGICAL ILLNESS AS CORRELATES OF MARITAL DISRUPTION

Susan L. Jones
Kent State University

Although the rate of divorce among younger cohorts began to stabilize over the past decade, the rate of divorce increased 50% among people between the ages of 40 and 65 and 35% among people 65 and older (Weingarten, 1988). A contemporary phenomenon is that divorce is a significant factor in the lives of individuals over 40 years of age. Of particular importance and the focus of this chapter is the fact that marital partners may well have spent more than half of their adult lives together and thus the social and psychological stresses of divorce in later life are much more traumatic (Jones & Jones, 1988). Specifically, the purpose of this chapter is to examine physical and psychological illness as antecedents, correlates, and consequences of marital distress and divorce in long-term marriages.

First presented is literature linking marital distress and physical and psychological illness along with possible explanations for this consistently found relationship (i.e., the *selection* and the *protection/support* hypotheses). Next, literature is presented on conceptual and methodological issues in the study of marriage and divorce, with particular emphasis on long-term marriages. Empirical data are then presented concerning marital distress and physical and psychological illness in long-term marriages. The chapter closes with a discussion on future directions for research in the area of marital status, divorce, and illness.

THEORETICAL AND EMPIRICAL PERSPECTIVES
Marital Status and Illness

A large number of well-known investigations since the end of the nineteenth century (e.g., Dayton, 1936; Durkheim, 1897; Odegaard, 1946) has shown a strong link between marital status and physical or psychological well-being. More recently, epidemiologists continue to demonstrate this association (Coombs, 1991; Ross, Mirowsky, & Goldstein, 1990). With few exceptions, the overall positive effect is strong and consistent. Compared with married people, single individuals have higher levels of depression, anxiety, and other forms of psychological distress (Bowling, 1987; Gore & Mangione, 1983; Gove, Hughes, & Style, 1983; Mirowsky & Ross, 1989). In fact, Gove et al. (1983) found that marital status was a stronger predictor of mental health than education, income, age, race, or childhood background. Furthermore, single individuals have more physical health problems than married persons. Single individuals experience higher rates of acute conditions, chronic conditions, days of disability, and lower perceived health status (Anson, 1989; Berk & Taylor, 1984; Hafner, 1986; Riessman & Gerstel, 1985; Tcheng-Laroche & Prince, 1983).

Although the association between marital status and illness is well established, the explanation for the association is not clear. Two major hypotheses are generally put forth (Coombs, 1991; Hafner, 1986; Ross et al., 1990). First is the *selection* hypothesis. That is, the claim is made that there is a selection of healthy people into marriage and this accounts for the association. It is further argued that those who experience illness are physically or psychologically less desirable and, therefore, are less likely to marry than their healthier counterparts. Furthermore, if such people do get married, they are more likely to have higher rates of divorce. These individuals divorce because of psychological immaturity, which precludes them from assuming the responsibilities involved in marriage (Coombs, 1991).

The second hypothesis is the *causation* or *protection/support* hypothesis. Here, the argument is made that a conflictual marriage can cause illness, whereas an emotionally satisfying marriage protects or buffers the person from illness. Thus happily married people—because of the emotional support attained in the marriage—are less likely to suffer either psychological or physical illness. However, if the marriage becomes conflictual—and the emotional support is replaced by negative emotion—the marriage in and of itself can promote illness (Ross et al., 1990).

In what follows, empirical studies are reviewed that use each of these hypotheses as causal explanations linking marital status and illness. Important here is the understanding that the hypotheses are not mutually exclusive but rather represent a continuum. Although studies claim to support one or the other hypothesis, this is actually an artificial distinction, and exclusive emphasis on either hypothesis presents only a partial picture of what the actual association between marital status and illness means. Nevertheless, to present an accurate summary of the literature that follows the thrust of the authors, studies are organized according to one or the other of these hypotheses. The ambiguity of causal explanations are subsequently discussed, however, to provide a more comprehensive picture of the association between marital status and illness.

As stated above, the selection hypothesis assumes that the association between marital status and physical or psychological health is spurious and artificial because each variable is dependent on emotional maturity. Emotionally mature or physically healthy individuals more readily involve themselves in interpersonal relationships that lead to marriage. Furthermore, they are more favorably regarded by potential mates and, overall, they deal with the stress of relationships more easily (Coombs, 1991).

For example, considering physical illness, Brown and Giesy (1986) showed that people with spinal cord injuries are less likely to be married. They conclude that people with physical health problems have trouble finding and keeping marriage partners because of their physical illness. Considering psychiatric illness, the selection hypothesis has been most successful in explaining marital status in schizophrenic and alcoholic populations (Gotlib & McCabe, 1990). For example, Eaton (1975) concluded that the highest rates of hospitalization for schizophrenic disorders are for never-married individuals. Bachrach (1975) found that unmarried individuals had a higher proportion of psychiatric admissions for schizophrenia than did married people. Turner, Dopkeen, and LaBreche (1970) found that healthier schizophrenics or preschizophrenics are more likely to marry or stay married than less healthy individuals.

In a classic early study conducted by Odegaard (1946) of 526 hospitalized schizophrenic patients, it was found that the prepsychotic personality was the only significant distinguishing characteristic between the single and married individuals. Single patients had twice the rate of prepsychotic schizoid characteristics.

Similarly, Gittelman-Klein and Klein (1968) found that premorbid personality was a stronger predictor of subsequent pathology than current marital status. Their conclusion was that marital status has no independent theoretical prediction of schizophrenia outcome. These findings were reconfirmed in a later report (Coombs, 1991; Rosen, Klein, & Gittelman-Klein, 1971). Both Robertson (1974) and Reich and Thompson (1985) reported comparable findings for treatment of alcoholism (i.e., that marital status had no independent theoretical prediction for alcoholism). The major point is that premorbid personality affects marital status, which may in turn affect the illness outcome.

In contrast with the selection hypothesis is the *causation* or *protection/ support* hypothesis, which poses that marriage either protects the individual from illness or is an etiological factor in the development of the illness. The life-style associated with marital status produces different levels of risk and/or stress, resulting in different levels of either physical or emotional illness. Stated differently, this hypothesis assumes that, compared with the married, unmarried individuals experience physical and emotional pathology more often because they are lacking continuous companionship with a spouse who provides emotional support and buffers them against the stresses of daily living (Coombs, 1991).

Using this hypothesis, it would be argued that marriage protects against spinal cord injuries because married people engage in fewer risky activities than unmarried people. Considering psychiatric illness, the finding that married people have lower rates of emotional disturbance than do unmarried individuals is the result of the increased social support available from the spouse (Gerstel, Riessman, & Rosenfield, 1985; Mirowsky & Ross, 1989). One of the most comprehensive investigations of the causation hypothesis was conducted by Pearlin and Johnson (1977). They examined the relationship between life strains and psychological distress in a large sample of married and unmarried people. They found that a greater proportion of unmarried versus married individuals experienced life strains such as economic hardship, social isolation, and so forth. Furthermore, these life strains affected the unmarried more severely than the married.

The protection/support hypothesis may be used to explain the association between marital status and schizophrenia as well as the association between marital status and alcoholism. Marriage may reduce the adverse effects (e.g., hospitalization) of schizophrenia, a finding that is consistent for both men and women. Several studies show that the married as compared with the unmarried have less severe symptoms (Chapman, Day, & Burnstein, 1961; Counts & Devlin, 1954; Jenkins & Gurel, 1959; Marks, 1963; Sherman, Moseley, Ging, & Bookbinder, 1964). In a similar vein, fewer married than unmarried individuals develop schizophrenia (Gittelman-Klein & Klein, 1968; Turner et al., 1970). Marital status was found to be the third most important variable (following education and occupation) in predicting the length of hospital stay among first-admission, middle-class schizophrenics (Turner et al., 1970). Alcoholism and treatment outcomes for alcoholism also affirm the protection/support hypothesis. Studies consistently find more alcoholism and problem drinking among the unmarried than the married. For example, Woodruff, Guze, and Clayton (1972) found that of the 59 ever-married alcoholics in their treatment group, 49% were divorced. In a similar manner, Miller (1976) studied chronic problem drinkers and found that 70% of drinkers were separated or divorced, whereas only 15% were married and 6% were never married. Other studies further support this hypothesis by showing that the lowest percentage of heavy drinkers are married individuals, both in the United States (Cahalan, Cisin, & Crossley, 1969) and in Canada (Layne & Whitehead, 1985).

The protection/support hypothesis also explains treatment outcomes for alcoholism. In an early study (Voegtlin & Broz, 1949), patients were followed for over 10 years. The research found that 50% of the married alcoholics continued to abstain, whereas only 34% of the divorced and 26% of the never-married did so. A later study (Gove, 1973) supported these findings by showing that single men are more than three times as likely as married men to die of cirrhosis of the liver.

For both men and women, marriage is the largest predictor of overall happiness (Bradburn, 1969; Bradburn & Capiovitz, 1965; Campbell, 1981; Glenn, 1975; Glenn & Weaver, 1988; Gurin, Veroff, & Feld, 1960; Schmoldt, Pope, & Hibbard, 1989). Married people are happier and, according to the protection/support hypothesis, the happiness is due to the emotional support that is shared within the marital relationship (Campbell, 1981). As mentioned above, Ross et al. (1990) showed that marriage protects the individuals from stress because of the moderating effect of social support, particularly the emotional element of social support. Emotional support is the sense of being cared about, loved, esteemed, and valued as a person (Ross et al., 1990). Emotional support decreases depression, anxiety, and physical illness (Blazer, 1982; Gerstel et al., 1985; Hanson, Isacsson, Janzon, & Lindell, 1989; House, Robbins, & Metzner, 1982; Pearlin, Lieberman, Menaghan, & Mullan, 1981).

Although marriage may protect an individual from physical or emotional illness, if the marriage is conflictual, not only is the protective mechanism dissipated but a detrimental effect may be produced (Jones & Jones, 1988; Ross et al., 1990). It is not enough just to have someone around. That is, the mere presence of a spouse does not guarantee an emotionally supportive relationship. Evidence also shows that the beneficial effects of marriage may be lessening over time (Glenn & Weaver, 1988). It is better to live alone than in a marriage characterized by a lack of consideration, caring, esteem, and equity (Aneshensel, 1986; Jones & Jones, 1988).

Gove et al. (1983) show that the emotional benefits of marriage depend on the quality of the marriage. The 62% of married people who report being very happy with the marriage are less distressed than the unmarried. The 4% who say they are not too happy or not at all happy with the marriage are more distressed than unmarried of all types (Gove et al., 1983).

Although marriage generally protects and improves physical and psychological health, it is important to note that it protects men's psychological and physical health more than women's (Bird & Fremont, 1991; Gove, 1984; Ross et al., 1990). Women in unhappy, unsupportive marriages, compared with more happily married women, generally have higher cholesterol levels, more illness, more illness symptoms, increased levels of depression, and decreased immune system functioning (Gore, 1978; Kiecolt-Glaser et al., 1987). An unhappy marriage has been called a disability that is analogous to a minority status, economic deprivation, or physical illness (Renne, 1970).

In summary, the above literature review shows that both the selection hypothesis and the protection/support hypothesis have been used in explaining the epidemiology, course of illness, and outcomes for several physical and psychological illnesses. Important here is the conclusion that the selection and protection/support hypotheses are not mutually exclusive. That is, both pre-illness individual factors and marital support are powerful influences in these illnesses. The dual role of these two hypotheses are particularly evident in the explanation of the etiology of schizophrenia and alcoholism. Above, it was shown that researchers using both the selection and protection/support hypotheses find that indices for severity of schizophrenia and alcoholism are less for the married than the unmarried. Because of the cross sectional nature of the studies, it is nearly impossible to clearly outline a causal link for either hypothesis. Important for future research is the move toward understanding the conditions under which the selection hypothesis, compared with the protection/causation hypothesis, more clearly explains the causal link between marital status and illness.

Marital Research: Conceptual Issues

In an excellent review article on quantitative research in marital studies (Glenn, 1990), several conceptual issues involving studies of marital stability and instability are discussed. First, Glenn points out that theoretical perspectives on the topic tend to use some variant of social exchange theory. However, empirical research on this topic has not been highly theoretical. These studies tend to be driven by practicality rather than global theoretical propositions. Unfortunately, however, family theorists and family therapists seem to read and publish in parallel journals, with the result that neither systematically uses information from the other.

A second major issue involves the unit of analysis. Some researchers have viewed marital quality as an individual phenomenon (i.e., how the married persons feel about their marriage). Other researchers have emphasized the relationship between the two individuals as the unit of analysis instead of, or in addition to, the separate feelings of the two spouses. This latter "adjustment" school was prominent at the beginning of the 1980s (Spanier & Lewis, 1980). Later in the 1980s, however, emphasis again turned toward the measurement of individual evaluations (e.g., Fincham & Bradbury, 1987).

A third issue pointed out by Glenn (1990) involves definition of the dependent variable: the distinction between "marital quality" and "marital success." Marital quality is defined as how good the marriage is from the point of view of one or both spouses, whereas marital success refers to what happens to a marriage over time. A weakness of many previous studies is that only married persons were sampled. The point is that causal analysis on cross sectional data should not be conducted on a closed (married only) population with little variance on the dependent variable.

Once it is recognized that the divorced sample must be included, it is important to view the entire divorce sequence as a process with implications for social, psychological, legal, and parenting behavior (Kitson, 1990; Kitson, Babri, & Roach, 1985). Unfortunately, however, discussions of the process of divorce tend to focus on the *postfiling* period (i.e., after the couple decides to divorce and are in the court proceedings). Rarely is attention on the prefiling period leading to the marital breakdown.

The Long-Term Marriage

In Chapter 9, Coyne and Fiske convincingly argue the importance of focusing on the couple when studying health and chronic illness. In a similar manner, emphasis on the long-term married couple is especially relevant for several reasons. Long-term marriages are increasing in the United States because people are living longer (U.S. Bureau of the Census, 1989). As individual longevity increases, it is probable that marriages of long duration will also increase if one assumes that the rates of marital dissolution do not dramatically increase in the foreseeable future. Thus if one assumes that the divorce rate essentially remains the same, the potential for a couple to remain married well into later life is probable (Sporakowski & Axelson, 1989). In addition, Coyne and Fiske clearly point out that it is in middle and old age when chronic and catastrophic illness are having their greatest impact. Therefore, studying long-term marriages is important for our understanding of health in adulthood.

Although there is consensus that the study of marital stability and divorce in long-term marriages has been grossly neglected (Ade-Ridder & Hennon, 1989; Weingarten, 1988), there is much less consensus about what constitutes a long-term marriage (Sporakowski & Axelson, 1989). Some studies have defined long-term marriages as those lasting in excess of 40 years, whereas several studies also have defined "long-term" as 18, 20, or 25 years (Ade-Ridder & Hennon, 1989). Overall, the heterogeneous nature of studies—their samples, variables, and modes of assessment—has provided a diverse mix of findings and conclusions about long-term marriages such that few, if any, consistent conclusions are possible as this point.

In research on long-term marriages, the variables studied most frequently (although there is unevenness in the choice of variables) are marital happiness or satisfaction or adjustment, intimacy, personality, and an analysis of problems or tasks across the life cycle. Many of the studies are conducted by therapists, and the trend is to use instruments developed specifically for the study rather than standardized instruments (Sporakowski & Axelson, 1989).

Information about long-term marriage indicates that positive marital quality is highly correlated with health, morale, and need satisfaction as well as congruence between spouses on problems, tasks, and needs. There is little, if any, evidence that emotional intimacy increases over time in the marriage (Sporakowski & Axelson, 1989). Considering divorce, studies also suggest that divorce is more traumatic for women than for men (Jellinek & Slovik, 1981; White & Bloom, 1981) because women suffer greater financial losses and are less likely than men to remarry (Gerstel et al., 1985).

In sum, an increasing number of older individuals are ending marriages by divorce rather than through the demise of their spouse; as a result there is a great need for research in this area. What we know about the impact of divorce has been learned from people within short-term marriages; our knowledge of how people cope with divorce in later life is still in its infancy. Before meaningful findings can be isolated, however, several problems uniquely related to the study of long-term marriages have to be overcome.

First, there has to be agreement about what constitutes a long-term marriage. No doubt, this difference in measurement in several studies has been largely due to availability of subjects; however, it may be useful to follow the lead of gerontological literature, in which there are the "young" old (under 75) and the "old" old (over 75). Analogously, there could be the "young" long-term marriage (20 to 35 years) and the "old" long-term marriage (35 years and over). Important here is that the designation is driven by the length of marriage and not the age of the couple. Older couples may be in second or third marriages of short duration, whereas relatively young couples may have married very young and be in an "old" long-term marriage. The variable of interest here is length of marriage and it must not be confused with age.

A second and closely related issue is the fact that longitudinal studies are needed to sort out the causal relationship between marital distress and physical or psychological illness. These studies would capture the overall process leading up to the marital distress and divorce as well as the development of an illness. Such studies would also allow for viewing illness as either antecedents or consequences of the marital distress. Most studies in the literature are cross sectional, and it is usually unclear whether the marital distress preceded the illness or whether the illness preceded the marital distress.

A third problem is that the focus must be on the couple as well as the individuals. As mentioned above, a long-standing conflict has been the degree of relative emphasis on "couples" issues versus "individual" issues in data collection (Glenn, 1990). The two units of analysis need not be seen as mutually exclusive. Crucial to the collection of data, however, is that data are collected from both individuals within the relationship and that analyses must match respondents with their spouses. Individual data can then be assessed systematically so that conflicting individual responses between the couple can be compared to assess gender differences in the marriage. Data about couples as a unit are then possible and can be compared with the individual responses. The point is that, conceptually and methodologically, the couple must be seen as composed of two individuals who together constitute a unit greater than two individuals, and each must be assessed.

A criticism of both short- and long-term marriage research cited in the literature is that various researchers choose different variables to study and that standardized instruments are not used. Rather, clinically specific instruments are constructed for use in each particular study. It would be useful to decide on a number of important individual and couple variables to study and to systematically assess these variables across studies. However, it may be premature to assume that the standardized instruments that were constructed for other uses and populations are appropriate for assessment in long-term marriages. It remains an empirical question whether there are unique factors in long-term marriages that contribute to marital distress or positive marital quality.

Conclusions: Theoretical and Empirical Material

Although research on marriage, divorce, marital status, and illness have received considerable attention over the years, a potentially causal relationship between marital status and illness or between divorce and illness is far from understood. We know even less about long-term marriages and divorce following these marriages, and how they affect physical and psychological illnesses. Unfortunately, research in the areas of marital status and illness and of divorce and illness are not integrated. It is clear that there is a relationship between marital status and illness. In addition, specific consequences of divorce have been identified for both men and women. However, the sequential link between marital status, psychological and marital attributes leading to divorce and illness, and the link between divorce and illness are far from clear.

Divorce is also traumatic to the individual's psychological and physical well-being. We know that the psychological stresses of divorce in later life are more traumatic than with termination of the short-term marriage; however, the exact impact of this stress on the couple's physical and psychological health is not clear. One difficulty is that studies previously conducted have been heterogeneous in terms of definitions of long-term marriage, samples, variables, and modes of assessment. Other methodological shortcomings are the lack of longitudinal studies and assessment of only one individual in the marital relationship. It is clear that further research is needed to sort out the causal link between marital status and physical and psychological illness.

A CLINICAL PERSPECTIVE

In what follows, clinical material is presented that attempts to sort out the causal relationship by addressing some of the methodological shortcomings of the studies discussed above. Specifically, assessments were conducted before and after a decision to divorce or not divorce was made, both partners in the marriage were assessed, and a homogeneous sample of "young old" marriages was utilized. The following research questions are addressed:

1. What is the relationship between marital distress and physical or psychological illness in the marriage?
2. To what extent does divorce predict physical and/or psychological illness for individuals?

The Sample

Data were collected in a private practice setting from 1982 to 1991. The study sample consisted of 107 couples, married at least 20 years, who came to the author/therapist because of marital distress. The majority of the sample were between 40 and 49 years of age with the husbands being slightly older. Over half of the couples had been married between 20 and 24 years; another third had been married for 25 to 29 years, designating them as "young" long-term marriage (i.e., under 35 years).

Illness and Marital Distress

The presence of several physical or psychological illnesses was assessed during the initial sessions of treatment. Measures of previous inpatient or outpatient psychiatric treatment, abuse of alcohol, previous midlife crisis, physical ailments, and the existence of chronic illness were utilized. With the exception of alcohol abuse, few physical or psychological illnesses were reported. However, abuse of alcohol (i.e., "I know I'm drinking too much") was reported by 46% of husbands and 24% of wives.

Marital distress was operationalized by the presence of consistent conflictual process or content themes over time, as reported by the couple and evaluated by the therapist. A process theme is one that describes the process of fighting regardless of content (e.g., wife or husband gets angry and attacks, or one attempts to invoke guilt in the other). A content theme is one that describes specific content areas of conflict such as money, sex, or child discipline. Conflictual process themes were reported by over half of the husbands (51%) and two thirds (67%) of the wives. Conflictual content themes were also reported by over half of the husbands (51%) and three fifths (62%) of the wives.

Most important was the fact that alcohol abuse was found to be associated with conflict. For both husbands and wives, alcohol abuse was associated with both conflictual process ($p < .01$ for husbands, and $p < .001$ for wives) themes and content ($p < .01$ for husbands, and $p < .05$ for wives) themes.

The outcome of therapy was assessed by the therapist at the end of treatment and was defined in three categories: (a) The couple remained married and the conflict was resolved (i.e., a "complementary" relationship was established; 46%); (b) the couple remained married but the basic conflict was not resolved so that the conflict that brought the couple to marital therapy remained (21%); or (c) the couple dissolved the marriage through divorce (33%). Within the third category (divorce), two sublevels were distinguished. The couple may have had either a *conflictual* (16%) or nonconflictual (17%) divorce. A conflictual divorce here indicates a traditional "divorce court" based divorce in which one party files and the other party contests the divorce, using the traditional grounds for divorce as the reasons for separation. A nonconflictual divorce here indicates a no-fault divorce in which the parties mutually agree on the divorce settlement, often using only one attorney.

Once the couple made the decision to stay married or divorce, the author maintained contact with both individuals for a minimum of 10 months and up to 3 years, whether the couple remained in therapy or not. Illnesses were recorded as they occurred during the follow-up period. Most illnesses occurred within 1 year of termination of treatment.

Table 1 shows the number and percentage of physical and psychological illnesses reported by husbands and wives within the first 10 months after the decision to stay married or divorce was made. Percentages in this table are computed on the number of persons rather than on the number of couples. For example, in the 50 couples who remained married in a complementary relationship, four (8%) of the husbands developed a physical illness. Looking at the grand total in the same column, 6 (6%) of the 100 husbands or wives in the married-complementary group developed some type of illness.

The major finding is that those who divorced had the most illnesses (15, or 21%), whereas those who remained married in a complementary relationship (6, or 6%) had the least. Those who remained married in a conflictual relationship (6, or 14%) fell between the extremes. This linear trend is significant ($p <$ .001).

A comparison of husbands and wives in the type of illnesses they experienced shows that there were 13 men and 14 women who developed illnesses within the first 10 months post decision to remain married or divorce. Of these individuals, 9 out of 13 men developed a physical illness, whereas only 2 out of 14 women developed a physical illness. Analyses suggested that men were more likely to develop a physical illness, whereas women were more likely to develop a psychological illness ($p <$ .05).

Table 1   Percentage of Illnesses at Post Marriage Decision Point by Marital Outcome

| | Married Couples | | | |
Illness	Complementary (n = 50)	Conflictual (n = 22)	Divorced (n = 35)	Total (N = 107)
Husands				
Physical illness	4 (8%)	2 (9%)	3 (9%)	9
Psychological illness	0 (0%)	1 (5%)	3 (9%)	4
Wives				
Physical illness	1 (2%)	0 (0%)	1 (3%)	2
Psychological illness	1 (2%)	3 (14%)	8 (23%)	12
Grand total	6 (6%)	6 (14%)	15 (21%)	27

Note. N = 107 couples (214 people). Percentages are computed on the number of people rather than on the number of couples. Linear trend is significant ($p <$ .001).

In Table 2 is presented the mean number of illnesses (physical or psychological) per couple after the couple decided to stay married or divorce. The mean number of illnesses increases linearly with the degree of unfavorable marital outcome ($p < .001$, by linear t test for trend, shown in the unadjusted means column). By inspection, among those who divorced nonconflictually (no-fault divorce) or conflictually (traditional divorce), the mean number of illnesses per couple is higher among those who had a conflictual divorce.

Because illness, particularly physical illness, is known to increase with age, an analysis of covariance was conducted to adjust the above findings for the mean age of the couple. The mean age was a significant covariate in influencing the mean number of physical and psychological illnesses ($p < .05$, by analysis of covariance). However, with the possible exception of the group who remained married but had continued conflict (mean age 52), there was little variation in mean age among the marital outcome groups. Therefore, when the mean number of illnesses per couple was adjusted for mean age of the couple, the mean number of illnesses continued to show a linear relationship ($p < .001$) with degree of unfavorable outcome.

A comparison was also made in terms of illness development for those who divorced nonconflictually versus conflictually. The small sample size precludes a detailed quantitative analysis for the impact of conflictual versus nonconflictual divorce on physical or psychological illness and no table is presented. However, two major findings are apparent by inspection of the raw data: For those who divorce conflictually, compared with those who divorce nonconflictually, there is a greater number of illnesses and illness is more likely to occur during or shortly after the divorce process.

Table 2   Mean Number of Illnesses per Couple by Marital Outcome

Marital outcome	N	Mean age	Mean no. of illnesses per couple	
			Unadjusted for age	Adjusted for age
Married				
Complementary	50	46	0.120	0.138
Conflictual	22	52	0.273	0.208
Divorced	35	47	0.429	0.444
Nonconflictual	18	46	0.333	0.361
Confictual	17	48	0.529	0.530
Total	107	48	0.250	0.250

Note. $N = 107$ couples. Differences among means is significant by t test for linear trend ($p < .001$) in the unadjusted means column; this finding ($p < .001$) is not altered by performing the proper age adjustment in the adjusted means column.

Looking first at the 17 couples who had a conflictual divorce, an illness was diagnosed in 9 individuals either during the divorce process (seven illnesses: two physical and five psychological) or shortly thereafter (two physical illnesses). Of the 18 couples who experienced a nonconflictual (no-fault) divorce, no individuals became ill during the divorce process; however, 5 experienced a psychological illness shortly after the divorce was final. Certainly, these results are not conclusive. Nevertheless, the overall trend is suggestive of a relationship between marital stress and the emergence of physical and psychological illness.

Summary and Discussion

In summary, of the illness measures, alcohol abuse by either husband or wife is the only one related to marital distress. Divorce, particularly a conflictual divorce, is associated with the highest incidence of illness. Among those who become ill, husbands are more likely to develop a physical illness, whereas wives are more likely to develop a psychological illness.

The major identified illness that was found to be associated with marital distress was alcohol abuse. Alcoholism has been found to be associated with marital status within studies using the selection hypothesis (Gotlib & McCabe, 1990) and the protection/support hypothesis (Gerstel et al., 1985; Pearlin et al., 1981). Unfortunately, sorting out the direction of causation within the present study is not possible because the reporting of alcohol abuse and marital distress occurred simultaneously.

Although the direction of causation is not known between alcohol abuse and marital distress, the types of drinking patterns and marital distress related to alcohol abuse are similar to those that have been previously reported in the literature (Gotlib & McCabe, 1990). The husbands in the present study were more likely to abuse alcohol than wives, which is consistent with previous research. How alcohol abuse affects a marriage is not simple or straightforward. Some studies show that periods of sobriety are described in positive terms; that is, the marital tension decreased during these times. Because the alcoholic spouse is sober, effective communication is possible between the couple. In contrast, other studies showed that periods of sobriety were associated with increased levels of marital tension in which wives were particularly critical of their husbands (Gotlib & McCabe, 1990). It is as if the wife becomes aware that many of the marital problems do not disappear when the alcoholic husband is sober; on the other hand, the alcoholic spouse perceives increased marital satisfaction during intoxicated periods because of decreased perceived levels of criticism. Such as interpretation is supported by findings of the present study in that times of sobriety were described as both positive and negative by the nonalcoholic partner.

Because all individuals in the study were followed for a minimum of 10 months post decision to divorce or remain married, the longitudinal nature of the data allows at least some initial sorting out of the causal pattern in the association between marital status and illness. Consistently, marital status predicted illness status post decision to remain married or divorce. Furthermore, as previous research has shown (Ross et al., 1990), it is not enough to just have someone close by. The couples who remained married but for whom the conflict continued were at high risk for developing illness. Even worse, an intense amount of stress can occur if the breakup of the marriage is conflictual. Consistent with previous literature, those individuals involved in a conflictual divorce are more likely to be stressed during the divorce (Kitson, 1990) and this stress resulted in illnesses in the study population. Those individuals who divorced without conflict developed fewer illnesses and none did so during the divorce process.

DIRECTIONS FOR FUTURE RESEARCH

Although a consistent pattern has been established showing that married people are physically and psychologically healthier than unmarried people, the exact reasons for this relationship are unclear. Furthermore, research on divorce and the illness consequences of divorce has been conducted independently of research on marital status and illness so that an integration of findings concerning marital status and divorce and illness has not been accomplished. In addition, many other issues have not been addressed and methodological problems remain.

First, there needs to be a conceptual and methodological integration of physical and psychological illness as it is associated with marital status and divorce. Under what conditions is marriage beneficial to individuals and under what conditions is divorce the more positive alternative? If the benefit of marriage is the positive emotional support sustained in the relationship, how negative can this emotion become before it is detrimental? Or, under what conditions is divorce more beneficial than a conflictual marriage?

A second conceptual issue involves the artificial distinction between the selection hypothesis and the protection/support hypothesis. These two hypotheses are not mutually exclusive. Studies that attempt to explain the causal sequence using either hypothesis in isolation present only a partial picture of the dynamic nature of this relationship. The two hypotheses must be integrated into an overall research design to fully comprehend the dual role of illness as a cause and consequence of marital status and marital status as a cause and consequence of illness.

The major methodological pitfall of previous research is the paucity of longitudinal studies. Such studies are needed to establish causal links between marital status, illness, and several other variables. Prospective studies are needed that examine the overall trajectory of the marital process leading to a complementary relationship, a conflictual relationship within the marriage, or a divorce. The health and illness consequences of each marital status can then be studied in a causal fashion.

REFERENCES

Ade-Ridder, L., & Hennon, C. B., (Eds.). (1989). *Lifestyles of the elderly.* New York: Human Science Press.
Aneshensel, C. S. (1986). Marital and employment role strain, social support, and depression among adult women. In S. E. Hobfoll (Ed.), *Stress, social support, and women* (pp. 99–133). Washington, DC: Hemisphere.
Anson, O. (1989). Marital status and women's health revisited: The importance of a proximate adult. *Journal of Marriage and the Family, 51,* 185–194.
Bachrach, L. L. (1975). *Marital status and mental disorder: An analytical review.* National Institute of Mental Health (DHEW Publication No. ADM 75-217). Washington, DC: U.S. Government Printing Office.
Berk, M. L., & Taylor, A. K. (1984). Women and divorce: Health insurance coverage, utilization, and health care expenditures. *American Journal of Public Health, 74,* 1276–1278.
Bird, C., & Fremont, A. (1991). Gender, time use, and health. *Journal of Health and Social Behavior, 32,* 114–129.
Blazer, D. G. (1982). Social support and mortality in an elderly community population. *American Journal of Epidemiology, 115,* 684–694.
Bowling, A. (1987). Mortality after bereavement: A review of the literature on survival periods and factors affecting survival. *Social Science and Medicine, 24,* 117–124.
Bradburn, N. M. (1969). *The structure of psychological well-being.* Chicago: Aldine.
Bradburn, N. M., & Capiovitz, D. (1965). Correlates of well-being. In *Reports on happiness: A pilot study of behavior related to mental health* (pp. 8–60). Chicago: Aldine.
Brown, J. S., & Giesy, G. (1986). Marital status of persons with spinal cord injury. *Social Science and Medicine, 23,* 313–322.
Cahalan, D., Cisin, J. H., & Crossley, H. M. (1969). *American drinking practices.* New Haven, CT: College and University Press.
Campbell, A. (1981). *The source of well-being in America: Recent patterns and trends.* New York: McGraw-Hill.
Chapman, L. J., Day, D., & Burnstein, A. (1961). The process of reactive distinction and prognosis in schizophrenia. *Journal of Nervous and Mental Disease, 133,* 383–391.
Coombs, R. H. (1991). Marital status and personal well being: A literature review. *Family Relations, 40,* 97–102.
Counts, R. M., & Devlin, J. P. (1954). Sexual experience as a prognostic

factor in psychosis. *Journal of Nervous and Mental Disease, 120,* 364–368.

Dayton, N. A. (1936). Marriage and mental disease. *New England Journal of Medicine, 215,* 153–155.

Durkheim, E. (1897). *Le suicide: Etude sociologie* [Suicide]. Paris: Alcan.

Eaton, W. W. (1975). Marital status and schizophrenia. *Acta Psychiatrica Scandinavica, 52,* 320–329.

Fincham, F. D., & Bradbury, T. N. (1987). The assessment of marital quality: A reevaluation. *Journal of Marriage and the Family, 49,* 797–809.

Gerstel, N., Riessman, C. H., & Rosenfield, S. (1985). Explaining the symptomatology of separated and divorced women and men: The role of material conditions and social networks. *Social Forces, 64,* 84–101.

Gittelman-Klein, R., & Klein, D. F. (1968). Marital status as a prognostic indicator in schizophrenia. *Journal of Nervous and Mental Disease, 147,* 289–296.

Glenn, N. D. (1975). The contribution of marriage to the psychological well-being of males and females. *Journal of Health and Social Behavior, 19,* 157–165.

Glenn, N. D. (1990). Quantitative research on marital quality in the 1980s: A critical review. *Journal of Marriage and the Family, 52,* 818–831.

Glenn, N. D., & Weaver, C. N. (1988). The changing relationship of marital status to reported happiness. *Journal of Marriage and the Family, 50,* 317–324.

Gore, S. (1978). The effect of social support in moderating the health consequences of unemployment. *Journal of Health and Social Behavior, 19,* 157–165.

Gore, S., & Mangione, T. W. (1983). Social roles, sex roles, and psychological distress. *Journal of Health and Social Behavior, 24,* 300–312.

Gotlib, I. H., & McCabe, S. B. (1990). Marriage and psychopathology. In F. D. Fincham, & T. N. Bradbury (Eds.), *The psychology of marriage* (pp. 226–257), New York: Guilford Press.

Gove, W. (1973). Sex, marital status and mortality. *American Journal of Sociology, 79,* 45–67.

Gove, W. (1984). Gender differences in mental and physical illness: The effects of fixed roles and nurturant roles. *Social Science and Medicine, 19,* 77–84.

Gove, W. R., Hughes, M. M., & Style, C. B. (1983). Does marriage have positive effects on the psychological well-being of the individual? *Journal of Health and Social Behavior, 24,* 122–131.

Gurin, G., Veroff, J., & Feld, S. (1960). *Americans view their mental health: A nationwide interview study* (Joint Commission on Mental Illness and Health, Monograph Services, No. 4). New York: Basic Books.

Hafner, R. (1986). *Marriage and mental illness.* New York: Guilford Press.

Hanson, B. S., Isacsson, S., Janzon, L., & Lindell, S. E. (1989). Social network and social support influences mortality in elderly men. *American Journal of Epidemiology, 130,* 100–111.

House, J. A., Robbins, C. A., & Metzner, H. L. (1982). The association of social relationships and activities with mortality: Prospective evidence from the Tecumseh Community Health Study. *American Journal of Epidemiology, 116,* 123–140.

Jellinek, M. S., & Slovik, L. S. (1981). Divorce: Impact on children. *New England Journal of Medicine, 305,* 557–560.

Jenkins, R. L., & Gurel, L. (1959). Predictive factors in early release. *Mental Hospital, 10,* 11–14.

Jones, S. L., & Jones, P. K. (1988). Predictors of divorce in long-term marriages. *Archives of Psychiatric Nursing, 2,* 267–273.

Kiecolt-Glaser, J. K., Fisher, L. D., Ogrocki, P., Sout, J. C., Speicher, C. E., & Glaser, R. (1987). Marital quality, marital disruption, and immune function. *Psychosomatic Medicine, 49,* 13–34.

Kitson, G. (1990). The multiple consequences of divorce: A decade review. *Journal of Marriage and the Family, 52,* 913–924.

Kitson, G., Babri, K., & Roach, M. J. (1985). Who divorces and why. *Journal of Family Issues, 6,* 255–293.

Layne, N., & Whitehead, P. (1985). Employment, marital status and alcohol consumption of young Canadian men. *Journal of Studies of Alcohol, 46,* 538–540.

Marks, J. (1963). Predicting outcomes in schizophrenia. *Journal of Abnormal Psychology and Social Psychology, 66,* 117–127.

Mirowsky, J., & Ross, C. E. (1989). *Social causes of psychological distress.* New York: Aldine de Gruyter.

Miller, P. M. (1976). *Behavioral treatment of alcoholism.* Oxford, England: Pergamon Press.

Odegaard, O. (1946). Marriage and mental disease: A study in social psychopathology. *Journal of Mental Science, 92,* 35–39.

Pearlin, L., & Johnson, J. S. (1977). Marital status, life strains and depression. *American Sociological Review, 42,* 704–715.

Pearlin, L., Lieberman, M. A., Menaghan, E. G., & Mullan, J. T. (1981). The stress process. *Journal of Health and Social Behavior, 22,* 337–356.

Reich, J., & Thompson, W. D. (1985). Marital status of schizophrenic and alcoholic patients. *Journal of Nervous and Mental Disease, 173,* 499–502.

Renne, K. (1970). Correlates of dissatisfaction in marriage. *Journal of Marriage and the Family, 32,* 54–67.

Riessman, C. K., & Gerstel, N. (1985). Marital dissolution and health: Do males or females have greater risk? *Social Science and Medicine, 20,* 627–635.

Robertson, N. C. (1974). The relationship between marital status and the risk of psychiatric referral. *British Journal of Psychiatry, 124,* 191–202.

Rosen, B., Klein, D. F., & Gittelman-Klein, R. (1971). The prediction of re-hospitalization: The relationship between age of first psychiatric treatment, contact, marital status and premorbid social adjustment. *Journal of Nervous and Mental Disease, 152,* 17–22.

Ross, C. E., Mirowsky, J., & Goldstein, K. (1990). The impact of the family on health: The decade in review. *Journal of Marriage and the Family, 52,* 1059–1078.

Schmoldt, M. S., Pope, C. R., & Hibbard, J. H. (1989). Marital interaction and the health and well-being of spouses. *Women and Health, 15,* 35–56.

Sherman, L. J., Moseley, E. E., Ging, R., & Bookbinder, L. J. (1964). Prognosis in schizophrenia. *Archives of General Psychiatry, 10,* 123–130.

Spanier, G., & Lewis, R. (1980). Marital quality: A review of the seventies. *Journal of Marriage and the Family, 42,* 825–839.

Sporakowski, M. J., & Axelson, L. V. (1989). Long-term marriages. In L. Ade-Ridder & C. B. Hennon (Eds.), *Lifestyles of the elderly* (pp. 9–28). New York: Human Sciences Press.

Tcheng-Laroche, F., & Prince, R. (1983). Separated and divorced women compared with married controls: Selected life satisfaction, stress, and health indices from a community survey. *Social Science and Medicine, 17,* 95–105.

Turner, R. J., Dopkeen, L. S., & LaBreche, G. P. (1970). Marital status and schizophrenia: A study of incidence and outcome. *Journal of Abnormal Psychology and Social Psychology, 76,* 110–116.

U.S. Bureau of the Census. (1989). Household and family characteristics: March 1988. *Current Population Reports* (Series P-20, No. 437, Ma7). Washington, DC: U.S. Government Printing Office.

Voegtlin, W. L., & Broz, W. R. (1949). The condition reflex treatment of chronic alcoholism: X. An analysis of 3,125 admissions over a period of ten and a half years. *Annals of Internal Medicine, 30,* 580–597.

Weingarten, H. R. (1988). The impact of late life divorce: A conceptual and empirical study. *Journal of Divorce, 12,* 21–39.

White, S. W., & Bloom, B. L. (1981). Factors related to the adjustment of divorcing men. *Family Relations, 30,* 349–360.

Woodruff, R. A., Guze, S. B., & Clayton, P. J. (1972). Divorce among psychiatric outpatients. *British Journal of Psychiatry, 121,* 289–292.

III

FAMILIES AND INTERVENTION

11

OVERVIEW

Kathleen A. Laing
Kent State University

As was demonstrated in Sections I and II of this volume, a significant data-based knowledge has begun to accumulate on the relationship between family factors and a diverse range of health-related issues. Consideration of family factors was shown to be of prime importance whether studying health cognitions, developing preventive physical and psychological health programs, or examining the impact of chronic and terminal physical illness. The authors of Section III extend the focus on family factors and health to the context of providing treatment to individuals and families confronted with physical illness.

The authors in Section III discuss, from diverse perspectives, the treatment of individuals presenting with a wide range of physical illnesses. Drotar (Chapter 12), a psychologist, begins this section with a focus on intervention planning with families confronted with chronic pediatric illness. His emphasis is on the necessity of an adequate theoretical base to guide family-centered interventions. Campbell, a physician, focuses on the treatment of physical illness in general. He and his colleagues, McDaniel and Seaburn (Chapter 13), discuss the exciting new field of family systems medicine, which utilizes a biopsychosocial approach to illness. Lastly, Walker (Chapter 14), a family therapist, addresses treatment of families with a member who is infected with HIV. She describes a family systems therapy model that has evolved out of her extensive work with individuals and families at various stages of HIV infection. Although the authors of these chapters represent a broad range of health professions and focus on vastly different patient populations, a common theme underlying each of their chapters is the recognition that consideration of family factors is imperative for optimal patient care.

Drotar describes and critiques current theories of family adaptation to childhood chronic illness. In his review of the literature, Drotar indicates that these theories have received only partial empirical support. He also demonstrates how these theories provide little guidance for intervention planning with families of children with chronic illness. Consequently, Drotar argues that conceptual models of family adaptation to childhood chronic illness need to be refined to guide family-centered interventions with this population.

One of the major contributions of Drotar's chapter is his formulation of a unique theoretical approach to the study of family adaptation to childhood chronic illness. He proposes that, to enhance the heuristic value and clinical relevance for theories of family adaptation to childhood chronic illness, the tasks and interactions by which families socialize their children to the demands of managing a chronic condition need to be delineated. Drotar describes specific family socialization tasks associated with childhood chronic illness and draws on research and clinical experience to examine how families manage these socialization tasks. He also describes threats to family socialization practices that are frequently imposed by childhood chronic illness. In contrast with existing theories of adaptation initially discussed by Drotar, this shift in focus to the family socialization process has direct implications for intervention. Drotar concludes his chapter by insightfully expanding on these implications to offer specific suggestions for developing interventions with families of children with chronic illness.

As described by Campbell, McDaniel, and Seaburn, the field of family systems medicine emerged out of the integration of family therapy, systems theory, and modern medicine. Consequently, illness is conceptualized not only in terms of biological factors but also in terms of individual, family, patient-provider, and larger social contextual factors. Within this biopsychosocial approach, family systems medicine emphasizes the family as the primary context for understanding health and illness.

In a thorough review of the empirical literature on family interventions in health care, Campbell, McDaniel, and Seaburn present evidence that supports the family systems medicine approach to medical care. However, their review also reveals that relatively few empirical studies have been conducted on family interventions, particularly family therapy, with physical illness. Thus Campbell and his colleagues pinpoint a need for additional empirical research in which family interventions are developed and evaluated in medical settings.

Collaboration between physical and mental health professionals is an integral part of providing a comprehensive, biopsychosocial approach to health care. Campbell, McDaniel, and Seaburn delineate three models of collaborative relationships and present an interesting case vignette that further elucidates the range of collaborative relationships that exists between physical and mental health professionals. The authors also provide insight into barriers to effective collaboration that can arise if differences in theory and practice between these two helping professions are not acknowledged and negotiated. Walker narrows the focus from illness in general to terminal illness, specifically AIDS, the most serious infectious disease epidemic of modern times. Walker provides unique insight into the social and psychological impact of HIV on infected individuals and their families. Although the impact of terminal illness on families was addressed in Section II of this volume, Walker raises important issues that result from a cultural bias that uniquely associates AIDS with deviance and sin. This pervasive social stigma frequently generalizes beyond the person with AIDS to his or her family and is also often internalized by family members and the patients themselves. Thus family systems interventions are an important component of treatment, and an understanding of the social and psychological impact of HIV infection is imperative if efficient intervention programs are to be developed for individuals with this terminal illness and their families.

One of the major contributions of Walker's chapter lies in her formulation of a family systems therapy model for individuals infected with HIV. Walker's model of therapy is characterized by several principles, which address such issues as goals for therapy, the tasks of the therapist, and process and resistance issues. In addition, Walker describes steps that individuals with AIDS or ARC frequently progress through on their way to acceptance of the illness and preparation for death, as well as patterns that have frequently emerged in couples therapy when one of the partners is HIV-positive. This formulation of a family systems therapy model for individuals infected with HIV represents a significant contribution to the family therapy and illness literature and will no doubt be quite valuable to the increasing number of professionals who are seeing individuals at various stages of HIV infection in their practices.

Taken together, the authors in this section go beyond the well-established fact that families and health are interrelated and illustrate how a consideration of family factors can be incorporated into distinct forms of health care. As demonstrated by Campbell, McDaniel, and Seaburn, family interventions can be incorporated into medical care, resulting in improved patient physical health. Family factors can also be a major focus in psychological treatment, as illustrated by Walker, leading to improved mental health. Finally, Drotar illustrates how attention to family influences within theoretical models can improve professional guidance to families regarding both physical and mental health issues. Thus consideration of family influences in theory, medical care, and mental health care can have a positive impact on patient health.

The chapters in this section also illustrate that the incorporation of family factors into treatment can take a variety of forms. For example, the chapters vary in the amount of emphasis placed on altering family interactions in treatment. Consistent with a family systems perspective, an underlying theme of all three chapters is that people are products of their social context and that any attempts to understand individuals must include an appreciation of their families. However, a family systems perspective also contends that the most effective way to treat people is to alter family interactions. Walker clearly places the most emphasis on changing dysfunctional family structures, patterns of interaction, and narratives. In a similar vein, given that family systems medicine evolved, in part, out of family therapy and systems theory, changing dysfunctional patterns of interaction is a form of family intervention addressed by Campbell, McDaniel, and Seaburn. However, family systems medicine emphasizes the family context in general, and thus family-centered interventions are not necessarily focused on altering patterns of interaction alone. Finally, although Drotar makes a number of insightful suggestions for family-centered interventions, he does not specifically address interventions designed to alter dysfunctional family structures and patterns of interaction.

The three chapters in this section also exemplify the interrelationships among theory, research, and clinical practice. As demonstrated in each of these chapters, the development of a coherent body of knowledge facilitates applied interests. All interventions described in Section III are based on theoretical models that have gained at least partial empirical support. In addition, Drotar specifically illustrates how the development of efficacious interventions can be hindered by the lack of an empirically supported theoretical model. Difficulties can also arise when attempts are made to carry out theoretical principles in clinical practice, as demonstrated by Campbell and his colleagues. Thus, to continue the process of developing efficacious family-centered interventions with physical illness, treatment must continue to be based on theory and validated with applied empirical research.

From their unique perspectives, all of the authors in this section illustrate the importance of addressing mental health as well as physical health issues in interventions with families confronted with physical illness. It is hoped that collaboration between physical and mental health professionals will become the norm as professionals with diverse training and experience move away from a mind–body dualism and work together to assist families in need of support in mastering the demands placed on them by physical illness. Only then will interventions with these families be truly comprehensive.

12

INTEGRATING THEORY AND PRACTICE IN PSYCHOLOGICAL INTERVENTION WITH FAMILIES OF CHILDREN WITH CHRONIC ILLNESS

Dennis Drotar
Case Western Reserve University School of Medicine
MetroHealth Medical Center, Cleveland, Ohio

Large numbers of children, adolescents, and young adults are affected by chronic physical conditions. Moreover, psychological disorders that can accompany these conditions may warrant specialized psychological intervention (Cadman, Boyle, Szamari, & Offord, 1987; Gortmaker & Sappenfield, 1984). Several factors heighten the need to refine conceptual models of family adaptation to the stress of childhood chronic illness in order to guide family-centered intervention with this population. Childhood chronic illness imposes strenuous emotional burdens on parents, siblings, and extended family members that can constrain their quality of life (Drotar, Crawford, & Bush, 1984). Moreover, the quality of family functioning is a salient influence on the child's ability to negotiate the stressful demands of treatment regimens, socialize with physically healthy peers, and function effectively in school or at work (Pless, Roghmann, & Haggerty, 1972). For these reasons, effective intervention for children with chronic physical disorders should address family influences.

In considering the need for family-centered intervention, it is important to recognize that children and adolescents with a chronic illness present with psychological disorders identical to those encountered among physically healthy children. In addition, they can demonstrate a wide range of illness-related adjustment problems (Drotar & Bush, 1985). Various family members may also have difficulties coping with the stresses of childhood chronic illness, for example, a mother who becomes depressed about her child's chronic condition and finds it increasingly difficult to maintain her responsibilities for his or her care, or a sibling who is extremely resentful of the time and attention that his or her chronically ill brother or sister receives.

Although many families of children with chronic illness undergo considerable psychological distress, they may not receive the mental health services they need because of limited accessibility to services and the problems of integrating mental services with pediatric care (Sabbeth & Stein, 1990). Because practitioners who work with children with chronic physical disorders are often burdened by multiple demands on their time, they would benefit from theory to help them focus their intervention efforts and identify families who would benefit most from intervention. However, limitations in theory have hampered the development of interventions for families of children with chronic illness. In particular, several critical, unanswered questions concerning intervention pose a formidable agenda for theories of family adaptation to chronic illness. First, which families and children are likely to be most vulnerable to stress and in need of supportive intervention? Who are more resilient? Second, at what point in the course of the child's illness or developmental stage is intervention likely to be most effective? Finally, what form should intervention take to be most useful and accepted by families?

This chapter, which addresses the application of models of family adaptation to the stresses of childhood chronic illness to clinical practice, has several purposes: (a) to describe and critique theories of family adaptation in childhood chronic illness; (b) to describe implications of these theories for intervention with families of children with chronic illness; (c) to suggest ways to develop family-centered theory and research concerning chronic childhood illness; and (d) to suggest new directions for intervention.

THEORIES OF FAMILY ADAPTATION
TO CHILDHOOD CHRONIC ILLNESS

Although there is no single well-articulated theory of family adaptation to childhood chronic illness, two conceptual frameworks are especially relevant: the Family Adjustment and Adaptation Response model (Patterson, 1988) and the Family Resource and Resistance Factor model (FRRF; Varni & Wallander, 1988).

Family Adjustment and Adaptation Response Model

The initial ABCX Family Crisis Model postulated that A (the stressor event) interacted with B (the family's crisis-meeting resources) and C (the family's definition of the event) to produce X (the crisis) (Hill, 1958). The Double ABCX Model of Family Behavior (McCubbin & Patterson, 1982) elaborated processes by which families achieve pre-crisis adjustment and post-crisis adaptation and is applicable to childhood chronic illness. Salient features of this model included the concept of pile-up of demands on family resources and the identification of coping strategies used by the family, especially the need for family members to modify perceptions of their situation in order to adjust and adapt to a crisis.

The most recent extension of the Double ABCX Model, the Family Adjustment and Adaptation Response (FAAR) model (Patterson, 1988), emphasizes the meanings that family members attribute to stressors and level of resources for balanced family functioning. These meanings may be situational (e.g., the family's subjective definition of demands and capabilities) or global (i.e., how the family views the relationship of family members to one another, the community, etc.; Reiss, 1981). In a time of crisis, such as the diagnosis of a chronic illness in a family member, stressors or demands on family members may exceed their capabilities. In such situations, family members may attempt to restore equilibrium by (a) acquiring new adaptive resources and/or coping behaviors, (b) reducing the pile-up of demands, or (c) changing the way they perceive their situation.

According to the FAAR model, families use many resources and capabilities for meeting demands, including financial, personal (e.g., self-esteem, knowledge, and skills), systems resources (e.g., cohesion, organization, and communication skills), and community resources (e.g., schools, churches, medical care, and social support). Some general resources, (e.g., family cohesion) can be used to meet most demands, whereas others such as support groups are stressor or demand specific. Coping behavior, which is a major family resource in the FAAR model, is defined as action to either reduce demands or acquire resources, or by changing the meaning of a situation to make it more manageable.

The FAAR model assumes that some families are much more vulnerable than others to crises. For example, specific family resource problems such as conflicted patterns of interaction may develop into chronic strains that can trigger a crisis. On the other hand, families with very high resources are assumed to be resilient to most stresses.

Although the FAAR model was not developed from research or clinical experiences with childhood chronic illness, variations of this framework have been tested with this population. Patterson (1985) hypothesized that the level of family compliance with treatment for cystic fibrosis would be negatively associated with the pile-up of family demands in the past year and the family's subjective appraisal of the difficulty of demands but positively associated with both family systems resources (e.g., cohesion and expressiveness) and personal resources (mother's time, parents' education, and parental coping efforts). Partial empirical support was obtained for this model. Contrary to prediction, neither the frequency of intrafamilial strains nor the total pile-up of demands related to family compliance. On the other hand, the family resource, expressiveness, correlated positively with compliance, whereas active recreation orientation correlated negatively. Paternal educational level and lack of maternal employment also related positively to compliance, but these correlations were low, and the complete regression equation that was tested was not specified by the theory.

Family Resource and Resistance Factor Model

Varni and Wallander (1988) have proposed an alternative framework that is directly applicable to children with a chronic illness. Developed to account for individual variation in psychological adaptation among children with a chronic illness (Drotar, 1981), this model integrated stress and coping theory from several sources (Lazarus & Folkman, 1984; Moos & Schaefer, 1984; Pless & Pinkerton, 1975). The distinction between risk factors that are hypothesized to increase the probability of adjustment problems in children with chronic illness versus resistance factors that are expected to decrease the likelihood of psychological disturbance is central to this framework. Risk factors include disease or disability parameters (e.g., severity of handicap, presence of medical problems, central nervous system involvement, and visibility of handicap), the child's functional independence, and psychosocial stressors that encompass several domains such as handicap-related problems, major life events, and daily hassles. Wallander, Varni, Babani, Banis, and Wilcox (1989) have suggested that a diminished level of the child's functional independence is the prototypical chronic strain for families of children with chronic conditions.

The Varni-Wallander model assumes that the impact of risk factors is moderated by three broad types of resistance or coping resource factors. These include (a) stable intrapersonal factors (e.g., temperament and perceived competence); (b) stress-processing or coping ability factors (e.g., cognitive appraisal and coping behaviors); and (c) social-ecological influences such as the quality of family relationships, utilitarian resources such as money, and so on.

Partial empirical support for this model, especially for the predictive power of family resources, has been obtained in a series of cross-sectional studies (Varni, Wilcox & Hanson, 1988; Wallander, Varni, Babani, Banis, Dehaan, & Wilcox, 1989; Wallander, Varni, Babani, Banis, & Wilcox, 1989). Wallander, Varni, Babani, Banis, Dehaan, and Wilcox (1989) hypothesized that psychological and utilitarian family resources (e.g., income and maternal education) would predict child adaptation (e.g., behavior problems and social adjustment). The combination of utilitarian and psychological family resources accounted for significant variance in psychological adjustment, but less so for behavioral problems (16%–18%) than for social competence (42%). Although these findings provided some support for the model, they were limited by a cross-sectional design, failure to demonstrate independence of predictor variables, and reliance on maternal report to assess independent and dependent measures.

This model has now been tested (with somewhat different results, not all of which were predicted) with several samples of children with different chronic conditions. For example, in a study of children with congenital or acquired limb deficiencies (Varni, Rubenfeld, Talbot, & Setoguchi, 1990), family functioning and child temperament (greater emotionality) and their interaction predicted children's behavior problems; contrary to hypothesis, age, sex, socioeconomic status, and physical status did not. Wallander, Varni, Babani, Banis, Dehaan, and Wilcox (1989) also found that mothers of children with different chronic disabilities reported more problematic adaptation than expected for a general sample. Yet, contrary to prediction, the quality of maternal adaptation did not relate to children's disability status or chronic disability-related strain.

IMPLICATIONS FOR INTERVENTION AND LIMITATIONS OF THEORIES OF FAMILY ADAPTATION TO CHILDHOOD CHRONIC ILLNESS

Neither the FAAR nor the Varni-Wallander model have focused explicitly on interventions for families under stress. Nevertheless, certain implications for definition and targeting of interventions with families of children with chronic conditions can be derived from each of these models.

Defining Psychological Intervention

In the FAAR and Varni-Wallander models, psychological intervention can be defined as an added resource or support that reduces the negative effects of stressors or demands of a chronic illness. Support may include information about the child's condition, medical treatment, generalized support and advocacy, or direct help with financial resources as well as specialized psychological intervention designed either to ameliorate or prevent adjustment problems in children or family members (Drotar & Bush, 1985). Patterson (1988) described one role of intervention as helping family members acquire resistance capabilities, which may include specific coping behaviors, positive appraisals of their child's chronic condition, or support groups.

In the Varni-Wallander model, risk factors such as severity of disability and disease-related psychosocial stressors are assumed to be fixed and hence not amenable to direct intervention. On the other hand, resistance resources such as intrapersonal factors (e.g., problem-solving ability), social-ecological factors (e.g., social support), and coping strategies are considered to be modifiable targets of intervention.

Targeting Interventions to Families of Children with Chronic Illness

Efficient deployment of limited resources for psychological intervention would be facilitated by a conceptual framework that sets priorities for families who are most in need of intervention and also considers individual differences in families' response to intervention.

The models of family adaptation reviewed thus far both predict that families who have a high frequency of stressors, demands, or risk factors relative to frequency of resistance or resources would be at greatest risk for problems and hence might receive priority for interventions. Unfortunately, the applicability of this concept is limited by several problems. For example, both the Varni-Wallander and the FAAR models imply that families with a high ratio of risk versus resistance factors (or demands vs. resources) can be identified readily by a simple count of resources and risk factors. However, assigning equal weights to risk and resistance factors assumes that resources and demands operate in a simple additive fashion to produce psychological disturbance, which is only one of several possible causal models (Garmezy, Masten, & Tellegen, 1985). Perhaps even more important, one cannot quantify risk and resistance factors (or demands and resources) as meaningful units that can be balanced on the same scale (Hobfoll, 1988, 1989).

The families of children with chronic illness are so heterogenous that any single intervention plan is not likely to be equally effective with all types of families. Theories of family adaptation have not addressed individual differences in family response to intervention. However, Affleck, Tennen, Rowe, Roscher, and Walker (1989) assessed individual differences in mothers' response to a support program designed to aid their adaptation to the transition from hospital to home care of high-risk neonates, some of whom had chronic problems such as bronchopulmonary dysplasia. Participation in the support program did not lead to any significant effects on 6-month outcomes, independent of severity or need for support. However, positive effects of the program on maternal responsiveness, perceived control, and sense of competence were evident only for mothers who responded that they needed the most support prior to their children's discharge from the hospital. Perhaps the most interesting finding was that at low levels of need for support, participation in the program actually had negative effects on maternal sense of competence, perceived control, and responsiveness.

Clinical experience also suggests that level of family functioning may also influence the acceptability of interventions to families. For example, families with high levels of functioning and excellent relationship resources are often able to utilize information and guidance from professionals to help them communicate more effectively and develop strategies to contain specific stressors related to the child's condition. On the other hand, more dysfunctional families may be so preoccupied with stress that they cannot use professional guidance to facilitate management or anticipation of problems (Drotar, 1991).

Defining Illness-Related Demands as Targets of Intervention

Concepts of stress or demand are central not only to models of family adaptation to chronic illness; illness-related stress may also be a focus of intervention with families (Drotar et al., 1984). Indices of illness severity that have been used to operationalize illness-related stressors in testing models of family adaptation have not shown a consistent relationship to child or family adjustment (Drotar, 1981). Moreover, the concept of illness severity or burden does not adequately define the characteristics of the child's treatment regimen, the tasks that families must manage to complete these regimens, or the characteristics of the illness course.

The demands that are imposed on families by a specific chronic condition at any particular point in time depend on the illness course. For example, the psychological and physical demands of medical treatment imposed on families of children who have been newly diagnosed with cancer are very different from those for children and adolescents with cancer in remission (Koocher & O'Malley, 1981).

Individual differences in illness progression also influence the demands that family members experience. For example, some illnesses (e.g., cystic fibrosis) are characterized by a chronic adaptational phase in which the condition is stable, followed by gradual deterioration. Others such as ulcerative colitis have an episodic course in which stable periods characterized by a low level or absence of symptoms are followed by unpredictable periods of acute flare-up (Rolland, 1987). Conditions with an episodic course might be expected to generate very different levels of family strain because of uncertainty than are stable conditions (Dolgin, Phipps, Harow, & Zeltzer, 1990; Jessop & Stein, 1985).

NEW DIRECTIONS: FAMILY SOCIALIZATION TASKS IN CHILDHOOD CHRONIC ILLNESS

To enhance their heuristic value and clinical relevance, theories of family adaptation to childhood chronic illness should define and consider the tasks and interactions by which families socialize their children to the demands of the management of a chronic condition. This shift in emphasis would have several advantages: First, a process-oriented approach would enhance our understanding of how families help their children learn to manage important developmental tasks concerning their chronic illness, such as learning coping strategies that ensure freedom from disruptive anxiety, effective adherence to regimens, and health-related behaviors (Johnson, 1985). Increased focus on how family members help children learn key illness-related responsibilities would enhance the quality of professional guidance to families concerning such issues as children's readiness to assume independent responsibilities for their physical treatment (Wysocki, Meinhold, Cox, & Clarke, 1990). Finally, a greater theoretical concern with the family experience of raising children with chronic illness would facilitate the development of interventions concerning the day-to-day child-rearing problems that family members identify as demanding or stressful.

What specific family socialization tasks are required by childhood chronic illness? Families of children with chronic illness have the same basic responsibilities to nurture and discipline their children as other families. Moreover, they need to assume considerable responsibilities in three other areas: (a) ensuring that the children receive medical treatment and care, (b) helping the children learn effective self-care and management of the physical treatment of their illness, and (c) facilitating the children's ability to cope with the psychological and social burdens of their illness.

Family Responsibilities
to Ensure Children's Medical Treatment

Parents have primary responsibility to ensure that their children receive necessary treatments for their chronic illness. This complex set of tasks includes administration of physical treatments designed to prevent additional illness-related complications, management of acute symptoms or illness-related crises, and communication with the children's health care provider at times of acute medical crisis and for routine care (Johnson, 1985). In most medical treatment programs, helping family members to assume responsibility for the children's medical treatment is the top priority. However, the demands on family members to teach children to learn to manage the physical and psychological demands of their illness are also considerable.

Helping Children Learn Effective Self-Care
of Their Chronic Condition

Parents are called on to help their children learn to assume responsibility for the proper timing and method of administering medication and other treatments for their chronic conditions. Teaching children to monitor their health and symptoms and to adhere to day-to-day treatment-related responsibilities is an important family task. Parents also need to teach their children to discriminate clinically relevant symptoms from those that are not, and to administer appropriate preventive treatments. For example, children with asthma need to learn to recognize the early signs of an asthmatic attack and to administer medication in a timely fashion; children with diabetes need to recognize symptoms of low blood sugar and administer glucose. To effectively recognize symptoms, children with chronic illness must learn appropriate levels of vigilance that stop short of counterproductive anxiety.

Children with many chronic conditions also must learn to accept and cope with treatments that constrain their activities and choices. For example, children with phenylketonuria (PKU) or diabetes must learn to restrict food choices in accord with a special diet. Conditions such as hemophilia or asthma require children to learn to restrict their activities to prevent symptoms and additional physical complications.

Helping Children Cope
with the Psychological Demands of Chronic Illness

Family members, especially parents, have the primary responsibility for helping their children learn to cope effectively with the psychological distress stimulated by the children's emotional reactions (anger, anxiety, or sadness) to their physical symptoms and medical treatment. In many cases, even assiduous adherence to a treatment regimen will not prevent illness-related crises involving hospitalization or surgery that require children to cope with physical pain and immobilization. Moreover, in such situations, children must learn to manage the difficult transitions from a relatively well to a more dependent, ill state and back again. Parents and family members provide the direct emotional support that is necessary to lessen the children's illness-related distress, help them accept the emotional demands of their condition, and facilitate their ability to learn effective coping strategies with psychological distress.

Family members are also primary influences on children's learning to construct a personal meaning of their chronic condition, including a positive sense of self-esteem and mastery in response to illness-related constraints (Taylor, 1983). In addition, children may also learn attitudes and beliefs about their chronic illness (e.g., personal susceptibility to symptoms; or costs and benefits of adherence to treatment regimens, learned from their parents and other family members; Brownlee-Duffeck, et al., 1987; Janz & Becker, 1984).

Finally, family members have the primary responsibility to help children with chronic illness learn to (a) maintain social relationships in the face of illness-related interruptions or restrictions, (b) cope with social threats such as teasing, (c) explain their medical condition or treatment regimen to peers, and (d) deal with peer pressure concerning their treatment regimen (LaGreca, 1990).

Family Management of Socialization Tasks
in Childhood Chronic Illness

How do families manage responsibilities for their children's socialization? Clinical experience and research suggest that parents initially assume responsibilities to administer their children's physical treatment, monitor their children's condition, and communicate with health providers (Johnson, 1985). However, sharing family responsibilities is a complex and stressful process, partly because the norms for assumption of various tasks at various ages are not well established (Anderson, Auslander, Jung, Miller, & Santiago, 1990; Wysocki et al., 1990). Parents of children with chronic illness are often uncertain about how much to protect their children from physical pain and psychological distress versus fostering their independence (Chesler & Barbarins, 1988). Child-rearing demands are a source of significant stress for many parents of children with chronic conditions (Hausenstein, 1990).

Unfortunately, parent–child relationships and child-rearing practices have received surprisingly little attention from chronic illness researchers. However, research concerning family socialization has identified direct training and reinforcement, modeling and vicarious learning, and attributional processes as important aspects of social learning (MacCoby & Martin, 1983). Specific social learning experiences, especially parental reinforcement, may influence the development of adaptive versus maladaptive response to illness-related pain and discomfort (Walker & Zeaman, 1989). In a recent study, Walker and Zeaman (1992) found that parental encouragement of illness behavior could be measured reliably, that mothers and children had similar perceptions of family interactions during episodes of child illness, and that children may learn specific illness behaviors in response to particular symptoms. Direct training and contingent reinforcement can influence children's response to painful events (Ross & Ross, 1987).

Hauser et al. (1986) have suggested a framework of family interaction that places primary emphasis on the family's ability to promote autonomous or differentiated functioning in chronically ill children. This model distinguishes between constraining behaviors that impede or undermine functioning versus enabling behaviors that promote independence. Constraining behaviors may be cognitively (e.g., withholding or indifference) or affectively constraining (e.g., devaluing). In a similar fashion, behaviors may be cognitively (e.g., focusing, problem solving) or affectively enabling (e.g., empathy). Although initial tests of this model did not confirm hypothesized relationships between constraining behaviors and the presence of diabetes (Hauser et al., 1986), this framework suggests intriguing hypotheses concerning social learning experiences in childhood chronic illness.

A third line of relevant research with families of children with chronic conditions concerns the identification of specific behaviors (e.g., reinforcement, criticism, and collaboration) that encourage adherence to medical treatment. These positive family support behaviors, which have been shown to relate to adherence among adolescents and adults with diabetes (Schaefer, McFaul, & Glasgow, 1986), should be studied in other chronic conditions.

Threats to Family Socialization Practices Imposed by Childhood Chronic Illness

Parents who are primarily responsible to help their children learn to cope with physical and psychological stressors of chronic illness are themselves burdened by multiple demands. Mothers may be especially burdened because they are often primarily responsible for caring for all of the children in the family and managing the household as well as the children's chronic condition. Hobfoll's (1988, 1989) model of conservation of resources suggests that because mothers of children with chronic conditions experience multiple demands and potential threats (e.g., possible deterioration in their children's condition, or loss of emotional support from other family members), they would be especially vulnerable to high levels of stress that could disrupt their ability to provide competent nurturing and support for their children. In support of this notion, studies have consistently found that mothers of children with chronic illness experience high levels of stress (Goldberg, Morris, Simmons, Fowler, & Levison, 1990; Hausenstein, 1990) and depressed mood (Jessop, Riessman, & Stein, 1989; Kovacs et al., 1985), relative to controls.

IMPLICATIONS FOR INTERVENTION

This discussion of an expanded model of family adaptation to childhood chronic illness has several implications for designing intervention and research for this population.

Targeting Interventions

Because mothers of children with chronic conditions appear to be especially vulnerable to stress, family-centered interventions should logically focus on this group. A range of intervention strategies could be used to help mothers reduce their level of personal threat and enhance their resources (Hobfoll, 1988, 1989). For example, intervention can focus on offsetting resource loss through advocacy to help parents obtain financial benefits or respite care for their children. Parents may also benefit from individual or group interventions to help them redefine or reevaluate the nature of the threats that are posed by the children's chronic conditions (Fiese & Sameroff, 1989; Hobfoll, 1989). A third type of intervention would involve direct training or education for mothers and family members to help them manage their children's treatment regimen or to help the child learn strategies to cope with illness.

In practice, interventions with the mothers of children with chronic conditions combine several different approaches. The "Sharing the Experience of Parenting" (STEP) model illustrates a comprehensive approach provided by lay intervenors (family consultants) through home visits and biweekly calls (Stein,

Jessop, & Ireys, 1988). The intervention was designed to enhance maternal resources by providing information support (e.g., sharing information about child behavior, parenting, and coping), affirmational support including identification of the mothers' competence and feedback about their parenting skills, and emotional support through the family consultants' availability to listen to problems and help mothers negotiate problems. The family counselors also provided practical support by serving as a link for mothers to access services such as housing, recreation, and medical care. Finally, mothers were encouraged to play an active role in identifying problems and unmet needs concerning their children's care and to clarify solutions to these problems. Preliminary evidence in a controlled clinical trial indicated that this intervention successfully engaged economically disadvantaged mothers of children with chronic conditions (Stein et al., 1988).

Timing of Intervention

Clinical experience and stress theory (Hobfoll, 1988) suggests that psychological intervention may be most accepted by families if it coincides with periods of greatest stress. Predictable stress points for families of children with chronic illness include the diagnosis of a chronic condition, changes in the children's illness status requiring hospitalization and/or extraordinary treatments, or deteriorations in condition resulting in a loss of functional independence. Each of these situations engenders specific psychological threats and requires family members to learn specific responsibilities for the children's care appropriate to that stage of the condition. For this reason, interventions are needed to help families cope with the emotional demands of these stress points and learn to deploy family resources to care for the children's physical and psychological needs. The study by Delameter et al. (1990) of family-based self-management training for children with diabetes is an interesting example of such an intervention. Following standard in-hospital diabetes education, children who were newly diagnosed with IDDM were randomized to conventional follow-up, supportive counseling, or self-management training that focused primarily on enhancing utilization of data obtained from self-monitoring of blood glucose. All interventions took place during the first 4 months following diagnosis, with booster sessions at 6 and 12 months. Self-management training was associated with better metabolic control 1 and 2 years later. However, it was not clear whether these interventions had any effects on family adaptation.

Developmental transitions (e.g., the beginning of school, onset of adolescence, or transition from adolescence to adulthood) also pose stresses to families of children with chronic illness who may need additional support to learn to manage the socialization demands of a new developmental phase (Ireys & Burr, 1984). For the most part, psychological interventions in childhood chronic illness have not focused on developmental transitions. However, Satin, LaGreca,

Zigo, and Skyler (1989) described a multifamily intervention that focused on helping adolescents with juvenile diabetes express feelings about their illness and enhance communication about the management of this condition, especially assertive diabetes-related communication. One interesting component of this particular intervention model was a parent simulation exercise in which adolescents taught their parents how to manage diabetes by reviewing management skills and serving as instructors while their parents actually carried out aspects of the regimen. Adolescents who participated in their family group demonstrated clinically significant improvements in metabolic control that were maintained at 6-month follow-up (Satin et al., 1989). Again, the effects of intervention on family functioning were not assessed.

Most empirical studies of interventions with families of chronic conditions focused on illness-related stress points or developmental transitions have involved a single chronic condition, juvenile diabetes, and should be generalized to other conditions. In addition, alternative approaches to reducing stresses on parents of children with chronic conditions such as discussion and parent education groups (Gonzalez, Steinglass, & Reiss, 1989; Telleen, Herzog, & Kilbane, 1989) and peer led groups (Toseland, Rossiter, & LaBreque, 1989), also need to be evaluated.

A final type of stress-point intervention, and one that has not been evaluated, to my knowledge, could focus on helping families manage the identifiable, chronic day-to-day stresses or hassles associated with illness management. Clinicians who provide ongoing guidance and support to parents of children with chronic illness often focus on such day-to-day problems as helping children understand and manage their own emotional reactions to their illness, negotiating family responsibilities for children's physical treatment, or dealing with the reactions of siblings or other family members to the stresses imposed by the children's condition (Chesler & Barbarins, 1988). Other possible targets of intervention might include specific child-rearing issues such as management of the children's fears (Dolgin et al., 1990), or reactions to painful events (Ross & Ross, 1987).

Process-oriented studies of family interactions and of management of various illness-related developmental tasks would help to formulate targeted anticipatory guidance concerning such issues as management of distress and pain (Dolgin et al., 1990), independence, and self-care (Anderson et al., 1990).

Targeting Intervention to Family Problems

Prior research has suggested the need to assess family members' appraisal of stressors and supports to identify families that might benefit most from psychological intervention (Affleck et al., 1989). Interventions that are tailored to specific resource problems demonstrated by families of children with chronic conditions should also be assessed in controlled studies. For example, children who are most vulnerable to recurrent physical crises are often from multi-problem families who may need an intensive intervention approach designed to stabilize the children's physical condition and prevent further depletion of family resources. For example, Golden, Herold, and Orr (1985) described an individualized intervention approach for families of children with diabetes who had at least two hospitalizations for ketoacidosis, which reflects an extreme and potentially life-threatening problem in metabolic control. The investigators assessed whether the cause of the children's hospitalization reflected misinformation or lack of education, problematic family allocation of responsibilities or more serious psychological and family dysfunction. Interventions were tailored to problems identified in the assessment and included the following: additional education; transferring responsibility for managing the children's insulin to another family member; additional support for families who did not manage the children's insulin properly (provided by school staff who monitored glucose levels and provided supplementary insulin); and ongoing public health nurse supervision of those families who were judged to have inadequate coping skills. These individualized intervention plans were generally associated with improvement in the children's condition.

Finally, investigators should identify factors that influence families' acceptance and utilization of psychological interventions. Some families of children with chronic conditions have difficulty accepting psychological interventions because they feel stigmatized or criticized (Sabbeth & Stein, 1990). Practitioners have important opportunities to assess family members' reactions to various clinical interventions that are offered in pediatric settings and to contribute pilot data concerning new interventions that appear to have positive effects.

REFERENCES

Affleck, G., Tennen, H., Rowe, J., Roscher, B., & Walker, L. (1989). Effects of formal support on mothers' adaptation to the hospital to home transition of high risk infants. The benefits and costs of helping. *Child Development*, *60*, 488–501.

Anderson, B. J., Auslander, W. P. F., Jung, K. C., Miller, J. P. & Santiago, J. V. (1990). Assessing family sharing of diabetes responsibilities. *Journal of Pediatric Psychology*, *15*, 477–492.

Brownlee-Duffeck, M., Peterson, E., Simonds, J. F., Goldstein, D., Kilo, C., & Hoette, S. (1987). The role of health beliefs in regimen adherence and metabolic control of adolescents and adults with diabetes mellitus. *Journal of Consulting and Clinical Psychology*, *55*, 139–144.

Cadman, D., Boyle, N., Szamari, P., & Offord, D. R. (1987). Chronic illness, disability and mental and social well being: Findings of the Ontario Child Health Study. *Pediatrics*, *79*, 805–813.

Chesler, M. A., & Barbarins, O.A. (1988). *Childhood cancer and the family: Meeting the challenge of stress and support.* New York: Brunner/Mazel.

Delameter, A. J., Bubb, J., Davis, S. G., Smith, J. A., Schmidt, L., Whie, N. A., & Santiago, J. V. (1990). A randomized prospective study of self-management training with newly diagnosed diabetic children. *Diabetes Care, 13,* 492–498.

Dolgin, M. J., Phipps, S., Harow, E. & Zeltzer, L. K. (1990). Parental management of fear in chronically ill and healthy children. *Journal of Pediatric Psychology, 13,* 733–744.

Drotar, D. (1981). Psychological perspectives in childhood chronic illness. *Journal of Pediatric Psychology, 6,* 211–228.

Drotar, D. (1991). The family context of failure to thrive. *American Journal of Orthopsychiatry, 61,* 23–34.

Drotar, D., & Bush, M. (1985). Mental health issues and services. In N. Hobbs & J. H. Ferrin (Eds.), *Issues in the care of children with chronic illness* (pp. 514–550). San Francisco: Jossey-Bass.

Drotar, D., Crawford, P., & Bush, M. (1984). The family context of childhood chronic illness. Implications for psychosocial intervention. In M. G. Eisenberg, L. C. Sutkin, & M. A. Jansen, (Eds.), *Chronic illness and disability through the life span: Effects on self and family* (pp. 103–132). New York: Springer.

Fiese, B. H., & Sameroff, A. J. (1989). Family context in pediatric psychology: A transactional perspective. *Journal of Pediatric Psychology, 14,* 293–314.

Garmezy, N., Masten, J., & Tellegen, A. (1985). The stress and competence in children: A building block for developmental psychopathology. *Child Development, 55,* 97–111.

Goldberg, S., Morris, P., Simmons, R. J., Fowler, R. S., & Levison, H. (1990). Chronic illness in infancy and parenting stress: A comparison of three groups of parents. *Journal of Pediatric Psychology, 15,* 347–358.

Golden, M. D., Herold, A. J., & Orr, D. P. (1985). An approach to prevention of recurrent diabetic ketoacidosis in the pediatric population. *Journal of Pediatrics, 93,* 195–200.

Gonzalez, S., Steinglass, P., & Reiss, D. (1989). Putting the illness in its place. Discussion groups for families with chronic medical illnesses. *Family Process, 28,* 69–87.

Gortmaker, S. L., & Sappenfield, W. (1984). Chronic childhood disorders: Prevalence and impact. *Pediatric Clinics of North America, 31,* 175–189.

Hausenstein, E. J. (1990). The experience of distress in parents of chronically ill children. Potential or likely outcome? *Journal of Clinical Child Psychology, 19,* 356–364.

Hauser, S. T., Jacobson, A. W., Wertlieb, D., Weiss-Perry, B., Follansbee, D., Wolsdorf, J. I., Herskowitz, R. D., Houlihan, J., & Rajapark, D. C.

(1986). Children with recently diagnosed diabetes: Interacting within their families. *Health Psychology, 5,* 273-296.

Hill, R. (1958). Generic features of families under stress. *Social Case Work, 39,* 139-150.

Hobfoll, S. E. (1988). *The ecology of stress.* Washington, DC: Hemisphere.

Hobfoll, S. E. (1989). Conservation of resources: A new attempt at conceptualizing stress. *American Psychologist, 44,* 513-524.

Ireys, H. T., & Burr, C. K. (1984). A part and apart: Family issues for young adults with chronic illness and disability. In M. G. Eisenberg, L. L. Sutkin, & M. A. Jansen (Eds.), *Chronic illness and disability through the life span: Effects on self and family* (pp. 184-205). New York: Springer.

Janz, N. K., & Becker, N. H. (1984). The health belief model: A decade later. *Health Education Quarterly, 11,* 1-47.

Jessop, D. J., Riessman, L. K., & Stein, R. E. K. (1989). Chronic childhood illness and maternal mental health. *Journal of Developmental & Behavioral Pediatrics, 9,* 147-158.

Jessop, D. J., & Stein, R. E. K. (1985). Uncertainty and its relation to the psychological and social correlates of chronic illness in children. *Social Science & Medicine, 20,* 993-999.

Johnson, S. B. (1985). The family and child with chronic illness. In D. C. Turk & D. D. Kerns (Eds.), *Health, illness, and families: A life span perspective* (pp. 183-219). New York: Wiley.

Koocher, G. P., & O'Malley, J. E. (1981). *The Damocles Syndrome: Psychosocial consequences of surviving childhood cancer.* New York: McGraw Hill.

Kovacs, M., Finkelstein, R., Feinberg, T. L., Crouse-Novak, M., Paulauskas, S., & Pollock, M. (1985). Initial psychological responses of parents to the diagnosis of insulin-dependent diabetes mellitus in their children. *Diabetes Care, 8,* 568-575.

LaGreca, A. M. (1990). Social consequences of pediatric conditions: Fertile area for future investigation and intervention. *Journal of Pediatric Psychology, 15,* 285-307.

Lazarus, R. S., & Folkman, S. (1984). *Stress, appraisal & coping.* New York: Springer.

MacCoby, E. E., & Martin, J. A. (1983). Socialization in the context of the family: Parent-child interaction. In P. H. Mussen (Ed.), *Handbook of child psychology: Vol. IV. Socialization, personality, and social development* (pp. 1-102). New York: Wiley.

McCubbin, H. L., & Patterson, J. M. (1982). Family adaptation to crises. In H. L. McCubbin, A. E. Cauble, & J. M. Patterson, *Family coping & social support.* Springfield, IL: Charles C Thomas.

Moos, R. N., & Schaefer, J. (1984). The crisis of physical illness: An overview and conceptual approach. In R. N. Moos (Ed.), *Coping with physical illness: Vol. 2. New perspectives* (pp. 3-25). New York: Plenum Press.

Patterson, J. M. (1985). Critical factors affecting family compliance with cystic fibrosis. *Family Relations, 34*, 79–89.

Patterson, J. M. (1988). Families experiencing stress: I. The family adjustment and adaptation response model. II. Applying the FAAR model to health-related issues for intervention and research. *Family Systems Medicine, 6*, 202–237.

Pless, I. B., & Pinkerton, P. (1975). *Chronic childhood disorder: Promoting patterns of adjustment.* Chicago: Yearbook Medical Publishers.

Pless, I. B., Roghmann, P. J., & Haggerty, R. J. (1972). Chronic illness, family functioning and psychological adjustment: A model for the allocation of preventive mental health resources. *International Journal of Epidemiology, 1*, 271–280.

Reiss, D. (1981). *The family's construction of reality.* Cambridge, MA: Harvard University Press.

Rolland, J. S. (1987). Chronic illness and the life cycle: A conceptual framework. *Family Process, 26*, 203–221.

Ross, D. M., & Ross, S. B. (1987). *Childhood pain: Current issues, research and management.* Baltimore, MD: Urban & Schwarzenberg.

Sabbeth, B., & Stein, R. E. K. (1990). Mental health referral: A weak link in comprehensive care of children with chronic physical illness. *Journal of Developmental & Behavioral Pediatrics, 11*, 73–78.

Satin, W., LaGreca, A. M., Zigo, M. A., & Skyler, J. S. (1989). Diabetes in adolescence: Effects of multifamily group intervention and parent simulation of diabetes. *Journal of Pediatric Psychology, 14*, 259–277.

Schaefer, C. C., McFaul, K. D., & Glasgow, R. E. (1986). Supportive and non-supportive family behaviors: Relationships to adherence and metabolic control in persons with Type 1 diabetes. *Diabetes Care, 9*, 179–185.

Stein, R. E. K., Jessop, D., & Ireys, H. (1988). Prevention of emotional problems in children with chronic illness. In L. Bond & B. Wagner (Eds.), *Families in transition: Primary prevention programs that work* (pp. 286–308). Beverly Hills, CA: Sage.

Taylor, S. E. (1983). Adjustment to threatening events: A theory of cognitive adaptation. *American Psychologist, 38*, 1161–1173.

Telleen, S., Herzog, A., & Kilbane, T. L. (1989). Impact of a family support program on mothers' social support and parenting stress. *American Journal of Orthopsychiatry, 59*, 410–419.

Toseland, R. W., Rossiter, C. M., & LaBreque, M. S. (1989). The effectiveness of three group intervention strategies to support family caregivers. *American Journal of Orthopsychiatry, 59*, 420–429.

Varni, D., Rubenfeld, L. A., Talbot, D., & Setoguchi, R. (1990). Family functioning, temperament, and psychological adaptation in children with congenital or acquired limb deficiencies. *Pediatrics, 84*, 323–330.

Varni, J. W., & Wallander, J. L. (1988). Pediatric chronic disabilities: Hemophilia and spina bifida, as examples. In D. K. Routh (Ed.), *Handbook of pediatric psychology* (pp. 190–221). New York: Guilford Press.

Varni, J. W., Wilcox, K. T., & Hanson, V. (1988). Mediating effects of family social support on child psychological adjustment in juvenile rheumatoid arthritis. *Health Psychology, 7*, 421–431.

Walker, L. S., & Zeaman, J. C. (1989, August). Mother and father reinforcement of child illness behavior. Paper presented at annual meeting of American Psychological Association, New Orleans, LA.

Walker, L. S., & Zeaman, J. C. (1992). Parental response to child illness behavior. *Journal of Pediatric Psychology, 17*, 49–71.

Wallander, J. L., Varni, J. W., Babani, L., Banis, H. T., Dehaan, C. B., & Wilcox, K. T. (1989). Disability parameters, chronic strains, and adaptation of physically handicapped children and their mothers. *Journal of Pediatric Psychology, 14*, 23–42.

Wallander, J. L., Varni, J. W., Babani, L., Banis, H. T. & Wilcox, K. T. (1989). Family resources as resistance factors for psychological maladjustment in chronically ill and handicapped children. *Journal of Pediatric Psychology, 14*, 157–173.

Wysocki, J., Meinhold, P., Cox, D. J., & Clarke, W. L. (1990). Survey of diabetes professionals regarding developmental changes in self-care. *Diabetes Care, 13*, 63–68.

13

FAMILY SYSTEMS MEDICINE: NEW OPPORTUNITIES FOR PSYCHOLOGISTS

Thomas L. Campbell
Susan H. McDaniel
David B. Seaburn
University of Rochester School of Medicine

Family systems medicine is a relatively new and exciting field of health care that developed from the integration of "family therapy, systems theory and modern medicine" (Bloch, 1983). An essential component of family systems medicine is a collaborative health care team consisting of medical providers and mental health professionals, including psychologists. This chapter briefly reviews the field of family systems medicine, including its basic premises and the research that supports this approach. Some of the opportunities for psychologists and other mental health professionals to work within a family systems medicine model are described and illustrated with a clinical case example. Although this chapter is written primarily for clinical psychologists, the ideas and suggestions apply equally well to other health professionals and therapists who work in medical settings.

BASIC PREMISES OF FAMILY SYSTEMS MEDICINE

Family systems medicine represents a major departure from the traditional biomedical approach of modern medicine in that it considers all patient problems within the larger social and family context. Other terms have been used to describe similar models, including family-centered medical care (Doherty & Baird, 1983), family-oriented primary care (McDaniel, Campbell, & Seaburn, 1990), and medical family therapy (McDaniel, Hepworth, & Doherty, 1992). These family systems approaches to health care share the following basic premises (McDaniel et al., 1990):

1. Family systems medicine is based on the biopsychosocial model. The traditional biomedical model assumes that disease can be reduced to "measurable biological variables" (Engel, 1977, p. 130). The task of the health care provider using a biomedical approach is to identify and treat the simplest biological factors, such as infectious or toxic agents, that are viewed as the primary cause of the disease. Illness is conceptualized solely from a biological vantage point, and social and psychological factors are largely ignored. This biologically based model has been extremely successful in the treatment and even eradication of many diseases, especially infectious diseases. Yet, as Baird and Doherty (1990) have stated, "Focusing only on the biological level represents a cultural bias disguised as scientific theory" (p. 397).

The biopsychosocial model, as proposed by Engel (1977), places illness within a larger framework involving multiple systems. To understand an illness, the health care provider must not only attend to the biological factors (molecules, cells, and organs) but also to the person, the family, the patient–provider relationship, and the social context (see Figure 1). These various elements are interrelated in such a way that changes in any one level can have an effect on the others, so that there is continuous and reciprocal feedback across the levels.

2. Family systems medicine focuses on the family as the most important context within which illness occurs. A family systems approach to health care is based on a biopsychosocial approach but emphasizes the family level or context as the primary arena in which medical care issues are addressed. Four key concepts are essential to this family orientation.

First, the family is the primary source of many health beliefs and behaviors. The initial appraisal of physical symptoms is usually made within the family and is based on family beliefs about health. Most families have a health expert who often makes an initial health assessment and decides whether a physician should be contacted. Most health behaviors, including smoking, diet, and exercise, are developed within the context of the family, which has a strong influence on whether the behavior is maintained or changed (Doherty & Campbell, 1988).

Second, the stress that a family feels when going through developmental transitions can become manifest in physical symptoms. Marriage, birth of the first child, adolescence, leaving home, midlife, death of a parent, and retirement are all normal and stressful developmental transitions that can make family members more vulnerable to illness (Carter & McGoldrick, 1988). Research on stressful life events has demonstrated how many of them occur at transitions in the family life cycle and are associated with increased illness (Campbell, 1986).

Third, somatic symptoms can serve adaptive functions within the family and be maintained by family patterns. Physical symptoms can often be under-

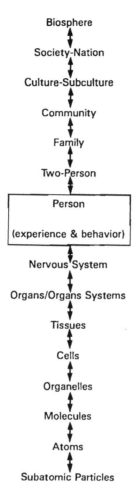

FIGURE 1 Systems hierarchy. From G. L. Engel, "The Clinical Application of the Biopsychosocial Model, *American Journal of Psychiatry, 137,* 535–544. Copyright May 1980 by The American Psychiatric Association. Reprinted with permission.

stood as a barometer of the pressure felt within a family. A young adult's difficulty "leaving home" and living independently may be exacerbated if he or she develops a disabling illness or if the young adult is needed to care for an ill family member. In a child, symptoms such as abdominal pain or wheezing may help stabilize a distressed marriage by keeping the parents focused on the child rather than on marital difficulties. Getting well can threaten the family's homeostasis, so that family members may encourage the patient to maintain his or her sick role.

Fourth, families are a valuable resource during an illness. Medical providers do not treat illness; they recommend treatment that is usually carried out in the home by the patient and family members. Health care providers must collaborate and rely on the assistance of the family in the management of most chronic illnesses (McDaniel, et al. 1990).

3. Family systems medicine requires collaboration between health care providers and mental health professionals. Even the best trained, family-oriented physician cannot meet the needs of all the families in his or her practice. Studies have demonstrated that over one half of all medical visits are for problems that are primarily psychosocial in nature (Katon, 1985) and that 15% to 40% of patients in primary care have a diagnosable mental disorder (Hoeper, Nyez, & Cleary, 1979). The medical care system has been termed the "de facto" mental health care system (Regier, Goldberg & Taube, 1978) because the vast majority of patients with mental health disorders is treated solely in the medical sector by non-psychiatrists, most of whom have inadequate training to deal with these problems. Many well-trained physicians want to develop good working relationships with psychologists and other mental health professionals to whom they can confidently refer their patients with serious emotional and relational problems.

4. Family systems medicine providers are seen as "a part of" rather than "apart from" the treatment system. A traditional biomedical approach views medical providers as objective outsiders who assess, diagnose, and treat their patients' illnesses. This approach fails to acknowledge how physicians may influence and be influenced by their patients' behavior. For example, when treatment does not go well, physicians may blame their patients and label them as "difficult" or "noncompliant." A systems perspective encourages health care providers to observe their interactions with patients and how their behavior contributes as much to what transpires as their patients' interactions with them.

These basic premises form the foundation upon which a family systems approach to health care can be developed. Family systems research is beginning to support the validity and effectiveness of this approach.

RESEARCH ON FAMILY INTERVENTIONS IN HEALTH CARE

Over the past two decades, there has been an increasing amount of research that demonstrates that families have a powerful influence on health and illness (reviewed in Campbell, 1986; Doherty & Campbell, 1988; McDaniel et al. 1990). However, little research has been conducted on family interventions with physical illness, and most of these studies are case reports or series. Only a few randomized controlled trials of family interventions have been published (see Table 1).

Expressed Emotion and Family Psychoeducation

Research on family interventions in mental health has been very productive, particularly studies of expressed emotion and family psychoeducation in schizophrenia. McFarlane (1991) has suggested that schizophrenia is similar to many chronic medical disorders and can serve as a model for developing family interventions for physical illnesses.

Research from the family therapy field on expressed emotion has shown how negative family interactions can influence mental health. The concept of expressed emotion (EE) developed from early observations (Brown, Birley, & Wing, 1972) that schizophrenic patients who returned to families that were emotionally overinvolved and hostile (high EE) relapsed at a much higher rate than patients returning to a more supportive or neutral environment. The two important components of expressed emotion are the degree of emotional overinvolvement and the frequency of critical comments. Numerous studies have shown that high EE strongly predicts relapse in schizophrenia (Leff & Vaughn, 1981; Vaughn & Leff, 1976; Vaughn, Snyder, Jones, Freeman, & Falloon, 1984) and depression (Gilhooly & Wittick, 1989; Hooley, Orley, & Teasdale, 1986; Hooley & Teasdale, 1989) and has led to the development of family interventions designed to lower EE. Several randomized controlled studies (Falloon et al., 1982; Hogarty et al., 1986; Leff, Kuipers, Berkowitz, Eberlein-Vries, & Sturgeon, 1982) of different types of family psychoeducation have demonstrated a dramatic reduction of relapse by lowering EE in the families of schizophrenic patients. Some of the common elements of these family psychoeducational interventions include (a) having a nonblaming, empathic stance that seeks to understand and validate the illness experiences of the family; (b) intensive education about the illness, particularly its biological basis; (c) teaching of coping skills and problem solving around specific problems that occur with the disorder; and (d) enhancing social support and increasing contact with other families dealing with the same illness.

Studies are currently being conducted to examine the role of family expressed emotion in physical health and illness (Vaughn, 1989). One study found that family expressed emotion, measured by a self-report instrument, was a

Table 1   Randomized Controlled Trials of Family Interventions in Physical Illness

Study	Illness	Intervention	Results
Clark et al., 1981	Asthma	Family education management of illness	Less fear and better
Baranowski et al., 1982	Cardiovascular risk factors	Multifamily support groups	More supportive behaviors to change diet and exercise
Saccone & Israel, 1978	Obesity	Spouse reinforcement	Increased weight loss
Wilson & Brownell, 1978	Obesity	Family involvement	No effect
Brownell et al., 1978	Obesity	Spouse involvement	Maintained weight loss
Pearce et al., 1981	Obesity	Spouse involvement and maintenance	Greater weight loss
Brownell et al., 1983	Obesity	Mother involvement	Group with mother and daughter seen separately lost the most weight
Morisky et al., 1983	Hypertension	Family support	57% reduction in overall mortality
Earp et al., 1982	Hypertension	Family involvement in home visit	No effect
Lask & Matthews, 1979	Asthma	Family therapy and thoracic gas volumes	Improvement in symptoms
Gustafsson et al., 1986	Asthma	Family therapy	Improvement in overall pediatric assessment

better predictor of cardiovascular risk behaviors (smoking, diet, and exercise) than measures of social support (Franks, Campbell, & Shields, 1992). A family psychoeducational approach has been adapted for use with groups of families coping with different chronic medical problems (Gonzalez, Steinglass, & Reiss, 1989). It appears to be quite effective but has not been tested in a rigorous manner. Clark et al. (1981) were able to demonstrate improvement in the self-management of asthma with an educational family intervention. However, the outcome measures were limited to self-reports of behaviors, with no assessment of disease activity or severity.

Social Support Interventions

Social support has been found to be as powerful a factor in physical health as family expressed emotion is in schizophrenia. Several carefully controlled prospective studies have demonstrated that low social support results in higher mortality and that family members are the most important source of social support (Cohen & Syme, 1985). In a recent review, House, Landis, and Umberson (1988) concluded, "The evidence regarding social relationships and health increasingly approximates the evidence in the 1964 Surgeon General's report that established cigarette smoking as a cause or risk factor for mortality and morbidity from a range of diseases. The age-adjusted relative risk ratios are stronger than the relative risks for all cause mortality reported for cigarette smoking" (p. 543). For middle-aged adults, the spouse is the most important source of social support, whereas for the elderly, the presence of adult children has the greatest impact on health. Social supports have similar influence on the onset and course of specific health conditions such as pregnancy (Nuckolls, Kaplan, & Cassel, 1972), heart disease (Ruberman, Weinblatt, Goldberg, & Chaudhary, 1984), and hip fractures (Cummings et al., 1988). Spousal support is also associated with implementing healthy behaviors such as smoking cessation (Mermelstein, Cohen, Lichtenstein, Baer, & Kamarck, 1986) and weight reduction (Barbarin & Tirado, 1984).

Social support can be thought of as being provided from within or outside the family. Interventions designed to enhance social support have either focused on increasing extrafamilial supports through support groups or increasing the support provided within the family, especially by a patient's partner (Gottlieb, 1988). Most of the work on support groups has been individually focused and has not included the family. An exception to this is the study of Baranowski, Nader, Dunn, and Vanderpool (1982), who studied the effectiveness of family support groups in changing dietary and exercise behaviors. The family members who participated in the support groups reported that they were more supportive of changes in family member's diet and exercise than those in the control group.

Intervention studies developed to enhance intrafamily supports have come

largely from behavioral psychology and have involved using spouses as rein-
forcers of healthy behaviors, especially for weight loss and smoking cessation.
Several randomized trials have examined the effectiveness of spousal support in
weight reduction programs. An early study (Saccone & Israel, 1978) found that
spouses were more effective at reinforcing eating behavior changes than were
therapists. A similar study (Wilson & Brownell, 1978) was unable to demonstrate an improvement in weight loss when the spouse was involved. In a third
study (Brownell, Heckerman, Westlake, Hayes, & Monti, 1978), obese men
who received support from their wives continued to lose weight after the end of
the 10-week study and lost significantly more weight over the next 6 months
than the control group. This study suggests that the spouse can continue to
reinforce behavior changes after the end of the intervention. Observational
studies have found that some spouses interfere with attempts at weight loss by
offering food or criticizing dieting behaviors (Stuart & Davis, 1972).

Pearce, LeBow, and Orchard (1981) demonstrated that instructing spouses
not to interfere with a behavioral treatment program for obesity was as effective
as involving the spouse.

The impact of family support in obesity treatment appears to depend on the
life stage of the family. Brownell, Kelman, and Stunkard (1983) examined the
effect of involving mothers in the treatment of adolescent obesity. The adolescents in the groups in which the mothers and adolescents met separately lost
more weight then those in groups in which the mothers and adolescents met
together or the mothers were not involved.

Spousal involvement has also been studied in smoking cessation programs.
Observational studies (Coppotelli & Orleans, 1985; Mermelstein, Lichtenstein,
& McIntyre, 1983) have shown that spousal or partner support is associated
with successful smoking cessation and that nagging or critical partner behavior
is associated with relapse of smoking. However, interventions studies designed
to improve spousal support for smoking cessation have been ineffective (Mermelstein et al., 1986). In these trials, spousal support predicted successful quit-
ting, but the interventions were unable to improve the level of support or cessation rates. The researchers concluded that it is difficult to change spousal
behaviors within the context of a smoking cessation program and that more
intensive interventions are necessary to improve spousal support.

An Integrated Approach

The most effective family intervention in physical illness involved a very simple
approach to providing family education and enhancing family support for hypertensive patients. Morisky et al. (1983) at Johns Hopkins studied the impact
of three different educational interventions (brief individual counseling, family
education during a home visit, and small patient group sessions) on appointment
keeping, weight control, blood pressure, and overall mortality in black, inner-

city hypertensive patients. The family intervention consisted of a single home visit during which a significant family member (usually the spouse) was educated about hypertension and encouraged to support the patent's medical regimen (taking medication, keeping appointments, and losing weight). At 2- and 5-year follow-ups, the experimental groups had a significant improvement in all outcome measures, including compliance with appointments and medication, lowering of systolic and diastolic blood pressure, and overall mortality. At 5 years, the experimental groups had a 57% reduction in overall mortality compared with the control group. Family education and support, either alone or in combination with other interventions, appeared to be more effective than the other interventions, but the groups were too small to detect any significant differences between experimental groups.

This landmark study demonstrated that a very simple family intervention can have major impact on overall mortality. Unfortunately, because of the design of the study and the number of patients in each group, the effective ingredients of the interventions could not be determined. A similar study (Earp, Ory, & Strogatz, 1982) failed to demonstrate any effect of family involvement in the control of hypertension, but the follow-up period was briefer (6 months) and the intervention was not as intensive. Morisky's study is a major breakthrough in the field of family intervention and may be analogous to the work on family psychoeducation in schizophrenia. The family intervention was included in the study because a study of the hypertensive patients in their clinic indicated that 70% of them expressed a desire for family members to learn more about hypertension. Most surveys of families with chronic illness indicate that one of their greater needs is to receive more information about the illness. Thus research on social support and health is beginning to have an influence on the care of medical patients, perhaps analogous to the influence of the research on expressed emotion on the care of patients with schizophrenia. However, it is surprising that similar interventions have not been tested with other chronic illnesses.

Family Therapy Interventions

Although many studies have found an association between overall family dysfunction and numerous physical illnesses (Campbell, 1986), only a few investigators have developed family interventions designed to change dysfunctional patterns of family interaction in chronic physical illness. From their carefully articulated Psychosomatic Family Model (Minuchin, Rosman, & Baker, 1978), Minuchin et al. (1975) at the Philadelphia Child Guidance Center used structural family therapy to change the patterns of interaction they observed in psychosomatic families. They report considerable success in using this intervention in 48 cases of diabetes, asthma, and anorexia nervosa. As a result of their work, the psychosomatic family model has become the most influential model of families and chronic illness, and structural family therapy the most widely promoted family intervention in physical illness (Griffith & Griffith, 1987). Recently, Minuchin's work has come under considerable criticism for conceptual and methodological problems (Campbell, 1986; Coyne & Anderson, 1988; Kog, Vandereyecken, & Vertommen, 1985). By their own admission, these families were a highly selective group that were not representative of families with these illnesses (Rosman & Baker, 1988). In addition, their results represent a series of cases without any controls.

Despite this interest in family therapy for physical disorders, there are only two randomized controlled trials of family therapy in physical illness, both for asthma. Using the psychosomatic family model, Gustafsson, Kjellman, and Cederblad (1986) were able to demonstrate a greater improvement than the controls in overall health of nine children with severe asthma whose families received eight monthly sessions of structural family therapy. In a similar study, Lask and Matthews (1979) in England randomly assigned 33 families with 37 asthmatic children to experimental and control groups. The families in the experimental group received a total of 6 hours of family therapy designed to improve the families' coping skills in dealing with acute attacks. At the end of 1 year, the children who received family therapy reported less wheezing and slightly improved pulmonary function testing. Of note is that these researchers used a psychoeducational approach that focused on problem solving and coping with the illness rather than on changing family structure or functioning. In both studies, the benefits of therapy were quite modest and the generalizability of these studies to other families with asthma is not clear.

In summary, family interventions designed to improve the support of a significant family member (usually the spouse) for complying with a medical treatment (e.g., taking medication or losing weight) appears to be quite effective in improving health outcomes. On the basis of this research, the National Heart, Lung and Blood Institute of the National Institutes of Health (Working Group on Health Education and High Blood Pressure, 1987) recommended that the following be used as part of a basic strategy in improving compliance in patients with hypertension.

Enhance support from family members—identify and involve one influential person, preferably someone living with the patient, who can provide encouragement, help support behavior change, and, if necessary, remind the patient about the specifics of the regimen. (p. 4)

Research on the effectiveness of family therapy in medical conditions shows only modest results and needs more study. However, it is well demonstrated that providing mental health services in conjunction with medical care improves overall health and reduces overall health costs (termed the *offset effect*; Mumford, Schlesinger, Glass, Patrick, & Cuerdon, 1984; Schlesinger, Mumford, Glass, Patrick, & Sharfstein, 1983). There is a need for research comparing the cost-effectiveness of family therapy with other forms of psychotherapy provided in the medical setting.

THE ROLE
OF THE FAMILY-ORIENTED PSYCHOLOGIST
IN THE HEALTH CARE SETTING

As described above, one of the basic premises of family systems medicine is the need for close collaboration between the medical providers and therapists to provide a comprehensive, biopsychosocial approach to health care. Much has been written about different models of collaborative care (Glenn, 1987; Glenn, Atkins, & Singer, 1984) and the challenges involved in collaboration (McDaniel & Campbell, 1986). These collaborative relationships can be thought of as ranging from consultation (for mysterious or "stuck" cases) to co-therapy (for especially difficult cases such as somatic fixation or dysfunctions around chronic illness) to referral (for serious psychiatric disorders or time-consuming cases; McDaniel et al., 1990; McDaniel et al., 1992; see Figure 2).

For a *consultation*, the consultant is available to provide information, suggestions, and support to the consultee but generally does not provide direct care to the patient or family. In a *referral*, the referring provider asks the specialist to provide treatment or therapy for a specific problem that the patient or family is having. In *co-therapy*, the physician and therapist work jointly together on the presenting problems, negotiating a division of labor consonant with their respective skills. It is crucial that the psychologist in a medical setting negotiate with the medical provider the kind of collaborative relationship that is requested in each case.

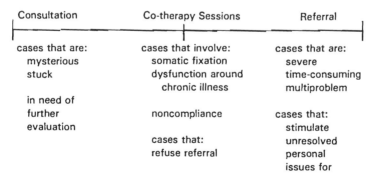

FIGURE 2 Types of collaborative relationships between primary care providers and mental health specialists. From S. H. McDaniel, T. L. Campbell, and D. Seaburn, *Family-oriented primary care*, Springer-Verlag, 1990. Reprinted with permission.

Consultations are usually framed as questions by the consultee to the consultant, such as "What is the best way to screen this patient for depression?" "Do you think this patient's pain could be psychogenic?" or "How could I work more effectively with this patient (or family)?" Consultations may be very brief and informal, such as an "informal hallway" consult in the hospital or office when therapists and physicians work in the same setting. A more formal consultation usually requires meeting with the physician, the patient, and the family. Consultations can be particularly helpful when the physician is feeling "stuck" in caring for a patient and when there are problems in the doctor-patient-family relationship, as illustrated in the following case example from one of the authors' practices (Campbell & McDaniel, 1987).

The Bunker family (see Figure 3) did not like visiting physicians or other health care providers. Mrs. Bunker was a 61-year-old housewife and mother of eight who suffered from severe chronic obstructive pulmonary disease (COPD) due to her smoking. She had been hospitalized many times and on one admission had needed to be put on a respirator for several days. She used oxygen to help her breathe at night. Her other medical problems included intermittent chest pain due to inflammation of her stomach and esophagus and nerve entrapments at

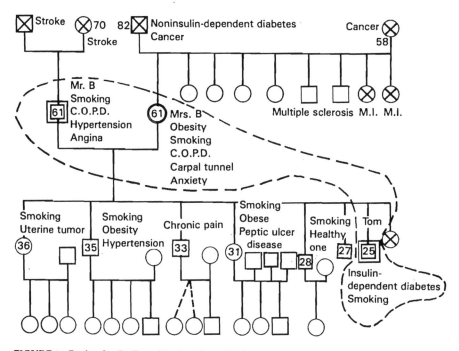

FIGURE 3   Bunker family. From M. Crouch, and L. Roberts, (Eds.), *The family in medical practice*, Springer-Verlag, 1987. Reprinted with permission.

both of her wrists (carpal tunnel syndrome) for which she refused surgery. Despite the severity of her lung disease, she continued to smoke one pack of cigarettes a day (reduced from two) and took benzodiazepines (Librium) for her anxiety.

Mr. Bunker was a 63-year-old electrician with hypertension, chronic obstructive pulmonary disease, and coronary artery disease. He smoked one and a half packs of cigarettes per day. Despite adjustments in his medication, he continued to have several episodes of chest pain a week. He had difficulty making office appointments due to his demanding job, and frequently requested refills of his medications over the phone.

Tom Bunker was the youngest son and the only child living at home with his parents. He was 25, unemployed, and had been diabetic for 12 years. He checked his own blood sugars at home and kept a detailed record of his insulin dosages and blood sugar levels. Although his diary indicated he was in good diabetic control, his blood sugars and glycosylated hemoglobin (a measure of chronic diabetic control) measured in the office were always very elevated (indicating very poor control). He smoked two packs of cigarettes a day and had tried numerous times to quit, without success.

The Bunkers' family physician, Dr. C. liked the Bunker family but found them very frustrating to care for. They rarely came in for medical appointments, often canceling because of "family emergencies" and then would request medication refills by the phone. They were very concerned about each other's health and often stated how important it was for another family member to see the doctor. All of them recited how bad smoking was for their health and how much they wanted to quit. Several attempts to quit smoking as a family had been unsuccessful.

For several years, Dr. C. told the family how concerned he was about their health problems and the effects of their smoking. He continually urged them to come in for more frequent appointments and at each visit stressed the importance of smoking cessation. Over the years, he felt increasingly powerless and frustrated and began seeing the family less frequently.

After one of Mrs. Bunker's hospitalizations for her COPD during which Dr. C. became furious with her for continuing to smoke, Dr. C. realized that he needed help with the case and consulted with Dr. M., a family therapist and psychologist with whom he had worked in the past. She helped him to take a step back and look at the family and his relationship to them from a systemic perspective. She pointed out how the family members were caught up in a vicious pattern in which each worried about the other while being irresponsible and hopeless about his or her own behavior. Each family member would say to the other: "I cannot change, but you have to change because you are so sick," and to the physician: "I cannot be helped because I cannot do what I need to do to help myself, but you must help my mother/father/son." Dr. C. began to see how he was being inducted into the family in that he shared their hopelessness and frustration about others not changing. With Dr. M's help, he formulated the following strategy with the family.

First, Dr. C. recognized that the repetitive theme for this family was that everyone was waiting for someone else to change first, so he decided to be the first person in the treatment system to change his own behavior, in a sense, to "stop smoking" and do something different, completely independently of whether it produced change for anyone else (i.e., the family). Second, Dr. C. decided to use his time differently. Rather than treating this family as needed, he set up regular meetings with each of them. He convened a family meeting to discuss everyone's current health status, their concerns for each other, how they were unable to change despite good intentions, and his sadness about that. He informed the family that he needed to have family meetings every 6 months to efficiently keep track of all their health problems. Third, by shifting the way he thought about this family, Dr. C. became more curious about them, realizing they had a lot to teach him. This family had learned how to appear healthy while actually being quite sick, and the risks of changing were very great. Dr. C. used the individual and family sessions to better understand what the risks were for each family member to change his or her health behaviors. Finally, he negotiated with each family member one or two small but realistic goals for treatment over the next 6 months.

Dr. C.'s brief consultation with a trusted colleague and therapist allowed him to become "unstuck" with this family by seeing them from a different perspective and feeling less responsible for getting them to change and less reactive to their helplessness. Because he no longer viewed them as therapeutic failures, Dr. C. began to enjoy seeing the Bunker family again. No longer facing predictable challenges about their smoking, family members came in for medical visits more regularly. Over several years, each of the Bunkers began to make some significant changes in his or her health behaviors. Tom discovered a comprehensive diabetes management program at the local hospital and joined it on his own. Mr. and Mrs. Bunker went to a hypnotist to help them stop smoking and, after numerous unsuccessful attempts, eventually stopped smoking at the same time. Dr. C. expressed genuine surprise and pleasure at each of these changes.

In co-therapy, both the physician and the therapist meet with the family together and negotiate a division of labor on the basis of their respective skills. The physician focuses more on the biological processes and the medical issues, whereas the therapist attends more to the psychosocial processes. Co-therapy treatment teams are sometimes essential in treating cases of somatization or somatic fixation, in which the patient or family is inappropriately fixated on somatic problems (McDaniel, Campbell, & Seaburn, 1989). These are very common and frustrating cases because the patient or family are often reluctant to address any psychosocial issues. The simultaneous involvement of medical and mental health providers facilities an integrated biopsychosocial approach to these problems. The patient or family's view of the problem is elicited and the treatment team negotiates a shared understanding and treatment for the symptom that utilizes the family's strengths and areas of competence.

Collaborative health care teams in which family physicians and family therapists form a primary health care team and see patients together on a regular basis have been described by Glenn (1987) and others (Dym & Berman, 1986). Although both the medical providers and patients have reported high levels of satisfaction with these collaborative models, no outcome studies have been published. This type of collaboration seems to be particularly useful when the medical problems are chronic or severe and are intertwined with the family difficulties, as demonstrated with the Bunkers.

Several months after stopping smoking, Mr. Bunker began coughing up bloody sputum and was discovered to have lung cancer. He had the tumor and part of his lung removed, but the surgeon found that the cancer had spread to his lymph nodes. His post operative course was complicated by an infection of his incision and difficulty in eating, which led him to lose forty pounds and become quite emaciated. During his hospitalization, he worried constantly about how his wife was doing without him at home but refused to let her visit him, fearing it would upset her too much.

After Mr. Bunker returned home from the hospital, the anxiety in the Bunker household increased dramatically. Mrs. Bunker called Dr. C. daily with concerns about her husband, and Mr. Bunker worried about his wife's breathing and her return to smoking while he was in the hospital. Feeling overwhelmed by the severity of the family's medical problems and emotional difficulties, Dr. C. asked Dr. M. to see the family with him in co-therapy. He explained to the family that he needed some help from a colleague in dealing with their different health problems.

Dr. C. and Dr. M. met with the family at monthly intervals for four sessions lasting about three quarters of an hour. Dr. C. clarified Mr. Bunker's diagnosis, prognosis, and treatment plan with the family and explored with them some ways that they could become more involved in his medical care. Dr. M. helped the family share their feelings about what was happening to Mr. Bunker: their fears about the future, their sadness and grief about his dying, and their anger that this happened just as he was retiring and had given up smoking. Mr. Bunker was able to tell his family how they could be helpful to him, and what chores and activities he wanted to continue to do for himself. Mrs. Bunker agreed to come in for more frequent medical checkups, so she could remain well enough to care for her husband.

Seeing this family together in co-therapy allowed the physician and psychologist, as a collaborative team, to help the family with their medical as well as their psychosocial needs. On a number of occasions, the family had resisted referrals to a mental health professional, stating that they did not need counseling. Yet, they were very receptive and appreciative of the co-therapy sessions, where they were able to share their feelings in a medical setting.

Referrals by physicians to psychologists and other mental health professionals are the most common form of collaboration and involve referring a patient or family for the treatment or management of a specific problem (e.g., depression, eating disorder, or marital problem). It is important that the therapist recognize that the physician will continue to see and treat the family for other, often related health issues. Because different kinds of treatment are being provided simultaneously by each professional, communication and role clarification are essential.

During the 6 months after his surgery, Mr. Bunker became progressively weaker from his lung cancer and eventually died in the hospital from respiratory failure. During the last few weeks of this life, Dr. C. met regularly with the Bunker family to discuss his treatment and prognosis. Mr. Bunker decided with his family that he did not want to die at home, nor did he want any extraordinary life support measures to be taken to keep him alive.

Two weeks after Mr. Bunker's death, Dr. C. convened the family and asked Dr. M. to join him again. Dr. C. reviewed with the family the events surrounding his death and the preliminary autopsy results. With Dr. M.'s assistance, Dr. C. encouraged them to share their grief and sorrow over Mr. Bunkers's death. Several of the Bunker children expressed concern about Mrs. Bunker's physical and mental health since her husband's death. Dr. C. agreed to monitor her COPD more closely, and Dr. M. offered to meet Mrs. Bunker and the rest of the family to help them through the grief process. Although the children felt that only Mrs. Bunker needed some counseling, they agreed, at Dr. M.'s request, to join the counseling sessions to help their mother.

Dr. M. met with the Bunker family every 2 weeks for 12 sessions. The initial sessions dealt solely with the family's grief but, with time, other family problems arose and were addressed. These included Mrs. Bunker's drinking, which had increased since her husband's death, Tom's inability to get a job and leave home, and conflicts between other family members. During this time, Dr. C. continued to see the family for their health problems.

Dr. C. and Dr. M. communicated regularly by phone and letter about their respective work with the family. After one family session with Dr. M., Mrs. Bunker had an acute exacerbation of her COPD and required admission to the intensive care unit of the hospital. Dr. C. and Dr. M. used this crisis as an opportunity to mobilize the family's resources and resolve some chronic conflicts in the family. With Dr. C.'s support and participation, Dr. M. met with the family in Mrs. Bunker's room in the ICU to continue the family therapy.

This case illustrates the range of collaborative relationships between a family physician and family psychologist extending over several years. A consultation helped the physician to change his relationship with the family and freed the family up to change their own health behaviors. In co-therapy, the physician and therapist were able to work simultaneously on the medical and psychosocial issues the family was facing. The physician was able to help the psychologist understand the patient's medical problems. After Mr. Bunker's death, the family was referred to the family psychologist for grief counseling and family therapy, but the family physician continued to care for the family's medical concerns and collaborate with the therapist.

BARRIERS TO EFFECTIVE COLLABORATION WITH MEDICAL PROFESSIONALS

Establishing collaborative relationships with physicians and other medical providers is essential for psychologists and other mental health professionals working in medical settings. As McDaniel et al. (1992) have pointed out, working with medical patients without consulting and collaborating with their medical providers is analogous to doing marital therapy with only one spouse and is likely to be incomplete or even destructive. However, establishing and maintaining such collaborative relationships can be challenging and requires work. Physicians and therapists differ in their training, language, and theoretical models (McDaniel et al., 1990). Table 2 describes many of the differences in working styles and goals of medical professionals and mental health professionals. Collaboration requires skills in joining, networking, consultation, and systems assessment and intervention. To work in a medical setting, one must understand the medical culture.

In no area is the culture of medicine more evident than in its special language. Some have even humorously suggested that medical terms were invented to keep patients and nonmedical professionals from understanding what medical providers do (Seaburn et al., in press), analogous to the use of Latin in writing prescriptions in the past. It is helpful to remember that some of the language used by psychologists is as incomprehensible to physicians as the medical language is to nonmedically trained therapists. To work effectively with medical providers, it is necessary for the therapist to have a rudimentary understanding of common medical terms (such as myocardial infarction, dyspnea, and bronchospasm) and abbreviations (such as MI, COPD,

Table 2 Differences in the Working Styles of Primary Care and Mental Health Professionals.

Category	Primary care	Mental health
Language	Medical	Humanistic, psychoanalytic, or systems
Traditional paradigm	Biomedical	Psychoanalytic
New paradigm	Biopsychosocial	Family systems
Professional style	Action-oriented	Process-oriented
	Advice-giving	Avoids advice
	M.D. takes initiative	Patient takes initiative
Standard session time	10–15 minutes	45–50 minutes
Demand for services	Around the clock	Scheduled sessions (excepting emergencies)
Use of medications	Frequent	Infrequent
Use of individual and family history	Basic	Extensive
At risk for	Somatic fixation	Psychosocial fixation

From S. H. McDaniel, T. L. Campbell, and D. Seaburn, *Family-oriented primary care,* Springer-Verlag, 1990. Reprinted with permission.

and CHF), and to request clarification when a medical provider uses a term that the therapist is not familiar with. Physicians forget that nonmedical providers are not fluent in "medicalese." In a similar fashion, therapists must be careful about using obscure psychological language in their communication with physicians.

The different theoretical models or paradigms of health professionals and psychologists must be acknowledged and negotiated for successful collaboration to take place. Physicians, even those who use a biopsychosocial approach, are trained in a biomedical model in which the disease-causing agent (e.g., bacteria or toxic substance) or pathological process (e.g., tumor or inflammation) is identified and removed or treated. Physicians have difficulty when they apply this mechanistic and linear approach to psychosocial problems or dysfunctional families. The traditional medical and biopsychosocial models may lead to different assessment as well as treatment plans and goals. Other differences in working styles can cause conflicts between physicians and therapists. Physicians tend to see patients for brief appointments and are much more authoritarian and directive than therapists. Thus, for effective collaboration, mental health providers need to recognize and respect these differences between professions and communicate regularly with physicians to negotiate joint treatment plans.

CONCLUSION

Family systems medicine is an exciting new field with enormous opportunities for psychologists and other mental health professionals. It is based on a holistic approach to health care that integrates the mind and body and focuses on the family as the primary context for understanding health and illness. A substantial body of research supports the powerful impact of the family on health, but much more research is needed to better understand how families affect health and vice versa. Family-oriented psychologists can play an important role in developing and testing effective family interventions in health care.

Family systems medicine requires an interdisciplinary approach with close collaboration between medical providers and mental health professionals. This represents a challenge for both disciplines: to break down the traditional barriers that support a mind–body dualism and to learn from each other. Ransom (1988) has posed the question, "Why bother to work in such an unfamiliar setting, one fraught with limitations and difficulties, and destined to be controlled ultimately by physicians?" (p. 298). He answers his own question by arguing that psychologists and family therapists have an opportunity both to test and refine their ideas and techniques in a new setting and to influence the way in which medical care is delivered in this country.

REFERENCES

Baird, M. A., & Doherty, W. J. (1990). Risks and benefits of a family systems approach to medical care. *Family Medicine, 22,* 396–403.

Baranowski, T., Nader, P. R., Dunn, K., & Vanderpool, N. A. (1982) Family self-help: Promoting changes in health behavior. *Journal of Communications, Summer,* 161–172.

Barbarin, O. A., & Tirado, M. (1984). Family involvement and successful treatment of obesity: A review. *Family Systems Medicine, 2,* 37–45.

Bloch, D. A. (1983). Family systems medicine: The field and the journal. *Family Systems Medicine, 1,* 3–11.

Brown, G. W., Birley, J. L. T., & Wing, J. K. (1972). Influence of family life on the course of schizophrenic disorders: A replication. *British Journal of Psychiatry, 121,* 241–258.

Brownell, K. D., Heckerman, C. L., Westlake, R. J., Hayes, S. C., & Monti, P. M. (1978). The effects of couples training and partner cooperativeness in the behavioral treatment of obesity. *Behavior Research and Therapy, 16,* 323–333.

Brownell, K. D., Kelman, J. H., & Stunkard, A. J. (1983). Treatment of obese children with and without their mothers: Changes in weight and blood pressure. *Pediatrics, 71,* 515–523.

Campbell, T. L. (1986). The family's impact on health: A critical review and annotated bibliography. *Family Systems Medicine, 4,* 135–328.

Campbell, T. L., & McDaniel, S. H. (1987). Applying a systems approach to common medical problems. In M. Crouch & L. Roberts (Eds.), *The family in medical practice* (pp. 112–139). New York: Springer-Verlag.

Carter, E. A., & McGoldrick, M. (Eds.). (1988). *The changing family life cycle: A framework for family therapy.* New York: Gardner Press.

Clark, N. M., Feldman, C. H., Evans, D., Millman, E. J., Wailewski, Y., & Valle, I. (1981). The effectiveness of education for family management of asthma in children: A preliminary report. *Health Education Quarterly, 8,* 166–174.

Cohen, S., & Syme, S. L. (1985). *Social support and health.* New York: Academic Press.

Coppotelli, H. C., & Orleans, C. T. (1985). Partner support and other determinants of smoking cessation maintenance among women. *Journal of Consulting and Clinical Psychology, 53,* 455–460.

Coyne, J. C., & Anderson, B. J. (1988). "Psychosomatic family" reconsidered: Diabetes in context. *Journal of Marital and Family Therapy, 14,* 113–123.

Cummings, S. R., Phillips, S. L., Wheat, M. E., Black, D., Goosby, E., Wlodarczyk, D., Trafton, P., Jergesen, H., Winograd, C. H., & Hulley, S. B.

(1988). Recovery of function after hip fracture. The role of social support. *Journal of the American Geriatrics Society, 36,* 801–806.

Doherty, W. J., & Baird, M. A. (1983). *Family therapy and family medicine: Toward the primary care of families.* New York: Guilford Press.

Doherty, W. J., & Campbell, T. L. (1988). *Families and health.* Beverly Hills, CA: Sage.

Dym, B., & Berman, S. (1986). The primary health care team: Family physician and family therapist in joint practice. *Family Systems Medicine, 4,* 9–21.

Earp, J. A., Ory, M. G., & Strogatz, D. S. (1982). The effects of family involvement and practitioner home visits on the control of hypertension. *American Journal of Public Health, 72,* 1146–1154.

Engel, G. L. (1977). The need for a new medical model: A challenge for biomedicine. *Science, 196,* 129–136.

Falloon, I. R., Boyd, J. L., McGill, C. W., Razani, J., Moss, H. B., & Gilderman, A. M. (1982). Family management in the prevention of exacerbations of schizophrenia: A controlled study. *New England Journal of Medicine, 306,* 1437–1440.

Franks, P., Campbell, T., & Shields, C. (1992). Social relationships and health: The relative roles of family functioning and social support. *Social Science and Medicine, 34,* 779–788.

Gilhooly, M. L., & Whittick, J. E. (1989). Expressed emotion in caregivers of the dementing elderly. *British Journal of Medical Psychology, 62,* 265–272.

Glenn, M. (1987). *Collaborative health care: A family-oriented approach.* New York: Praeger Press.

Glenn, M., Atkins, L., & Singer, R. (1984). Integrating a family therapist into a family medicine practice. *Family Systems Medicine, 2,* 137–146.

Gonzalez, S., Steinglass, P., & Reiss, D. (1989). Putting the illness in its place: Discussion groups for families with chronic medical illness. *Family Process, 28,* 69–87.

Gottlieb, B. H. (Ed.). (1988). *Marshalling social support: Formats, processes, and effects.* Newbury Park, CA: Sage.

Griffith, J. L., Griffith, M. E. (1987). Structural family therapy in chronic illness. Intervention can help produce a more adaptive family structure. *Psychosomatics, 28,* 202–205.

Gustafsson, P. A., Kjellman, N. I., & Cederblad, M. (1986). Family therapy in the treatment of severe childhood asthma. *Journal of Psychosomatic Research, 30,* 369–374.

Hoeper, E., Nyez, G., & Cleary, P. (1979). Estimated prevalence of RDC mental disorders in primary medical care. *International Journal of Mental Health, 6,* 6–15.

Hogarty, G. E., Anderson, C. M., Reiss, D. J., Kornblith, S. J., Greenwald, D. P., Javna, C. D., & Madonia, M. J. (1986). Family psychoeducation, social skills training, and maintenance chemotherapy in the aftercare treatment of schizophrenia. I. One-year effects of a controlled study on relapse and expressed emotion. *Archives of General Psychiatry, 43,* 633–642.

Hooley, J. M., Orley, J., & Teasdale, J. D. (1986). Levels of expressed emotion and relapse in depressed patients. *British Journal of Psychiatry, 148,* 642–647.

Hooley, J. M., & Teasdale, J. D. (1989). Predictors of relapse in unipolar depressives: Expressed emotion, marital distress, and perceived criticism. *Journal of Abnormal Psychology, 98,* 229–235.

House, J. S., Landis, K. R., & Umberson, D. (1988). Social relationships and health. *Science, 241,* 540–545.

Katon, W. (1985). Somatization in primary care [Editorial]. *Journal of Family Practice, 21,* 257–258.

Kog, E., Vandereyecken, W., & Vertommen, H. (1985). The psychosomatic family model: A critical analysis of family interaction concepts. *Journal of Family Therapy, 7,* 31–44.

Lask, B., & Matthews, D. (1979). Childhood asthma. A controlled trial of family psychotherapy. *Archives of Disease In Childhood, 54,* 116–119.

Leff, J. P., Kuipers, L., Berkowitz, R., Eberlein-Vries, R., & Sturgeon, D. (1982). A controlled trial of social intervention in the families of schizophrenic patients. *British Journal of Psychiatry, 141,* 121–134.

Leff, J. P., & Vaughn, C. E. (1981). The role of maintenance therapy and relatives' expressed emotion in relapse of schizophrenia: A two-year follow-up. *British Journal of Psychiatry, 139,* 102–104.

McDaniel, S. H., & Campbell, T. L. (1986). Physicians and family therapists: The risks of collaboration. *Family Systems Medicine, 4,* 4–8.

McDaniel, S. H., Campbell, T. L., & Seaburn, D. (1989). Somatic fixation in patients and physicians: A biopsychosocial approach. *Family Systems Medicine, 7,* 5–16.

McDaniel, S. H., Campbell, T. L., & Seaburn, D. (1990). *Family-oriented primary care: A manual for medical providers.* New York: Springer-Verlag.

McDaniel, S. H., Hepworth, J., & Doherty, W. J. (1992). *Medical family therapy.* New York: Guilford Press.

McFarlane, W. R. (1991). Schizophrenia and psychoeducation: Model for intervention in family practice. *Canadian Family Physician, 37,* 2457–2465.

Mermelstein, R., Cohen, S., Lichtenstein, E., Baer, J. S., & Kamarck, T. (1986). Social support and smoking cessation and maintenance. *Journal of Consulting and Clinical Psychology, 54,* 447–453.

Mermelstein, R., Lichtenstein, E., & McIntyre, K. (1983). Partner support and relapse in smoking-cessation programs. *Journal of Consulting and Clinical Psychology, 51,* 465–466.

Minuchin, S., Baker, L., Rosman, B. L., Liebman, R., Milman, L., & Todd,

T. C. (1975). A conceptual model of psychosomatic illness in children: Family organization and family therapy. *Archives of General Psychiatry, 32*, 1031–1038.

Minuchin, S., Rosman, B. L., & Baker, L. (1978). *Psychosomatic families.* Cambridge, MA: Harvard University Press.

Morisky, D. E., Levine, D. M., Green, L. W., Shapiro, S., Russell, R. P., & Smith, C. R. (1983). Five-year blood pressure control and mortality following health education for hypertensive patients. *American Journal of Public Health, 73*, 153–162.

Mumford, E., Schlesinger, H. J., Glass, G. V., Patrick, C., & Cuerdon, T. (1984). A new look at evidence about reduced cost of medical utilization following mental health treatment. *American Journal of Psychiatry, 141*, 1145–1158.

Nuckolls, K. B., Kaplan, B. H., & Cassel, J. (1972). Psychosocial assets, life crisis and the prognosis of pregnancy. *American Journal of Epidemiology, 95*, 431–441.

Pearce, J. W., LeBow, M. D., & Orchard, J. (1981). Role of spouse involvement in the behavioral treatment of overweight women. *Journal of Consulting and Clinical Psychology, 49*, 236–244.

Ransom, D. C. (1988). Family therapists teaching in family practice settings: Issues and experiences. In H. A. Liddle, D. C. Breunlin, & R. C. Schwartz (Eds.), *Handbook of family therapy training and supervision* (pp. 290–302). New York: Guilford Press.

Regier, D. A., Goldberg, I. D., & Taube, C. A. (1978). The de factor U.S. mental health services system: A public health perspective. *Archives of General Psychiatry, 35*, 685–693.

Rosman, B. L., & Baker, L. (1988). The psychosomatic family reconsidered: Diabetes in context—A reply. *Journal of Marital and Family Therapy, 14*, 125–132.

Ruberman, W., Weinblatt, E., Goldberg, J. D., & Chaudhary, B. S. (1984). Psychosocial influences on mortality after myocardial infarction. *New England Journal of Medicine, 311*, 552–559.

Saccone, A. J., & Israel, A. C. (1978). Effects of experimental versus significant other controlled reinforcement and choice of target behavior on weight loss. *Behavior Therapy, 9*, 271–278.

Schlesinger, H. J., Mumford, E., Glass, G. V., Patrick, C., & Sharfstein, S. (1983). Mental health treatment and medical care utilization in a fee-for-service system: Outpatient mental health treatment following the onset of a chronic disease. *American Journal of Public Health, 73*, 422–429.

Seaburn, D., Gawinski, B., Harp, J., McDaniel, S. H., Shields, C., & Waxman, D. (in press). Family systems therapy in a primary care setting: The Rochester experience. *Journal of Marital and Family Therapy.*

Stuart, R. B., & Davis, B. (1972). *Slim chance in a fat world: Behavioral control of obesity.* Champaign, IL: Research Press.

Vaughn, C. E. (1989). Expressed emotion in family relationships. *Journal of Child Psychology and Psychiatry and Allied Disciplines, 30,* 13–22.

Vaughn, C. E., & Leff, J. (1976). The influence of family and social factors on the course of psychiatric illness: A comparison of schizophrenic and depressed neurotic patients. *British Journal of Psychiatry, 129,* 125–137.

Vaughn, C. E., Snyder, K. S., Jones, S., Freeman, W. B., & Falloon, I. R. (1984). Family factors in schizophrenic relapse. Replication in California of British research on expressed emotion. *Archives of General Psychiatry, 41,* 1169–1177.

Wilson, G. T., & Brownell, K. (1978). Behavioral therapy for obesity: Including family members in the treatment process. *Behavior Therapy, 9,* 943–945.

Working Group on Health Education and High Blood Pressure. (1987). *The physician's guide: Improving adherence among hypertensive patients.* Washington, DC: U.S. Government Printing Office.

14

FAMILY THERAPY IN THE CONTEXT OF AIDS

Gillian Walker
Ackerman Institute for Family Therapy, New York

In the next decade, family therapists will be seeing in their practices increasing numbers of people at various stages of HIV infection. The U.S. Public Health Service now projects a cumulative total of 270,000 cases by 1991, with projected 180,000 deaths; by 1992, 365,000 cases; and by 1993, 453,000 cases. The current reservoir of infection is enormous and deadly: Between 1 and 1.5 million Americans are thought to be infected currently (Needle, Leach, & Graham-Tomasi, 1989). Each of these people is involved with family, from the gay man struggling to reconcile his relationships with family of origin and family of choice, to the hemophiliac who has unknowingly infected wife and children but who cannot reveal his family's tragedy to outsiders who do not even know of his hemophilia, to the adolescent infected by a casual affair whose family must deal with his or her illness and impending death.

The first wave of infection was among gay men, intravenous drug users, and hemophiliacs. The growing number of women infected through sexual contact with HIV-carrying drug users represented the second wave of the epidemic. Therapists are already beginning to see the third generation of HIV-infected people: sexual partners of individuals who themselves were infected through heterosexual contact. The majority of this new generation will be infected in adolescence or early adulthood, an age of experimentation with sex and often with drugs and frequently characterized by reckless passion, a sense of omnipotence, and a belief in personal immortality. As a result, adolescents are one of the most difficult groups to persuade of the necessity for precautions.

Despite growing evidence of its ultimate fatality, early diagnosis and treatment of HIV infection—together with the improvement in medical treatment of opportunistic infections—result in increasing length of survival time. As a result, AIDS now must be thought of as a chronic disease whose length is indeterminate and whose course is uncertain. The period of time from infection with HIV and manifestation of symptoms may be as short as a few months or as long as 15 or more years. The symptomatic phase may be chronic-episodic, with periods of good health interspersed with acute medical crises; its course may be progressive as the patient loses more and more capacity for independent functioning; or AIDS may seem to be a "bolt from the blue," an unexpected diagnosis leading rapidly to death.

The uncertainties of AIDS pose problems for patients in terms of defining how they will order their lives and plan for the future. A period of good health may lead a patient to plan for a relatively normal life, only to have those plans disrupted by a sudden life-threatening opportunistic infection. Recovery from that infection may be confusing because, although the person may be physically well enough to resume normal activities, the psychological shock of a brush with death may be emotionally debilitating.

The roller coaster nature of AIDS illness also poses problems of organization for the caregiving family or partner who must constantly be ready to adapt to the changing needs of the ill person. In a family in which more than one family member is infected or at risk, the uncertainty is particularly hard. "Who will care for me if I am infected?" wonders a young wife who has single-handedly nursed her ill husband despite family ostracism. She is afraid to be tested herself and to have their 6-year-old daughter tested. Yet, without knowing her sero-status, how can she plan her life or form a new relationship? Another mother watches as five of her seven adult children take sick one by one and, one by one, die. As she grieves each new loss she wonders how she and her well daughter will care for her 12 orphaned grandchildren.

For the family therapist or health care professional, the challenge of dealing with the myriad human tragedies caused by this unpredictable and complex disease is immense. Furthermore, AIDS is not just another disease that leaves in its wake normal human tragedy. AIDS, like plague, leprosy, tuberculosis, and cancer before it, has become part of a cultural mythology. As Sontag (1979, 1989) suggests, the terror of incurable illnesses of frightening course is managed by associating them with sin and deviance. As a result, the occurrence of AIDS is shrouded in secrecy and shame. Finally, because of its uncertain transmission patterns, AIDS remains a spectral visitor in families long after the death of the index patient.

This chapter outlines some critical issues for therapists working with people with AIDS infection and their families and describes some principles of effective intervention. It includes a rationale for a family systems model of counseling, descriptions of countertransferences experienced by AIDS counselors, and of resistances to family intervention. The chapter underlines the importance of understanding how illness can generate psychological problems by creating shifts in critical relationship systems. Key interventive tasks are described, including the need for empowering families for identifying caregiving resources, for constructing positive narratives that counteract AIDS stigma, for future planning, and for supplying medical information and advocacy.

CREATING A SYSTEMIC THERAPY MODEL

The family therapist working with people with AIDS believes that effective counseling must conceptualize the family itself as the living system that provides care and that must endure and heal itself after the death of the person with AIDS. As a result, counseling goals include reconciliation of the ill person and his or her family, the mobilization of family and network resources, facilitation of the ill person's participation in the ongoing life of the family of origin or choice, and in the planning for its future. A systems approach to chronic illness views the family as the unit of intervention and the entire course of illness as the time frame for intervention.

A systems model for HIV-infected people and their families draws on the inherent resources, coping skills, and problem-solving abilities of families both to manage illness and to perform non-illness related tasks that are fundamental to a family's core sense of its own identity. The professional's role is primarily as a consultant who encourages families to identify and change illness meanings, define problem areas, and effect solutions. AIDS counseling should be pragmatic and problem-focused, but it also must leave room for the ventilation of feelings elicited by the illness. For some periods of time, the therapist's work may consist merely of bearing witness to the person's experience of illness. At other times, he or she must actively encourage the family to focus on the tasks of everyday life, in order to put "illness in its place." (Gonzalez, Steinglass, & Reiss, 1987).

HIV infection forces families to interface constantly with larger systems. Because this interplay shapes the course of the illness, a systems therapist can utilize those interacting systems as natural resources for illness management. A systems approach not only examines the levels of patient and family experience but also attempts to create an ecosystemic or holistic approach to intervention that coordinates both medical and psychosocial care for all family members. Families may need help in making their needs and beliefs about the illness clear to the medical team, in negotiating services, and in obtaining necessary medical information to ensure that they have the correct protocols or are able to make informed choices about treatment. The psychosocial functioning of individual family members who are not themselves ill may be affected by the disease. For example an adolescent whose parent is dying may begin to make trouble in school. A therapist with a systems orientation may realize that swift intervention into the school system can be as strengthening to the family and the dying person as helping the family more directly with the illness. Preventing the adolescent from dropping out of school may even have a preventive aspect because goal orientation may discourage unsafe experimentation with sex.

Another critical element of family systems theory, as applied to chronic illness, is the understanding of intricate recursive loops between context and illness. Family belief systems, history, structural organization, and the family's location within the larger culture will affect the biological course of the individual family members' illness and shape its subjective experience. In a similar fashion, the illness experience will reconfigure or rigidify family beliefs.

The experience of HIV infection cannot be separated from the deeply stigmatized societal meanings given to AIDS. Because AIDS is associated with those areas where society has the most complex ambivalence and dread, including drug usage, sexual deviance, and sexuality itself, both the ill people and the families have to deal with their beliefs about what is normal and what is deviant. Even families who have the flexibility to adapt to illness needs have to overcome powerful messages transmitted through the generations and from the larger culture if they are to fully embrace the sufferer. For example, to construct an affirmative meaning for the illness, parents of a gay man may have to challenge deeply held beliefs about the meaning of homosexuality, just as the gay man may find that illness causes old confusions and guilts to resurface. The meanings that family members are able to assign to their participation in the care of a family member with AIDS will be critical both to the quality of patient care and to the healing of their own system throughout illness and after the patient dies.

The family systems literature has identified ways in which the processing of the illness experience can have a transformative or reifying effect on family organization (Reiss, 1981). For some families, the illness crisis becomes a time of experiencing, questioning, and learning, as families open themselves to utilizing information from the other systems that interact with them to broaden their understanding of themselves, their capacities, and their deficiencies (Reiss, 1981). For example, those families of origin of gay men, who used the illness crisis to work through their prejudices about homosexuality, found that a deeper transformation of values had occurred. Other families who did not emphasize the acquisition of new experience, knowledge, and skills became "engaged in decoding the symbolic meaning of the crisis and subsequent disorganization" (Reiss, 1981, p. 193). These decodings were often tied to a reiteration of past beliefs that were organized to give meaning to the crisis. These meanings were critical to maintaining a sense of family cohesion as well as to the family's management of illness and its recovery.

Tasks for the Systemic Therapist

Family therapists working with families in which a person has AIDS need to examine their own values and biases. Family systems thinking tends to *homoge-*

nize human relationships; despite its claims to objectivity and neutrality, it has implicit beliefs about *normative* family structure and human behaviors. The experience of working with people who are infected with AIDS challenges such normative beliefs and allows us to interact with subcultures that function with very different value systems. Therapists need to become familiar with, and to respect the mores, beliefs, traditions, and sexual practices of the different cultures that have been most affected by the disease.

For example, family systems work with people with AIDS (PWAs) has to conceptualize family in the broadest terms. Family may include networks of kin and non-kin. Family may consist of a group of intimate friends and exclude family of origin. Ex-lovers may have the status of family members for a gay couple. Different family groups—family of origin and family of choice—may compete for legitimacy. Or a family may be constructed out of a group of caregiving volunteers and professionals. The therapist must be open to working with all of these variations on the theme "family."

Therapists have to remember that their own fears about contamination and stigma may distance them from clients and encourage a defensively moralizing stance. Families are powerful systems that constantly remind us of our connection to them: the remark of a teenager who reminds us of a son or daughter, or an argument between husband and wife that echoes our own. Remembering the vulnerability of one's own past sexual life, or the sexual lives of those we love, can evoke powerful countertransference responses in most therapists. When AIDS is at issue, we may defend ourselves by invoking the concept of *otherness* to deal with our terrors about the proximity of the disease. "He belongs to a community to which I do not belong." "She is promiscuous and careless." "He uses drugs. I do not. Therefore, I am safe."

The challenge to family therapists is to face our similarities with people we are counseling so that we can always be aware of the ill person's *ordinariness rather than otherness*. For example, it is easy to view drug users in terms of the otherness of their drug-using behavior rather than allowing ourselves to empathize with them as a child and a parent, and to experience with them what it feels like to die before one's children are even grown or to have harmed the person one has loved the most.

To help the client face the anguish of AIDS, therapists must find whatever is most positive, strong, and effective in the client's experience. The therapist not only creates a bond that is therapeutic for the client but also is forced to face the intensity of emotions engendered by working with AIDS patients and their families.

PRINCIPLES OF THERAPEUTIC INTERVENTION

In using family systems therapy to help people with HIV infection, the following principles have emerged:

Overcoming Resistance to Family Therapy

It is important that the therapist who wishes to work in a systems model be sensitive to the issues that the AIDS-infected patient brings to therapy and to realize that the patient may be reluctant to involve family members. For the homosexual or bisexual man, internalized homophobia may be exacerbated by feelings that contamination due to the illness is God's punishment for his sexual orientation and life-style. These feelings, with their resultant depression, low-ered self-esteem, and fear of external judgment, may have to be carefully pro-cessed by the therapist in individual sessions before the PWA feels confident enough in himself and in the therapeutic relationship to invite into a session others who he feels may echo his own negative feelings.

The family therapist must also recognize that although his or her own values may dictate a resolution of issues with the family of origin, reconnecting with the original family may be less important for the gay man than (and may even be in conflict with) maintaining a good relationship with his family of choice (i.e., his gay friendship network). Because statistics on family accep-tance of a homosexual orientation seem to indicate that approximately half of the families react with some negativity, disclosure is risky business, particularly at a time of intense vulnerability. When encouraging a client to disclose either sexual orientation or HIV infection, it is important for the clinician to weigh the possibility that the stress of reconnection with the family may precipitate a health crisis in the immuno-compromised client.

A suggestion of couples therapy may also meet with resistance. The PWA may be terrified that beneath his lover's apparent acceptance and compassion, he may find the blame and anger he secretly believes he deserves as punish-ment, or may find that his lover secretly wishes to protect himself by leaving. By the same token, the lover without AIDS may be reluctant to enter therapy with his partner precisely because he does have ambivalent feelings from which he wishes to protect his ill, and therefore vulnerable, partner.

Drug users may have explosively distanced themselves from their families after diagnosis. They may deny their illness, increase their drug use, or feel bitter that their family did not succeed in its implicit promise of ultimate rescue. The family, in turn, may feel overwhelming anger and impotence, as the rescue dance between drug user and family ends in this fatal illness. Outreach to the family and initial processing of their emotions may have to take place in the absence of the drug user. Later, as he or she comes to terms with the diagnosis and the family has worked through the initial flood of emotions, conjoint ses-sions can take place.

In couples in which one partner has led a secret bisexual life, diagnosis may bring such shame because of the unresolved issues of his sexual orientation and his feelings of guilt at having betrayed his spouse, that it may be difficult initially to engage him in therapy. Again, the therapist must be flexible and compassionate toward the PWA's fears, wish for secrecy, and decision not to tell people in his larger network.

The patient's right to confidentiality versus the right of the partner to know that he or she may be at risk, is a heatedly debated issue in a discourse where vulnerability to infection and the infected person's infectiousness vary greatly. For example, a client may telephone to tell the therapist that he is AIDS infected, wants couples therapy, and does not wish his partner to know. The family therapist may contract for an initial session to discuss disclosure. If the PWA refuses but brings his partner to a subsequent session and still refuses to disclose, current legal opinion stresses that the therapist has a duty to protect the partner by informing him. Once the partner is present in the session, both are considered the therapist's patients. However, the therapist's responsibility to inform partners becomes less clear when the therapist is seeing a single client.

Family therapists who work with AIDS must be more flexible about attendance at sessions than they might be in other situations. Sometimes the PWA or care partner/spouse may need to be seen alone for coaching or exploring emotions he or she is not ready to share with the other person. Members of the family of origin may be seen separately to prepare them for a conjoint family session. Careful work with process, use of positive connotations to diffuse tense situations, and a supportive, nonjudgmental, and inquiring stance are helpful here.

Parents may resist having young children included in the work for fear that a secret will be revealed. Nevertheless, families should be gently encouraged to invite children to join them in a session when it feels appropriate so that they may understand what is happening in the family. Children are often confused by the mixed messages they receive from relatives. They may not be told that a parent has AIDS because adults fear, correctly in many cases, that they would be ostracized at school were they to tell schoolmates. The child, having overheard a secret, is more likely to blurt out the truth to others than the child to whom the situation is explained. In addition, the mystery of the parent's illness and the apparent shame associated with it are bewildering to young children. Many, having no language and finding themselves in a situation where talking itself is experienced as potentially dangerous, become symptomatic. A therapy session is a safe place where feelings can be ventilated, the reasons for secrecy explored, and the underlying reasons for acting-out behavior allowed to surface.

Therapists should be careful to respect the denial system of the patient. Denial may be his or her best defense against illness itself and/or a psychological dysfunction. Yet, the therapist must be open to the patient's need to express feelings about illness and potential death, following the patient's lead and never forcing issues and in a delicate dance of covering and uncovering.

Denial may also be invoked by parents when they fear a child is infected, ill, or dying. The therapist must patiently work around taboo areas, focusing instead on practical problems of living with illness and secrecy, using metaphors or stories to introduce topics that could not be introduced directly, until the family decides to raise the issue themselves. In our early work, we were not attentive enough to this vulnerability and lost some families from therapy by moving too quickly into painful areas.

Because each situation is unique, because there are no answers, and because AIDS affects such diverse populations, we like to think of the therapist's role as that of a caring and thoughtful companion on a voyage. Although sometimes they may guide or use strategic interventions, therapists working with families of AIDS/ARC patients will not be exclusively strategic, systemic, or structural. They will use elements from all of these approaches to help the family through the illness.

CREATING A CONTEXT
FOR ONGOING THERAPY

The therapist should frame counseling as an ongoing process whose nature and frequency will be calibrated to meet the varying psychosocial demands of the disease. Most often, counseling consists of intermittent, brief, intensive work as the family or patient undergoes a physical or emotional crisis. Placing the individual PWA or family members in support groups provides a context for networking and problem solving that substitutes for ongoing intensive individual or family counseling and alleviates the burden for the therapist. Although counseling may be intermittent, the family should be encouraged to experience the agency as an ongoing refuge, available to them not only during the time when illness is active but also during its aftermath, that time when its shadow still affects family and individual functioning.

Family counseling can be conceptualized as following critical phases of the disease that present the family and individual with specific illness tasks. The first phase, that of diagnosis of either HIV infection or the opportunistic infections, which signal that the disease process is active, creates a crisis of acceptance and adaptation that may be accompanied by intense grief or denial.

At diagnosis, the HIV-infected person may experience a wide range of emotions. He or she may be wildly angry one week, vividly remembering past situations of abuse and powerlessness. In the next week, he or she may have buried illness in work. He or she may feel guilty and bargain with God by denying any sexual feelings or needs: "Sex is the last thing on my mind." Or he or she may deny illness or vulnerability to further infection by increasing promiscuity or unprotected drug use. If the client is gay, he or she may show an increase of homophobia, blaming sexual orientation as evidence of "badness"; or he or she may become heterophobic, making it difficult for him or her to relate to the straight professionals with whom he or she now has to deal. Women infected by sexual partners whom they did not know were infected may experience cycles of rage and depression and they will certainly worry for the future of their children. Immediate practical tasks include dealing with issues of sexuality and making decisions about disclosure to family members, especially sexual partners. This is always a painful experience requiring much patience on the part of the therapist as he or she helps the client work through complex emotions that inevitably include fears of rage and abandonment by the partner. The therapist also will inevitably worry about the partner's safety in the face of the client's reluctance to disclose. It should be remembered that, in the long run, it is far better for the client to have the experience of being in charge of disclosure than for the therapist to usurp this responsibility. The therapist can buy time by helping the client find strategies for keeping the partner safe from further risk of infection while he or she works through his or her fears. Because AIDS diagnosis is demoralizing, it is important to help the client again perceive him- or herself as a person of strength and courage. It is often helpful to have the client identify other instances where he or she has had the courage to take a difficult but morally correct course of action.

For women, the necessity to disclose infection to those family members on whom they may be ultimately dependent for help with their children becomes a major issue in the face of fears of community ostracism. Because most women depend on social networks for a sense of well-being, the experience of being isolated from a partner, friends, or family because of a diagnosis of HIV infection may be emotionally devastating.

Disclosure is also an issue for the gay man. He may wonder which friends he can trust and solve these problems by isolating himself when he desperately needs companionship. He may become dependent on a helping professional or volunteer. If he has had a traumatic experience coming out to his family of origin about being gay, he may wonder if he dares acknowledge the HIV diagnosis. Yet he, too, may be dependent on family help if he becomes severely ill. Support groups for HIV-positive persons may provide valuable information and a shared experience that has the effect of normalizing emotional response.

During the crisis of diagnosis and as the family becomes ready to absorb information, the therapist should be able to impart medical information about the illness itself—etiology, symptoms, expected illness course, uses and side effects of basic medications, conditions conducive to optimal living, and environmental determinants of exacerbation. Frequently, the initial contact with the therapist provides family members with their first opportunity to explore the medical questions that concern them. There are relatively few doctors specializing in infectious disease in the large cities where AIDS populations are concentrated, and many clients (particularly those from backgrounds of poverty) are fearful of pressing their doctors for information. As a result, they remain unaware of the potentially helpful protocols available to them both as anti-virals and as prophylaxis against the most common opportunistic infections. In addition, the therapist must attend to prevention issues particular to HIV infection, which clients may be reluctant to raise. Often the client reveals that many people in the family are at risk for infection and do not have access to HIV-prevention information. The family system then becomes a point of entry for introducing such information to a large number of people.

To raise these issues, the therapist must take the lead in setting the agenda for therapy, for example, helping clients practice safer sex and helping drug users prevent bloodborne infection by cleaning works. For other populations at risk for AIDS, the complex issues of safer sex practice must be explored. For many people—particularly those from African-American, Latino, and African-Caribbean families—sexuality is an intensely private issue. Couples will avoid dealing with issues of sexual transmission because they are embarrassed to talk about sex, uncomfortable with condom use, and ashamed to acknowledge their discomfort. The therapist must be prepared to raise these issues with sensitivity and to keep them in the forefront of therapy until complex sociocultural, gender, and psychological issues determining sexual practice are resolved.

After diagnosis, fears of contamination cause many couples to cease having sexual relations altogether. The clinician's job is to be positive about reduced-risk sex, helping the couple to discover new and more creative avenues for sexual expression and physical intimacy. This work involves both an explanation of feelings and fears and an educative approach. For other couples, negotiation of safer sex in the face of infection may be extremely hard. If the well "partner" is a woman from a minority group, she may have a hard time breaking cultural taboos against being assertive and knowledgeable in sexual areas. The therapist may have to coach her to become insistent on her right to sexual protection at the same time as she repeatedly challenges the infected partner's denial of his illness and ability to contaminate.

The symptomatic phase is accompanied by tasks of managing the intrusion of medical systems and of reorganizing the care system to manage the recurrent crises and calm periods that characterize the illness. For families, a central task is to create a meaning for life with illness that can encompass the vastly changing demands of the disease and provide space for the family to accomplish non-illness related tasks.

Another critical task is to alert family members to signs of deteriorating health or the onset of an opportunistic infection. The family may bring the AIDS patient for counseling, attributing symptoms of depression or anxiety to relationship issues or interpreting them as reactions to illness when, in fact, a subtle process of neurological infection or reaction to medications is involved. Because so many opportunistic infections involve the central nervous system (CNS), psychotic behaviors and symptoms such as loss of mental acuity, forgetfulness, deadening of affect, and psychomotor retardation, which may look like symptoms of psychological depression, may be due to the virus or to drugs used to treat the virus and not to the patient's psychological context.

As the PWA becomes increasingly ill and enters a terminal phase, the family or care network has to help him or her manage the increasingly debilitating and often frightening symptoms of AIDS and ultimately prepare for death. Life-prolonging measures have to be weighed against quality of life in the context of the patient's wishes. Although some patients may wish to deny the gravity of their situation until the end, a denial that must be respected, most patients will be comforted if they can participate in planning for the future of their children, family, or partner.

Future-oriented questions may be of particular use with AIDS patients and their families because chronic or terminal illness introduces a sense of "frozen time"—a sense that change and evolution must stop in order to preserve the fragile structure the family has achieved (Penn, 1983, 1985). The gradual introduction of a sense of future—even if it includes planning for the life after the ill person's death—is healing. In a sense, the "time-ice" begins to melt and the ill person and family members experience themselves once more as part of the changing flow of *living* systems. Asking the dying person to participate in planning an optimistic future for the people he or she will leave is an immensely healing experience.

When the person with AIDS has died, the family enters a period of bereavement and reorganization. For many families, the secrecy that accompanies AIDS complicates the mourning process, depriving the family of normal social supports that alleviate grief. Moreover, because the dead person may have left behind others who are infected, the grieving process may be quite different from that which follows death from other diseases. If the dead person has been the source of infection for a partner, or for children, the experience of loss and grief may be dominated by periods of anger and fear that preclude the normal work of mourning.

Reorganization following the loss of a person to AIDS may be a complicated process both for partners and for families. Boyd-Franklin's (1989) suggestion that therapy be framed as an ongoing process is useful here. In this model, during the "termination" process which closes each piece of work, the family is helped to understand that it is normal for crises to occur. They are sensitized to identify events that call for therapeutic help and are encouraged to return. Follow-up telephone calls are an important way of defining the counselor's ongoing commitment to the family's well-being.

Families should be actively encouraged to return for a periodic checkup, even after AIDS seems to have disappeared as an active presence in the family. Both the trauma of the AIDS disease process and events surrounding the cause of HIV infection (e.g., drug use by the deceased person or the cut-off from a gay child) may have traumatized the family. As a result, many of these families are highly vulnerable to destabilization following some relatively minor crisis or dislocation.

An example of the lengthy shadow that AIDS can cast over family life can be seen in the following case vignette:

When Bobby's mother died of AIDS, he and his three siblings went to live with different maternal relatives. His father was alive at the time but also dying of AIDS. Because Bobby's father had been a drug user who had infected Bobby's mother, he was ejected from the family and left to die alone. Bobby grieved for his father but could not speak of his feelings in his mother's family. Instead, during the time of his mother's dying, he got in trouble in school and started to steal. Everybody said he would end up just like his father. His mother's sister and her new husband decided to adopt Bobby after his mother's death. Bobby liked his new uncle and was proud that his uncle believed in him and would give him another chance. Bobby did well for the first three years after his mother's death. But then his aunt and uncle had a baby of their own. Bobby began to act out in school so badly that the family considered placement. During a follow-up telephone call, the adoptive parents made it clear that they had not connected this crisis with events related to AIDS. They had not understood that the traumatic disease process of AIDS had left the boy terrified of further displacement and loss. As Bobby found himself driven to act out by the terror of displacement by a biological child, he became caught up in a self-fulfilling prophecy that he would end up like his father, and that in the end he, too, would be cast out of the family. The family could not make these connections because, for them, the agonizing experience of AIDS was a sealed chapter in their lives. Unfortunately, this painful chapter needed to be re-opened if the meaning of Bobby's present experience and the behavior that resulted from it were to be understood.

Understanding Common Patterns in Couple's Treatment

Even though each therapy has its own rhythm, the particular issues that surround AIDS seem to create patterns that are common to treatment. If the therapist can anticipate these patterns, he or she will be better prepared for the upheavals inherent in this very difficult therapy.

The majority of people with HIV infection will be dealing with a primary couple relationship that is emotionally charged with AIDS-related fears of contamination and by a confusion of anger, guilt, blame, and love. In the therapy of couples where one or both partners are infected, there is usually a belief about which partner introduced HIV into the relationship. As a result of this belief and the emotions that accompany it, therapy often follows a predictable pattern.

In the initial phase of therapy, the couple presents with relationship problems (i.e., fighting, worry about how the PWA is coping with his disease, sexual problems ranging from lack of sexual activity and desire to conflicting wishes for more or less sex). Both partners are often protective of each other and the relationship. There may be some denial of deeper issues.

Frequently, therapy rapidly creates a "solution" as the presenting problem seems to be resolved. The couple becomes more intimate, often resuming sexual contact. This period of stability and increased intimacy seems to lead to a safety zone in which the partner with AIDS may feel a need to "confess," that is, to share with his or her partner previously secret past behaviors that may have led to the disease. Or the care partner may feel freer to openly confront his or her ambivalence about staying in the relationship. In one case, a man confessed that his previous lover had died of AIDS before his new relationship began. He had never told his new lover of the existence of that partner. In another case, a man confessed his varied extramarital relationships to his wife.

This confessional phase may be received with a display of rage or by the partner initially denying overt anger. As anger surfaces, other relationship issues become attached to it and a stormy period of reevaluation follows in which the whole relationship may be called into question. This reevaluation may be followed by a period of crisis. As self-punishment, the PWA may decide to leave the relationship or may have suicidal thoughts. He may increase his attempts to provoke the partner to kick him out. The partner may become depressed or violent or even leave for periods of time as he tries to make sense of what has happened. If the relationship survives this period of crisis, a reconciliation with a new level of intimacy may follow, with the care partner committed to seeing the AIDS process through.

Empowering the Family

The therapist should empower the family to believe in its own capacities for problem solution and illness management. By carefully helping family members explore and define beliefs about illness and death, hopes for alleviation or cure, and skepticism about the limits of medical interventions, the therapist encourages them to resume control of their lives in relation to illness. By addressing the way in which a family's shared and individual beliefs are implicated in illness, the therapist helps the family gain the confidence to see illness as a deeply personal event rather than as an event belonging to the professionals involved. The family members are encouraged to handle illness in a way that honors their deepest beliefs and to defend their decisions even when those decisions are at variance with advice offered by medical professionals.

Reframing Family Narratives

To make sense out of the chaos of our existence, people weave events into explanatory narratives. These narratives frequently depend on "labeling practices" including scientific classification and the objectification of individuals (White & Epston, 1990) as a way of organizing all information. These classifications are, in reality, only constructed ideas that are accorded a truth status but, as White has said, "These truths are normalizing in the sense that they construct norms around which people are incited to shape or constitute their lives" (White & Epston, 1990, p. 20), just as they also shape the information that the observer will observe. For example, in the conventional medical model, diagnosis is used as if it represents a person's total identity: "He is a manic-depressive, schizophrenic, obsessive-compulsive, narcissistic personality." The person is objectified when we construct a dominant narrative out of what seems to be deviant behavior. He or she is then assigned membership in a group considered as deviant, for example, hemophiliacs, AIDS victims, or homosexuals. This group membership represents a central identity around which we organize our understanding of all other behaviors.

By contrast, systemic therapists see behaviors not as fixed and classifiable, but as relative, flowing from the contexts which they, in turn, shape. Behaviors are, in turn, subject to change as new information changes those contexts. Nevertheless, certain behaviors may become fixed because the premises that are attached to them create dominant narratives that preclude the system's access to other information. As a result, a dominant narrative, particularly one that invokes classification, shapes the loop between the social system's view of an individual and the individual's perception of himself or herself in the social system. The knowledge that a person has AIDS immediately locates him or her within certain possible classifications, which then become dominant narratives, dictating how others perceive him or her and how the PWA perceives himself or herself. Such classifications include terminally ill, AIDS victim, drug addict, homosexual, and/or sexually promiscuous. The visibility of AIDS means that the infected person can no longer pass as "normal"; instead, he, for instance, must embrace a stigmatizing classification that reduces him "from a whole and usual person to a tainted and discounted one" (Goffman, 1986, p. 3). The stigmatized identity breaks "the claim that his usual attributes have on us" (Goffman, 1986, p. 5). If he once passed as "normal," he now experiences a denial of the respect people have usually accorded his uncontaminated identity. The stigmatized person now completes the recursive cycle by operating as if some of his own attributes warrant the stigma (Goffman, 1986). Stigma isolates the person with AIDS from surrounding systems and often extends to the family, as members become categorized, stigmatized, and isolated because of their association with him. The insistence on the use of the phrase "person with AIDS" (PWA) by the PWA Coalition was a response to the dehumanizing terms "AIDS victim" and "AIDS patient," which subsumed the person's identity in his illness designation.

For most families, the prevailing narrative about the AIDS illness and the ill person generates challenging problems. Because of the association of AIDS with behavior considered to be socially deviant, the illness narrative may become fixed and rigid. Feelings about drug use or homosexuality are often linked to feelings about the person dying. Families may believe that AIDS is a punishment for a family member's *choice* to be gay. Although the family may care for the ill person, they may continue to condemn his life choice. In this version, the ill person is subsumed in the category "gayness"; attitudes are defined by his participation in the category "gay." Illness is seen as punishment and equated with death, and the family role is identified as compassionate attendance while he dies. The message to the patient is that family members can be loving toward him as long as he is dying, but if he lives they will have problems with his life-style. These messages are powerful and, in turn, may define the patient's attitude toward the meaning of his own illness and impending death.

To open possibilities for new and different interactions among family members, the therapist constructs alternative narratives about the AIDS patient, offering an opportunity to escape the rigid category of "drug addict" or "homosexual" that has dominated family members' relationship with him. For example, the therapist does not focus on the family divisions created by the client's homosexuality but instead emphasizes other aspects of the family narrative. Asking a gay son, "Could you tell your father what you have learned from him?" elicits an affirmation of valued connections, creating what hypnotists have called a "yes set" in the father. If the father is to accept his son's affirmation of the positive qualities his son has learned by observing him, then he must say yes to the corollary, "I, as your son, am at least in part that which you have made me." The constructed narrative becomes one about the difficulties and successes of the father–son relationship. The message to the father is clear: "What is most important here is your son's role as a son and your role as a father—not whether or not he is gay." Reframing is one way of introducing alternative constructions that disrupt the tedious regularity of the problem focus and allow other patterns to emerge. Sometimes the family itself will spontaneously create new, transforming narratives out of the experience of AIDS.

A crucial aspect of our work is attending to the flow of meanings each person in the family assigns to the disease itself. Illness meanings are generated at all system levels, from the societal to the familial to the personal. The prevailing social narrative defining our relationship with AIDS is its silent, omnipresent fatality. The infected person lives in a culture where AIDS equals DEATH. Gay Men's Health Crisis (the largest AIDS social service agency in the world) and the PWA Coalition have constructed an alternative narrative in which the experience of AIDS is one of constructing a meaningful life in the face of a sometimes painful, chronic condition. This fundamental reframing of the disease allows space for living and for making life decisions that might not seem to matter if the AIDS process were constructed only as preparation for death.

Usually, the illness narrative dominates family life and obliterates the family's sense of itself as a surviving and functioning unit. Problems may loom so large that family members cannot see their capacity for resolving them. Often, the problem focus is so extensive that they cannot identify friends, relatives, or outsiders who could play a positive role in problem solution. The therapist works to enlarge the family's awareness of potential helpers, with the understanding that increasing the flow of information to the family and its sense of connectedness to a wider network will provide increased support and options.

Mapping the Family Illness Structure

The therapist maps the pre- and post-illness family structure to help the family return as much as possible to a pre-illness unit. To ascertain which problem behaviors occurred before diagnosis, the therapist takes a careful history of family development, exploring how family members have handled crises in the past and what options are open to them in the current crisis. *Circular questioning*, a technique developed by the early Milan team (Penn, 1982) to rapidly gather information about the structure and organization of a family without arousing resistance, forms the basis of the structured assessment interview. The questions induce family members into a method of systemic thinking in which they examine how beliefs influence behaviors. Thus, family members are able to identify illness-generated coping patterns and to seek a balance between illness needs and normative family needs and functions. Pre- and post-illness functioning is usefully mapped in such areas as school, work, marital satisfaction, parent–child relationships, extended family relationships, and drug and alcohol use.

One aspect of understanding the family's pre-illness structure is the mapping of the development of family coalitions. Rigid coalitions can be seen as a response to the threat of family disorganization under the extraordinary stress of AIDS. In essence, family members hold onto and reiterate the known, almost as though it were a mantra, in the face of uncertainty and potential loss. Unlike other chronic illnesses, AIDS assaults the family's position in the community as well as exacerbating conflict between family members. In families with the greatest resistance to changing coalition patterns, we have discovered that these patterns were established during similar experiences of illness in the previous generations. Only by addressing the past as it is reincarnated in the present have we been able to shift these dynamics (Sheinberg, 1983; Walker, 1983). As family structure becomes more flexible and as deeply felt emotional needs of healthy family members find avenues for satisfaction, illness meaning begins to change in the direction of alleviating psychological pain.

Another aspect of understanding the pre- and post-illness structure is to understand the structure of interpersonal relationships as they existed before illness and as they have evolved during the course of illness. One way of describing relationships which family therapists have considered useful is in terms of the balance of power between the participants. Relationships are considered symmetrical if both partners negotiate power issues from a relatively equal status. They are considered to be complementary if one partner is dominant in decisionmaking situations, the other submissive. Most stable couples relationships contain some areas of complementarity and other areas where the partners are relatively equal.

How power is distributed in a relationship may have particular significance during illness as the ill person experiences loss of autonomy and the well partner assumes increasing decisionmaking power. The roles that partners assume in critical relationships may be fundamental to their sense of identity. Physical illness creates an emotional disordering of relationships, which may be fiercely resisted.

Therapists who do not understand the structure of the couple's interaction, as it existed before the occurrence of illness, may find themselves sympathizing with a compelling series of complaints from the ill person, well partner, or family but unable to change the interpersonal context. For example, one PWA sought help because his well partner, who had always been helpless and dependent in their relationship, seemed to become even more dependant as the illness worsened. The ill man's repeated requests for help seemed to fall on deaf ears. In fact, the therapist was blind to the subtle ways by which the PWA sabotaged each competent act his partner made. Any shift in the time-honored complementarity of their relationship was experienced as a threat to its familiar structure, at a time when illness made their partnership seem particularly vulnerable.

For this PWA who had always been the dominant partner, admitting his new dependency might have threatened his use of control in the relationship as a psychological defense against his own fears of dependency. In fact, he had grown up as an overresponsible only child of an extremely needy, bitterly unhappy divorced mother. As a result, his childhood experience was one of either repressing his own needs to care for his mother or being punished psychologically if he demanded anything for himself. He brought a tremendous anger and fear to his adult relationships, which he concealed by being a devoted caretaker to dysfunctional partners. Were he to lose his role of caretaker and allow himself to experience the vulnerability of dependency just as the ravages of illness were also robbing him of a sense of control, deep-seated childhood terrors would clearly be re-evoked. On the other hand, if he refuses to give up control and to allow his partner to care for him, he may become exhausted and vulnerable to infection.

The paradox is obvious. As one sensitive but seemingly dysfunctional care partner put it, "If I take over more, he will lose the stubborn way he controls everything. And that stubbornness is what he uses to fight his illness. Things might go better for us, but I would worry for him." This man refused family therapy because he feared for his partner, were he to change the structure of their interaction. Individual therapy in a systems context allowed the therapist to understand the dance and gradually to help the AIDS patient retain control by giving him strategies for changing his partner's behavior. Because he had the illusion of retaining control because he was "orchestrating" his partner's caretaking of him, he could permit himself to be more comfortable with the new situation. As a balance for the loss of control in his relationship he dedicated himself to teaching others his profession.

In some instances, the PWA may have been subordinate in the pre-illness relationship. If AIDS has tipped the balance of power in the relationship too far in the direction of the dominant partner and increased the sense of powerlessness in the subordinate partner, the latter may have no other tactics to gain power except by using his illness to fight the dominant partner's attempts to control him by resisting needed medical help.

Identifying Family Resources

The therapist should help the family identify resources both inside and outside of the family. As systems therapists, we defined "family" in its broadest sense, as an intimate network surrounding the person with AIDS infection, which might include a lover, spouse, a tight group of friends, or the family of origin or procreation. By skillfully utilizing the network, we hoped that the professional or volunteer would find his or her task of caring for the ill or dying patient immeasurably lightened.

One technique that can inform the therapist of unexpected areas of strength and expand the family narrative is working with the family to create a family resource eco-map (Hartman & Laird, 1983). The eco-map resembles a genogram but is broader and includes family members past and present, extended kin systems, significant friends, and larger systems (medical, welfare, child protection, and volunteer agencies), with notations about the degree of involvement with the identified patient. The family or ill person is encouraged to analyze the interconnections among people in the system, to identify the positive effects of persons who might not be thought of as "family," to ascertain whether or not they represent potential resources for caregiving, and to pinpoint problematic interfaces between involved systems.

HIV diagnosis may mean that the family is separated from normal healing rituals, family gatherings, friendship groups, and church groups. Such isolation inevitably increases stress. The eco-map can identify systems that have been helpful to the family before diagnosis and with which reconnection would be healing. In addition, the eco-map identifies allied and conflicting systems as well as workers who have entered the family's life post-diagnosis and who may be dominating family life in a detrimental manner.

The therapist can serve as an organizer and facilitator of meetings attended by representatives of the various systems with whom the family is involved. These systems may include health-care professionals, schools, child welfare, foster care, homemakers, and volunteers. Clarifying roles and developing a unified treatment plan in collaboration with the patient and the family can increase efficiency of care provision, just as such a meeting can be empowering and comforting to the family.

A systemic crisis intervention approach allows the professional to develop hypotheses necessary for devising a parsimonious and pragmatic treatment plan that utilizes the resources of the natural unit as identified in the eco-map. In the following clinical example, a team was asked by a hospital social worker for a consultation family assessment with a PWA mother and her school-phobic son:

> *The hospital social worker had attempted to get the son to school but felt the boy's school avoidance was a regression due to his mother's illness. In the family interview, it became clear that the son was able to attend afterschool activities that began when his stepfather came home from work. The hypothesis developed in the family session, and confirmed by the boy, was that he stayed at home because his lonely mother was frightened of becoming ill when alone. Constructing an eco-map with the mother and son allowed the consultant to see that the mother had a large extended family who lived at some distance from her but within the same city. She had been out of touch with them after she was diagnosed with AIDS. She was ashamed of her infection, which had been caused by drug use. A severe bout of pneumocystis pneumonia had made her unable to work. As a result she had no money for a telephone. In light of this information, the boy's behavior could be understood as overresponsible rather than regressive. Because the social worker had interviewed family members separately, she had missed the simple explanation for what was being rapidly constructed as a psychological problem (i.e., regression) that was impossible to solve. A clear assessment led to a clear treatment plan. The first goal was to organize family and Medicare to get the mother a telephone so that she could resume contact with a potential support system of family members from whom she had isolated herself. If the mother was in contact with an active support system, the boy would be relieved of assuming total responsibility for his mother and could return to school.*

Mobilizing Extrafamilial Supports

AIDS isolates. The therapist should encourage the family to become connected to community support systems, which can relieve AIDS isolation. Many families and individuals feel alienated from normal social discourse as they struggle in secrecy with emotional issues unique to AIDS, including guilt, shame, and mutual blame. As they try to cope with the terrors of an illness whose ravages are trumpeted in the press, they find themselves enduring hostility, contempt, fear, and inadequate care. To obtain desperately needed medications, they must fight endless red tape, only to find that they perhaps will be refused it because they do not fit a particular protocol.

The gay community has responded to the epidemic by founding self-help organizations that provide invaluable support networks for the ill and their caregivers, disseminate information, and empower people to become active in decisionmaking about treatment. Political groups like ACT-UP converted despair into activism, whereas groups such as the PWA Coalition and Body Positive helped people develop strategies for living positively with illness. Many programs use community volunteers to develop networks providing information and ongoing support to drug users and their families. Mothers' groups exist in many major hospitals, as well as in voluntary agencies, and can alleviate the isolation that both HIV-infected mothers and their infected children experience. Support groups should be seen as an invaluable addition to family resources.

CONCLUSION

In summary, the territory covered by the family therapist who works with AIDS, ARC, or sero-positive clients is unimaginably broad. It is also uncharted territory. Family therapists are aware how family structure affects the process of illness. We know how coalition structures, in the present and in the past, affect a family's experience of and coping with illness. However, we do not yet know how to help a family live with the Damoclean sword of an illness that may strike more than one family member. For partners, sexual contact, no matter how "safe," always carries an underlying threat of contamination. Families live with the fear that an open cut or sore may come into accidental contact with the AIDS patient's bodily fluids. Education cannot entirely alleviate irrational elements in any of these fears.

We have not had much recent experience in helping families manage illness while dealing with social stigma, enforced secrecy, and isolation. Because the majority of devastating epidemic illnesses have been brought under medical control, the losses of multiple family members and the orphaning of a generation of children are catastrophes more usually experienced in wars. Moreover, as family members struggle to make sense of their experience and draw together to help both those who are ill and those who will survive, they must first deal with devastating feelings of rage, blame, and guilt.

What has been remarkable about the work we are doing with families where there is AIDS is that, given the horror of the illness in its physical and psychosocial reality, the overwhelming experience for therapists has been of the strength and courage of families. The beauty of transformations witnessed, and of moments of shared connection between therapist and family, seems to underline what is important in living. A couple may work through all the violent emotions elicited by the illness and arrive at an intimacy, self-knowledge, and care never before experienced. A grandmother, losing her daughter, will overcome her grief to comfort and raise her three small grandchildren, amazing us with her steadfastness and wisdom. A gay lover will stand by his dying partner in the face of massive family opposition and find that the transforming experience of love has eradicated the last vestiges of his internalized homophobia, liberating him to celebrate his identity as a gay man. A dying man makes peace with a father who abused him and from whom he was estranged and both are healed in the process. A young couple decides to proceed with an adoption after they learn that their baby has AIDS and struggles with great love and tenacity to raise their child.

People with AIDS have translated their experience into a political movement that bears important ideas for therapists. People with AIDS refused to be labelled as AIDS patients and, by doing so, drew our attention to the way that we unthinkingly dehumanize people through practices of diagnosis and labelling. They demanded that we broaden our view of family to include the many kinds of families affected by the epidemic. They demanded that patient rights to information, to rapid access to new medications, and to broader powers of decisionmaking about illness be respected. They demonstrated that the most effective social service programs were community-based, provided comprehensive care, and could be effectively led and staffed by nonprofessionals. Finally, we saw that those families who became involved politically were strengthened by a collective energy. This political energy transformed depression into an anger that fueled political activism, and the despair of a fatal illness into a belief that breaking the silence that is death would constitute the legacy that the person with AIDS would leave to future generations.

REFERENCES

Boyd-Franklin, N. (1989). *Black families in therapy: A multisystem approach.* New York: Guilford Press.

Goffman, E. (1986). *Stigma: Notes on the management of spoiled identity.* New York: Simon & Schuster.

Gonzales, S., Steinglass, P., & Reiss, D. (1987). *Family centered interventions for people with chronic disabilities.* Washington, DC: George Washington University Medical Center, Rehabilitation Research and Training Center, Department of Psychiatry and Behavioral Science.

Hartman, A., & Laird, J. (1983). *Family centered social work practice.* New York: Free Press.

Needle, R., Leach, S., & Graham-Tomasi, R. (1989). HIV epidemic: Epidemiological implications for family professionals. In E. Macklin (Ed.), AIDS and families: Report of the AIDS Task Force, Groves Conference on Marriage and the Family. In *Marriage and Family Review, 13,* 13–34.

Penn, P. (1982). Circular questioning. *Family Process, 21,* 267–280.

Penn, P. (1983). Coalitions and binding interactions in families with chronic illness. *Family Systems Medicine, 1,* 16–25.

Penn, P. (1985). Feed-forward, future questions, future maps. *Family Process, 24,* 299–310.

Reiss, D. (1981). *The family's construction of reality.* Cambridge, MA: Harvard University Press.

Scheinberg, M. (1983). Creating a context of observation and the separation of patterns in chronic illness families. *Journal of Strategic and Systemic Therapies, 5,* 409–425.

Sontag, S. (1979). *Illness as metaphor.* New York: Vintage.

Sontag, S. (1989). *AIDS and its metaphors.* New York: Farrar Strauss Giroux.

Walker, G. (1983). The pact: The caretaker parent/ill child coalition in families with chronic illness. *Family Systems Medicine, 1,* 6–29.

White, M., & Epston, D. (1990). *Narrative means to therapeutic ends.* New York: Norton.

15

FAMILY HEALTH PSYCHOLOGY: DEFINING A NEW SUBDISCIPLINE

T. John Akamatsu
Kent State University

The potential influences of family factors on health and illness are numerous and varied. In the foregoing chapters, many important issues have been reviewed and discussed by authors to provide an updated literature review and to point to future directions for a field that is currently in a seminal stage of development. In the initial section, health cognitions and prevention were discussed. In the second section, family and marital factors in chronic illnesses were covered. Finally, intervention issues were addressed in the last section. In utilizing this course of illness organization it was hoped that adequate coverage of this large domain would be insured so that initial steps could be taken to identify and define important elements in a new subdiscipline, family health psychology.

The purpose of this chapter is to discuss some of these elements, first, in terms of general considerations in defining the new subdiscipline, and then in terms of specific issues relevant to theory, research, and intervention. Material from the preceding chapters and from the discussion at the Forum conference are the major sources for this chapter.

GENERAL CONSIDERATIONS

Family Considerations

Clearly, there are myriad factors that could potentially influence health and illness, and it would be impossible to consider all of them simultaneously in studying health and illness phenomena. The family provides a way of organizing at least some of these factors and thus can facilitate our investigation of them. Within the family are subsumed genetic factors, developmental issues, and socialization processes that can have a direct impact on family members. In addition, external factors such as socioeconomic status, cultural diversity, the effects of poverty, and so forth, are also largely reflected in family characteristics. Because of this overarching quality, a family focus encompasses a number of different elements and allows consideration of multiple influences. This is true whether or not a systems view is adopted.

The importance of considering family systems issues in examining the role of the family in illness and health should remain a central tenet of the new subdiscipline. However, the difficulties inherent in studying the family system as a system pose a significant challenge to the researcher. For example, current statistical procedures have difficulty dealing with the nonindependent observations that characterize systemic perspectives. One solution to this dilemma is to remember that adopting a systems view does not necessarily mean that all components of the system need to be considered at once. Indeed, as suggested by Coyne and Fiske (Chapter 9), the couple may be a more appropriate unit of investigation. Carried one step further, it is also possible to study individuals from a family systems perspective. The systems view can be thought of as an organizing principle or perhaps as a latent variable underlying more easily measured phenomena. It is interesting to note that a current issue in family therapy in general concerns the dynamic of individual versus systems considerations (Nichols & Schwartz, 1991).

The way in which the family is defined is another critical consideration. Traditional definitions involving a married couple with children are no longer appropriate for a growing number of single parent, gay and lesbian, and blended family arrangements. In some subcultures, grandparents, other relatives, friends, or even local community figures may play prominent roles in the family system. In considering family data, it is important to recognize the definition of the family utilized by the investigator because generalization may be problematic.

The Influence of Work from Existing Disciplines

Many of the contributions from existing disciplines to family health psychology are highlighted in the foregoing chapters. Yet, there are risks in the wholesale adoption of theory, research, or interventions from existing disciplines. For example, family systems theory and family therapy were developed in the context of family pathology and its treatment. Such a context may not be appropriate for a family that is merely responding to stress in normative ways. Adopting a family therapy mode in this case may pathologize what are really normal, adaptive processes.

Conversely, a stress and coping approach may outline healthy pathways in the process of normal adaptation and provide beneficial symptomatic relief but may miss important systemic contributions to pathological family circumstances, including dysfunctional communication, problematic structural features, or behaviors that maintain the problem. For example, a family's overconcern for an infirm elder member may lead to that person's taking too much medication, resulting in confusion that is then interpreted as senile dementia (Weakland & Fisch, 1985). Moreover, positive effects of the illness on the family may be overlooked. These could include a disruption of family functioning that may make it more amenable to intervention, increased communication and expression of mutual concern during an illness crisis, and recommitment and reorganization within the family following an illness crisis.

Another shortcoming in existing disciplines has been a failure to address issues of diversity. Much of the literature on health risk factors, for example, is based on data collected from white men. Data from women and minority groups are sorely lacking. Gender and gender roles issues are highlighted by Coyne and Fiske (Chapter 9). Several authors in this volume conclude that women bear the brunt of the burden in coping with illnesses, highlighting the need for future emphasis on gender issues.

Similarly, with a few exceptions (e.g., Ho, 1987; McGoldrick, Pearse, & Giordano, 1982), family systems theory and family therapy are based largely on work with white middle-class families. Much of the health psychology literature also suffers from a lack of consideration of minority issues. In defining a new subdiscipline, it is important to assess which cultural differences do and do not make a difference in conceptualizing, assessing, and intervening with minority populations. It is hoped that if such issues are recognized and addressed from the onset, the subdiscipline can avoid some of the problems experienced by existing disciplines.

It is also important to include evaluation of the effects of larger societal and public policy issues in studying families and health and illness. Societal factors such as racism, poverty, and the economic environment as well as policy issues regarding health care, health insurance, and maternity leave are critical elements in understanding familial factors. As is discussed subsequently, future development in the theoretical, research, and intervention areas will be enhanced by consideration of societal and policy issues.

Lastly, the importance of interdisciplinary collaboration should be highlighted. As has been emphasized in a number of places in this volume, the existing disciplines have often worked in isolation, independent of other disciplines and often uninformed of developments in other areas. The lively discussion that characterized the Forum conference owed much to the diversity among participants. Clearly, family health psychology should capitalize on the integration of input from varied disciplines in pursuing knowledge in the new subdiscipline.

THEORETICAL DIRECTIONS

It is unlikely that one overarching theoretical model will emerge as preeminent in family health psychology. As seen in the foregoing chapters, the field is diverse and numerous theoretical underpinnings are represented in previous work from existing disciplines. Family systems theories, family adaptation to illness approaches, and family and health models have all had a role in bringing us to our current state of knowledge. In family health psychology, instead of a "true" theory, what may be more useful is a series of "sensitizing concepts" to guide future work in the area.

Such sensitizing concepts should be designed to help identify areas of study, relevant variables, and appropriate interventions. In addition, these concepts should lead to differential prediction and be empirically validated. In this way, a firm knowledge base can be established without an overarching grand theory that cover all components of the field.

Although it is obvious that existing theories cannot and should not be adopted in their current forms, they do provide useful information regarding potentially important sensitizing concepts that may be of value in family health psychology.

Contributions from Family Systems Theories

Family systems based theory provides some fruitful concepts for further exploration. Although it is not an intervention based model, Pratt's (1976) notion of the energized family may be useful in identifying characteristics of families who are particularly resilient in the face of illness. The flexibility and independence shown by members of energized families as well as the positive effects of support and encouragement for efforts at coping warrants further exploration. This work has particular relevance to the health promotion and prevention areas. Minuchin's (1974) model offers a means of identifying structural elements in the family system that may be of relevance in families dealing with chronic illness (e.g., Penn, 1983). The pattern of coalitions and alliances among family members and nature of the hierarchical organization within the family may provide useful insights into the functioning of such families.

Reiss's (1989) family paradigm approach emphasizes each family's unique nature, offers a system to categorize different families along common dimensions, and emphasizes the tailoring of interventions to the particular family, based on its unique attributes. The model may also be of value in suggesting ways to assess how families process information coming into the system and how this information is dealt with. Steinglass's life-history model (Steinglass, Bennett, Wolin, & Reiss, 1987), developed in the context of alcoholism, could be expanded to illuminate the effects of illness in general in disrupting family life cycle and development. Focus on these aspects of the family could provide sensitizing concepts that have not yet been widely applied in the existing literature.

Lastly, crisis theory (e.g., Parad, 1965), which views crisis as an opportunity or challenge that can lead the family in new directions, may also provide clues to adaptive elements in family functioning that will maximize the success in dealing with illness or making changes in health-promoting behaviors.

Contributions from Adaptation to Illness Models

Theoretical models from health psychology that emphasize the family's adaptation to stress or illness also provide useful concepts that deserve further investigation. The FAAR (Patterson, 1988) and the Varni and Wallander (1988) models (see Drotar, Chapter 12) are of particular value because they incorporate both stress and coping and family factors. Elaboration of these models such as Drotar's (Chapter 12) inclusion of family socialization factors may be productive. Hobfoll's (1988) model has also addressed family issues in terms of increased stress among mothers with children who have chronic illnesses. It is distinctive in its consideration of the role of conservation of resources in dealing with stress and in its testability but would need to be recast in family terms to be best used in family health psychology. This adaptation has, in part, been attempted in a more recent work (Hobfoll & Spielberger, in press).

Contributions from Family and Health Models

Family and health models also suggest useful concepts for further elaboration. Family aggregation approaches (Baranowski & Nader, 1985) indicate that health behaviors among family members tend to be similar, suggesting that family factors do have an influence on health behaviors. Although genetic and environmental factors underlie this process, the complex mechanisms of this influence deserve further study. On a similar note, concepts such as *intrafamilial transmission* of health beliefs among family members (Susman et al., 1982; see Gochman, Chapter 3) deserve further inquiry. In spite of evidence suggesting few familial effects on health beliefs, definitive conclusions cannot yet be drawn on the basis of available data.

Contributions from Social Ecological Models

Lastly, it will be important to utilize a social-ecological perspective (Bronfrenbrenner, 1979) in any conceptualization of the family and health and illness. Consideration of the interaction of the individual with the family, and the interaction of the family with larger systems (e.g., the health care system and social services system) as well as societal factors (e.g., poverty, racism, etc.) will provide a truly systemic perspective in developing sensitizing concepts. Mesosocial had macrosocial factors must be included in a complete rendering of important concepts with family health psychology.

RESEARCH DIRECTIONS

Definition of the Family

As previously discussed, definition of what constitutes the family as a unit of study is problematic. This is particularly true in research in which precise definition is a key concern. Possible definitions range from a strict traditional view of a marital pair and children, to one in which family members define for themselves who constitutes their family. It is not feasible or appropriate to attempt to develop a standard definition of the family. In fact, divergent definitions may be necessary, depending on the research question or the composition of the group that is being studied. It is important, therefore, for researchers to carefully specify the particular family unit that they are investigating, and their reasons for doing so, to ensure generalizability of results to the appropriate target groups.

Definitions of Illness and Health

In a similar manner, it is important to be careful in how illness or health is defined. In several of the foregoing chapters it was noted that different illnesses may require different conceptual models or intervention strategies. It is neither feasible nor appropriate to approach illness as a unitary phenomenon, nor does it make sense to develop a different conceptual model or intervention program for each individual illness that is studied. Rather, what is required is an organizational structure within which to categorize illnesses along dimensions that are relevant for research or intervention purposes.

Rolland's (1984) model, which includes the dimension of onset, course, outcome, and degree of incapacitation, is a good example of the kind of typology that can be utilized to facilitate definition of illnesses into meaningful dimensions (Kazak, Chapter 7). Coyne and Fiske (Chapter 9) suggest the addition of two dimensions: "the degree to which the patient's health or dysfunction depend on the couple's coping efforts and the degree to which the couple can affect ultimate outcomes" (p. 138). Alternately, Jacobs (Chapter 8) indicates that degree of predictability, degree of disability, stigma, degree of monitoring, and certainty of prognosis may be useful in categorizing illnesses in terms of assessing the degree of challenge faced by families that experience them. It is thought that rather than adopting one prescribed set of dimensions to define an illness, it is possible for the researcher to choose those particular dimensions that are most appropriate for the phenomenon under investigation. Again, specification of which dimensions define the illness and the reasons for selecting them are important.

Although it may be somewhat less obvious, there are also difficulties in defining health. A simple definition of the absence of pathology is used by many investigators interested in the impact of illness, and few definitions of a normal family have been put forth (Kazak, Chapter 7). From a health promotion or prevention perspective, such a definition may be unsatisfactory. Expanded definitions of health might include adherence to health-promoting behaviors or treatment regimens, or the active practice of prevention techniques. A more precise definition of health can facilitate the evaluation of interventions designed to promote it.

Measurement Issues

The nature and development of instrumentation is another important challenge facing researchers in family health psychology. To capture important features of the phenomena to be studied, the use of focus groups (see Coyne & Fiske, Chapter 9) is recommended. In this methodology, relevant participants (patients, spouses, or other family members) meet to discuss the problems and issues they face in dealing with the illness, or health promotion or illness prevention issue under investigation. Relevant sensitizing concepts may be used to guide the discussion. This approach provides a view of the situation from the perspective of the participants rather than a view that is overly biased by the experimenter's preconceived notions about what is going on or what is important to study.

The information garnered in the focus group can be used to construct questionnaires that reflect the relevant and meaningful dimensions that characterize the participants' experience. Questionnaires can then be administered and reevaluated. Such a strategy ensures that research is empirically driven, theory informed, and not overly influenced by any biases the experimenter may hold.

The issue of standardization of instrumentation versus the meaningfulness of the data collected by their use should also be kept in mind. It is difficult for knowledge in an area to progress if different instruments are utilized in each study because the comparability of findings across studies is difficult to determine. Yet, wholesale adoption of existing standardized instruments may fail to capture the unique aspects of the new situation of which they are being utilized (Coyne & Fiske, Chapter 9) or may even distort results. It is, therefore, important for researchers to make careful decisions about the instrumentation that is selected.

It is hoped that as research progresses, individually tailored instrumentation will proliferate to a point where some will be found to be meaningful to the phenomenon under investigation as well as useful to other investigators. The categorization of illnesses, as discussed above, may facilitate the development of such instrumentation. Illnesses that are categorized in comparable ways may be amenable to study by the same instruments. A similar facilitative effect can also occur as sensitizing concepts within the field are identified, explored, and elaborated.

Family Development and Life Course

Several authors in this volume have emphasized the importance of considering family developmental or life course factors in designing research on families and health and illness. Many of the findings in this area of research may be mediated or moderated by the developmental stage of the family. Thus, in constructing research questions, designing studies, and interpreting results, life course issues must be evaluated or controlled. Clearly, longitudinal designs are needed to help elucidate these developmental issues.

Although not directly addressed in the Forum conference discussion, it should be noted that many of the authors in this volume utilize longitudinal designs in their current work. As noted by Jones (Chapter 10), such designs have not always been used in previous research on marital factors and illness. This is true in the prevention area (Roberts & McElreath, Chapter 4) and in other literatures as well. Perhaps the lack of discussion of this issue at the meeting is indicative of a strong feeling among participants that such designs are obviously necessary in making causal statements and so must be utilized in future research in family health psychology.

INTERVENTION DIRECTIONS

Because of roots in clinical psychology, psychiatry, social work, and family therapy, there may be a tendency to pathologize families when considering health and illness issues and to approach interventions from that perspective. In family health psychology, it will be important to develop and utilize interventions appropriate for families ranging from "normal" families who have difficulty maintaining health-promoting behaviors or who experience stress because of illness, to families in which the situation is exacerbated by varying degrees of pathology. Goals for intervention in such families need to be differentiated.

General Goals for Interventions with Families

Most families do not require psychotherapy or family therapy in facilitating health promotion or in dealing with illness in a family member. Rather, more normative and developmental issues need to be addressed. It is very likely that families experience a sense of helplessness in confronting the health or illness problems they experience. Therefore, a very basic goal is providing the family with a sense of empowerment, the feeling that they can do meaningful things to deal effectively with the situation in which they find themselves. This is true whether the family faces a prevention issue (Roberts & McElreath, Chapter 4) or a serious illness such as AIDS (Walker, Chapter 14). The instillation of hope and reduction of anxiety also help to bring the family to the point where further changes can be made.

Subsequent goals include increasing the family's sense of responsibility for making those changes that are appropriate for them. Facilitating adherence to treatment regimens, increasing social support, and enhancing normative efforts at coping with stress are examples of such changes. Other families may require assistance with normative transitions in family life such as the death of an elderly parent. Increased communication, both within the family and with the professionals involved in treatment, can also be helpful. Assisting the family in understanding and working with the health care system in general and with the particular setting in which they find themselves can also be of great benefit. Education about the illness itself, its causes, course, and treatment can do much to reduce uncertainty among family members.

Family Systems Goals

Other families may require more extensive intervention if pathological elements are present. A family therapy orientation would be most effective in intervening in such cases. As with "normal" families, encouragement and facilitation of communication is viewed as an important goal. In pathological families, this goal is a much more basic one, however, because dysfunctional communication may exacerbate other aspects of family pathology. Moreover, communication styles and patterns of interaction may be diagnostic of the underlying factors that result in pathology and require intervention.

Subsequent goals include identification and eradication of patterns of blame because, from a systems view, such patterns can interfere with effective coping on the part of family members. Unspoken hostility, guilt, or overprotectiveness can do much to inhibit appropriate behavior change among family members. Contextual factors within the family that maintain dysfunctional behavior patterns need to be identified and modified. For example, overprotectiveness of the caretaking spouse may inhibit the development of appropriate autonomy in the identified patient following an illness. In sum, full-fledged therapy may be required in the most pathological families. However, it is important to utilize only those family therapy interventions that meet the criteria of effectiveness that are outlined below.

Assessment

Clearly, adequate assessment is required before effective interventions can be designed. Identification of individual and individual family differences is perhaps the primary assessment task. Exploration of the ways in which the individual or family is unique and different from others may provide more important data in selecting or designing subsequent interventions than the conventional emphasis on how the individual or family is similar to others.

Assessment of the type of intervention that is needed (e.g., supportive therapy, psychoeducation, or family therapy) reflects issues raised by Drotar (Chapter 12) in regard to the need to target interventions. Considerations of the timing of the intervention should also be made. Interventions may be most effective during the most stressful periods in the family's experience (e.g., initial diagnosis, changes in status requiring hospitalization or extraordinary treatment, or deterioration; Drotar, Chapter 12).

Assessment of the family's view of the situation can help to personalize the intervention to fit with the family's view of determinants of health and illness, their health beliefs, and any cultural or ethnic beliefs that might be relevant. Steps should be taken to ensure that the intervention is one that the patient and the family can accept, and to be sure it is something that the family can complete.

Lastly, family strengths should be assessed, again, to facilitate personalization of the intervention to be utilized. Such an assessment can also help diffuse any tendency to overpathologize families and to highlight the unique attributes that characterize the family.

Components of Effective Interventions

Although discussion of specific interventions is beyond the scope of this chapter, some general features or characteristics of effective interventions can be delineated.

First, interventions should be based on a reasonably well-articulated theoretical model. Or, if they are empirically derived, the sensitizing concepts that led to their development should be specifiable. Second, interventions should be based on empirical data that demonstrate their effectiveness in comparable situations. Third, outcomes associated with the use of the intervention should be evaluated systematically.

Interventions should facilitate accomplishment of the goals outlined above. The educational and empowering aspects of interventions are paramount. Interventions should be designed to enhance family functioning and reduce stress. Furthermore, they should enhance family communication both within the system and with treatment professionals. To be effective, interventions must be tailored to the individual family and must help the family to anticipate future events and their feelings and reactions to them (e.g., Koocher & MacDonald, Chapter 5).

Interventions at the social policy level can also assist families in achieving the goals outlined above. For example, at the mesosystem level, changes in hospital policy that humanize the treatment process, or changes in a school system's policy with regard to AIDS education can be of relevance to family health psychology. At the macrosocial level, changes in federal health insurance requirements, the availability of information on abortion to women receiving treatment in federally funded health clinics, and general policies regarding funding for research in AIDS or other illness are examples of foci for intervention.

CONCLUSIONS

What we hope is clear from the foregoing discussion is that the study of family issues in health and illness has reached a point at which it is possible to define characteristics of a new subdiscipline, family health psychology. To be most productive, it will be important to incorporate the best features of previous work from existing disciplines but not be overly tied to them. A more integrative and interdisciplinary perspective should be taken. Such a perspective should facilitate development of sensitizing concepts to guide research and the evolution of a full range of interventions appropriate for the varied interfaces of family and health and illness.

It will also be important to maintain a social-ecological perspective to ensure that sufficient attention can be paid to individual, family, and larger system dimensions. Investigation of the interplay among these levels of functioning may be a major distinctive feature of family health psychology. Particularly important will be developments at the mesosocial and macrosocial levels, including social policy relevant to issues of health care, economic factors, and diversity.

The development of interdisciplinary training programs is perhaps the next immediate step that needs to be taken. Such programs would ensure that the above objectives could be met by drawing on the expertise of professionals from different areas, but without the burden of overidentification with existing disciplines.

Although the difficulties involved in interdisciplinary endeavors are well known and have been discussed since early in the development of family theorizing (Auerswald, 1968), and although difficulties persist (Campbell, McDaniel, & Seaburn, Chapter 13), it is hoped that the process of defining a new subdiscipline will help to ensure that no dominant discipline will impose its conceptual framework on the field. Only in this way will it be possible to fully capture the wide range of elements that should constitute family health psychology.

REFERENCES

Auerswald, E. H. (1968) Interdisciplinary versus social ecological approach. *Family Process, 7*, 202–215.

Baranowski, T., & Nader, P. R. (1985). Family health behavior. In D. C. Turk & R. C. Kerns (Eds.), *Health, illness, and families* (pp. 51-80). New York: Wiley-Interscience.

Bronfrenbrenner, U. (1979). *The ecology of human development.* Cambridge, MA: Harvard University Press.

Ho, M. K. (1987). *Family therapy with ethnic minorities.* Newbury Park, CA: Sage.

Hobfoll, S. E. (1988). *The ecology of stress.* Washington, DC: Hemisphere.

Hobfoll, S. E., & Spielberger, C. D. (in press). Family stress: Integrating theory and measurement. *Journal of Family Psychology.*

McGoldrick, M., Pearse, J. K., & Giordano, J. (1982). *Ethnicity and family therapy.* New York: Guilford Press.

Minuchin, S. (1974). *Families and family therapy.* Cambridge, MA: Harvard University Press.

Nichols, M. P., & Schwartz, R. C. (1991). *Family therapy: Concepts and methods* (2nd ed.). Needham Heights, MA: Allyn & Bacon.

Parad, H. (1965). *Crisis intervention: Selected readings.* New York: Family Service Association of America.

Patterson, J. M. (1988). Families experiencing stress. I. The family adjustment and adaptation model. II. Applying the FAAR model to health-related issues for intervention and research. *Family Systems Medicine, 6,* 202-237.

Penn, P. (1983). Coalitions and binding interactions in families with chronic illness. *Family Systems Medicine, 1,* 16-25.

Pratt, L. (1976). *Family structure and effective health behavior: The energized family.* Boston: Houghton-Mifflin.

Reiss, D. (1989). Families and their paradigms: An ecological approach to understanding the family in its social world. In C. N. Ramsey (Ed.), *Family systems and medicine* (pp. 119-134). New York: Guilford.

Rolland, J. (1984). Towards a psychosocial typology of chronic and life threatening illness. *Family Systems Medicine, 2,* 245-262.

Steinglass, P., Bennett, L. A., Wolin, S. J., & Reiss, D. (1987). *The alcoholic family.* New York: Basic Books.

Susman, E. J., Hersh, S. P., Nannis, E. D., Strope, B. E., Woodruff, P. J., Pizzo, P. A., & Levine, A. S. (1982). Conceptions of cancer: The perspectives of child and adolescent patients and their families. *Journal of Pediatric Psychology, 7,* 253-261.

Varni, J. W., & Wallander, J. L. (1988). Pediatric chronic disabilities: Hemophilia and spina bifida, as examples. In D. K., Routh (Ed.), *Handbook of pediatric psychology* (pp. 190-221). New York: Guilford Press.

Weakland, J. H., & Fisch, R. (1985). The strategic approach. In S. Henao & N. P. Grose (Eds.), *Principles of family systems in family medicine* (pp. 74-89). New York: Brunner/Mazel.

INDEX

For Product Safety Concerns and Information please contact our EU
representative GPSR@taylorandfrancis.com Taylor & Francis Verlag GmbH,
Kaufingerstraße 24, 80331 München, Germany

Printed and bound by CPI Group (UK) Ltd, Croydon, CR0 4YY
11/04/2025
01843992-0012